Great American Woodies And Wagons

By Donald J. Narus

Editing and Design by
George H. Dammann

Crestline Publishing

Box 48, Glen Ellyn, Illinois 60137

Great American Woodies and Wagons

Copyright © By Crestline Publishing, Inc. 1977

Library of Congress Catalog Card Number 76-39875

ISBN Number 0-912612-13-4

Typesetting by Colonial Cold Type, Glendale Heights, Ill.
            Aaction Copy Preparation, Lombard, Ill.

Printed in U.S.A. by Wallace Press, Hillside, Ill.

Binding by The Engdahl Co., Elmhurst, Ill.

Cover Design by William J. Hentges, Warren, Mich.

Published by Crestline Publishing Inc.
            Box 48   Glen Ellyn
            Illinois   60137   U.S.A.

CRESTLINE AUTO BOOKS:

ILLUSTRATED HISTORY OF FORD
(1,400 Illustrations)

60 YEARS OF CHEVROLET
(1,650 Illustrations)

70 YEARS OF BUICK
(1,800 Illustrations)

70 YEARS OF CHRYSLER
(1,950 Illustrations)

THE DODGE STORY
(1,600 Illustrations)

AMERICAN FUNERAL CARS &
    AMBULANCES SINCE 1900
(1,900 Illustrations)

AMERICAN FIRE ENGINES
    SINCE 1900
(2,000 Illustrations)

ENCYCLOPEDIA OF AMERICAN STEAM
    TRACTION ENGINES
(1,200 Illustrations)

ENCYCLOPEDIA OF AMERICAN CARS,
    1930 - 1942
(2,000 Illustrations)

GREAT AMERICAN WOODIES AND
    WAGONS
(1,650 Illustrations)

Many Thanks

The author gratefully acknowledges contributions from the following individuals, organizations, institutions, publications and private enterprises, without whose cooperation and able assistance this undertaking would not have been possible. A very special thanks goes to my wife Lee. Her encouragement has been a continuous inspiration.

Chrysler Historical Collection, John Bunnel (Retired); Chrysler Historical Collection, Rob Chenny; National Automobile Collection, Detroit Public Library, James Bradley; Special Interest Autos, Bennington, Vt.; Auto-enthusiasts, Detroit; National Woodie Club, Hawthorne Ca.; Seventy One Society, High Point, N. C.; Ford Life, Silverado Publishing, Loren Sorenson; Ford Illustrated, Sunshine Publishing, Frank Taylor; D. B. Ventures, Detroit, Donald Butler, and Dragonwyck Publishing, Richard M. Langworth.

Also, The Packard Club; Brooks Stevens Associates, Brooks Stevens; Terry Hoeman, Columbus, Neb.; Tom Garrett, High Point, N. C.; Howard Schliehs, Lakewood, Ohio; The Crawford Auto and Aviation Museum, Cleveland; Will O'Neil, Hawthorne, Cal.; Bill Harris, Hyateville, Md.; Lynn Zettlemoyer, Orefield, Pa.; Ken Minch, Parma, Ohio; Bill Smee, Parma, Ohio; Ernest Klingenberg, Parma, Ohio, and Car Classics, Jack Pelzer, No. Hollywood, Cal.

Photo Credits

In addition to the individuals and organizations already mentioned, photographs were used from the author's own collection; from the vast files of Crestline Publishing, and from the collections of the following individuals and private enterprises:

Tom McPherson, Kitchener, Ontario; Frank Hamusek, Yorba Linda, Cal.; Patrick Van der Stricht, Brussels, Belgium; Hess & Eisenhardt, Cincinnati; and Don Scheuring, Parma, Ohio.

We have tried wherever possible to acknowledge the owners of the vehicles, whose photographs we used, in these captions. Many thanks.

FOREWORD

The "Station Wagon" is a literal interpretation of a need—that need being the transporting of a small number of people from a train station to the heart of a city, to a hotel or to a resort. Large conveyances were simply called "Station Buses," smaller ones, "Station Wagons" or "Depot Hacks," as the earlier wagons were referred to.

This book attempts to trace the history of the station wagon from its early beginnings at the turn of the century, to the present day. It shows, through a pictorial chronological sequence, the development of the station wagon from the early day of the "Woodies," a crude hard working utility vehicle, to the present day sleek "Station Wagon," the suburban housewife's answer to the busing problem. It also covers those off-shoots of the station wagon, the "Woodies," the glamour wagon sedans, and the convertibles.

We will talk about both wood and steel, but more so about wood. Wood has always been a part of the automobile, either functional or decorative. Early automobiles were nothing but wooden wagons and carriages with motors. When steel bodies were developed, wood continued to serve as the framework, the superstructure. Wood went on being used in building trucks long after it was no longer needed in passenger cars. It is still used today.

There is a certain romance to wood. Woodies conjure up African safaries, Long Island estates, the suburban railroad station along the main line, private schools, country clubs, and movie stars. Wood is also a sign of luxury. Example: The hand rubbed ornamental woods used in the dashboard and granish mouldings of the Rolls Royce or Mercedes Benz. Simulated wood veneer is used by all manufacturers in the top of the line models.

Woodies have always held a magnetism. They have always been the most expensive model in the line. But not necessarily, until recently, the most luxurious. They have been the toughest models to maintain; the hardest to repair; the insurance company's nightmare. But, they have been and still are the most attractive.

Journey back now to those thrilling days of yesteryear when out of the past comes the rumbling, chugging, sputtering, creeking and rattling old Woodie, the wind whistling through its windowless openings. Ain't it Bee-u-ti-fool!

The evolution of the Station Wagon as it is known today, began with the Express Body. This was a light truck vehicle. From this evolved the Depot Hack, which was the Express Body with the addition of seats. These seats were added in the usual conventional manner, one behind the other or in long opposing benches, one on each side set the length of the truck bed. Vehicles so arranged were also called "Jittneys." The express body usually had a fixed roof or top, so the addition of seats was a natural alteration, when the need for carrying more passengers arose.

The need for a Depot Hack evolved from the need to transport passengers in small numbers from the train depot or station, which was located outside the city, to the city. As the Depot Hack grew in popularity it began to become refined. The early models were for the most part do-it-yourself Jittneys. The conversions were done by owners themselves. Some dealers, seeing the potential of the Depot Hack, were enterprising enough to contract with local furniture manufacturers and cabinet makers to build whole bodies, as well as the conversions.

As the demand increased, some furniture manufacturers converted their facilities to building nothing but woodie bodies. With more and more demand came more and more body builders. Soon the auto manufacturer began advertising the Depot Hack, and began shipping chassis direct to the body builder who in turn shipped the finished product to the dealer. The train depot gave way to the train station, and the Depot Hack became known as the Station Wagon. Its primary duty however, remained the same—transporting passengers from station to city.

This 1906 Reo is a conventional "Depot Hack" woodie of the classic design. The design is rather advanced for the year and it is suspected that perhaps this body was added at a later date. The body builder is unknown.

One of the earliest examples of a Depot Hack was the 1899 Rapid. It had three seats set in the conventional manner, one behind the other. It also had a fringed surrey top. One of the earliest uses of the term "Station Wagon" was by Pierce Arrow in 1911. This "Station Wagon" was no more than a wooden box added to a touring car chassis. It had jittney type bench seats and could carry up to seven passengers.

Webster defines a Station Wagon as: "an automobile having an interior longer than a sedan, one or more folding or removable seats to facilitate trucking, and no separate luggage compartment." Now that's not bad, but we'd like to add: "a fixed top or roof, and a maximum carrying capacity of 10 passengers." In short it is a multi-passenger carrying utility vehicle. The Pierce Arrow certainly did fit Webster's definition as well as ours.

One of the earliest offerings of a station wagon type vehicle by an auto manufacturer was a 1912 Buick Wagonette and Express. It had opposing bench seats, which could be removed, an oiled duck canopy roof, and roll-up side curtains. It could carry 7 or 8 passengers easily. An interesting "Depot Hack" appeared in 1913 as the Stanley Mountain Wagon. Although it looked more like a bus it was classified as a wagon. Built for carrying passengers from train to mountain resort hotel, it was unique in that it had a folding canvas top. Seating was conventional and it could carry up to 10 passengers. But by our definition we would have to discount it: No fixed roof.

Depot Hack/Station Wagon type vehicles were put to other uses once their value was proven. One such use was by the Army. Here they were used as ambulances and personnel carriers. In 1917 Hudson was a supplier of such vehicles on a limited scale. Hudson had two different designs, both with opposing seats, fixed tops and roll-up side curtains. In 1918 White supplied the Army with Troop Carriers, which by definition, were Station Wagons. The seating arrangement in this wagon was a little unusual. Behind the driver's seat was a pair of facing conventional seats and behind these was another set of facing conventional seats.

The most popular chassis to be converted to or fitted with a Depot Hack/Station Wagon body was the Model T Ford. Various types, designs and styles of woodie bodies were used on the Model T. (Woodie—as defined by the author: A motor vehicle with a conventional sheet metal front end and a wooden constructed passenger compartment, framing and panels which are varnished or painted against the weather, rather than covered by sheet metal.) By the end of the decade, "Woodie Wagons" began to take on a conventional standardized look. When someone mentioned Depot Hack or Station Wagon, one would immediately know what he or she was talking about. They began to look familiar—even the do-it-yourselfers.

An 1899 Rapid. One of the earliest wagons on record with a familiar seating arrangement. It was used to transport guests from train station to hotel.

This 1906 Olds, although more unconventional looking, was nevertheless designated a "Wagonette." It could carry up to 18 persons which puts it out of the wagon definition, and classes it as a bus.

OLDS MOTOR WORKS, LANSING, MICHIGAN

A 1907 Logan. Logans were manufactured in Chillicothe, Ohio. This is the 6-passenger Depot Wagon. It sold for $1,150, and could be fully enclosed for bad weather.

1906 Duryea. This might have been the original surrey with the fringe on top. Seating was for eight. The driver's position was in the center seat. This unit sold for $1,250 as shown.

A 1907 Logan. This was called the Liveryman's Automobile Style No. 4. It was priced at $1,000. It was finished in optional Logan tan, dark green or black. Lettering was extra. Standard equipment included side lamps, tail lamp, horn and tools.

1906 Autocar. It was classified as a Depot Wagon, but this 12 passenger model would be more of a bus. It was powered by a 20 horsepower 2-cylinder opposed engine.

1906 Maxwell. This model was called the Tuxedo Park Station Wagon. It bears a strong resemblance to the Columbia, and may have been built by the same body builder. Three of these were in use at Tuxedo Park, N. Y. Note the emergency brake on the rear wheel.

1907 Columbia. This wagon was used by the Hotel Schenly in Pittsburgh. The all-weather curtains are in place. It was complete with luggage rack.

1907 White. This is the White Station Wagonette, outfitted for Japanese service. It had bench seats of the Jittney type.

1909 International Harvester. It was called the "Auto-Wagon." It was sold with one seat for $950, with additional seats costing $25 each. Brass lamps and the top were also optional. The second and third seats were removable. A choice of air or water cooled engines was available. This fine example is owned by Bob Griner of Rockville, Md.

This 1910 Buick, although described as a Special Motor Bus, bears a strong resemblance to what might be considered a Station Wagon. This is an early enclosed model with luggage rack. Wagon development surely wasn't consistent, and went from this closed model to open air wagons to closed weather-tite configurations.

1910 Buick. This early type Depot Hack had one conventional rear seat with an unconventional rear facing seat. There was cargo area behind the rear seat. It was logically used to carry the passengers' luggage.

1911 Pierce Arrow. This is one of the earliest usage of the term "Station Wagon." It was no more than a wooden box with jittney type facing seats. It could carry up to seven passengers.

A 1911 Buick. This is a more familiar design of the early type "Depot Hack," with conventional type "Woodie Sides." The seats were placed one behind the other, with an additional facing seat behind the driver.

1911 Autocar. It was the Autocar School Wagon, and was used for the training of commercial vehicle drivers. Note the ladder at the back for easier rear entry.

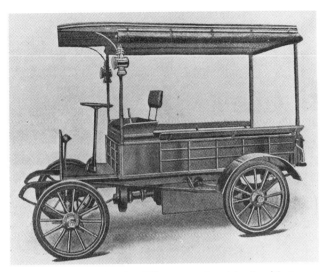

1911 Champion Electric. This was a depot hack with a conventional type woodie body. The body builder is unknown. Additional seats could be added.

The ever popular Model T Ford Depot Hack. It has the conventional seating arrangement and woodie body, but no roll-up side curtains. The body builder is unknown. This 1912 example is owned by D. B. Craft of Woodbridge, Conn.

A 1912 Buick Standard Express. With the addition of seats, this delivery wagon could be converted to a "Depot Hack." The body is wood with an oiled duck canopy. This was built on Buick's commercial chain-drive chassis.

This 1913 Stanley Mountain Wagon looks more like a bus, but was considered a "Depot Hack" type vehicle. It was used to carry hotel guests to and from the train depot. This is a unique car in that it is more an elongated touring car, complete with folding top. Owner is Carl Amsley of St. Thomas, Pa.

This 1912 Buick model is a combination Wagonette and Express. It has opposing Jittney type bench seats for passengers and it could be used to haul cargo. The body is wood, with an oiled duck canopy and roll-up side curtains. It is one of the earliest examples of a station wagon type vehicle being offered in an auto manufacturer's catalog.

The 1913 Buick Express Body. With the addition of seats it could be turned into a Depot Hack. Either two or three seats could be added.

This 1914 Model T Ford sports a homemade body. Many homemade bodies were built during this period, and the increasing number gave rise to professional body building shops such as Cantrell, York, Mifflinburg, etc.

A 1914 Ford Model T with a Seaman Body Co. express body. The addition of two extra seats converted this body into a Depot Hack. It came equipped with roll-up side curtains and a metal framed windshield.

This 1915 Model T Ford woodie is slightly different in that it has a wooden frame windshield, while most other models had metal frames. The wood frame on this wagon was painted a dark color to give it contrast against the light panels. This example is owned by Rippys Vetern Car Museum, Denver.

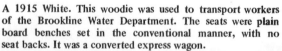

A 1915 White. This woodie was used to transport workers of the Brookline Water Department. The seats were **plain** board benches set in the conventional manner, with no seat backs. It was a converted express wagon.

This 1916 White was listed as a ¾-ton truck. It has the woodie type body, with roll-up side curtains and oiled duck top. It was used as an express wagon or, with the addition of seats, a Depot Hack.

The White Company
Cleveland, Ohio

A 1916 Vim ½-ton chassis equipped with an express body, complete with roll-up side curtains, fixed top and metal framed windshield. To convert to a Depot Hack, merely add seats.

This 1915 Studebaker model was called a Combination Passenger and Express Car. It sold for $875. There were jittney type bench seats which folded up out of the way to provide a larger cargo area. The body was of sheet metal with a very clean looking design. It had a capacity of 10 passengers. Studebaker claimed it had the clean cut lines of a pleasure car with the durability and all around efficiency of a "Carry-all."

A 1916 Ford Model T with a body by Parry Manufacturing of Indianapolis. This was the No. 204 Combination Passenger and Commercial Body. It was similar in design to the Studebaker but more austere.

This 1917 Ford Model T is a crude homemade express wagon. It bears a strong resemblance to a motorized Connestoga wagon. It is, however, an excellent example of what owners were doing to convert their touring cars. At this period in time, body builders for the most part, were not interested in building Depot Hacks. If an owner didn't live near a furniture manufacturer or cabinet maker, he did it himself.

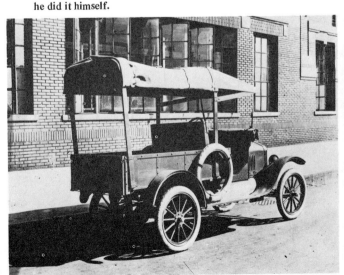

Hudson built a limited number of these 1917 woodies. They were used primarily by the military during World War I. It features jittney type bench seats, roll-up side curtains, a spotlight, a split windshield and dual side mounts. The body was probably built by Seaman Body Co. of Milwaukee.

A 1917 Hudson woodie ambulance. This is another version of the military woodie, built in limited numbers during World War I.

A 1917 Studebaker Combination Passenger and Express Car. It sold for $925, F.O.B. Detroit. It is illustrated here with its 10 passengers.

THE WHITE
COMPANY
CLEVELAND, OHIO

A 1918 White Army Transport. Note the unusual arrangement of seats. It was used primarily as a troop carrier. It was complete with fixed canvas covered top and roll-up side curtains.

A 1917 White ¾-ton truck chassis with an express body. It sold for $2,400, and could be converted to a Depot Hack. Although the driver's compartment was somewhat enclosed, it still lacked a windshield. The wheelbase was 133½ inches.

This is a 1918 Chevrolet Model "T" one-ton truck chassis. (Bet you thought only Ford made Model T's) This express body required the installation of extra seats to make it a Depot Hack. It sold for $1,325, with the added seats.

This 1918 Ford Model T Woodie body is more like a pick-up truck. It could be converted to a Depot Hack with the addition of seats and a fixed top. Note the two-piece windshield in a wooden frame. This appears to be a home-made job.

This 1919 Model T wagon is equipped with a side mount spare. It has three rows of seats, rear doors and roll-up curtains. The restoration on this model appears flawless.

A 1919 Ford Model T Depot Hack. This one features a side door for easier entrance into the rear seat area. It has a fixed roof with roll-up side curtains. The windshield is the wooden frame type.

A 1919 Model T with a body built by Columbia Body Corp. of Columbia, Pa. This was an early Suburban design. Note that some of the side curtains have been installed; also that there is a front and a rear door.

By 1920 a number of station wagon body builders had emerged. Such names as Cantrell, Mifflinburg, York, Martin, Parry (who later merged into Martin-Parry), Ionia, Cotton, Springfield, Baker-Rauling, Seaman, and Hercules would become synonymous with station wagons. The 1920 model depot hack was a little more refined and standardized. The bodies were given names, and every body builder

The 1920 Chevrolet Light Delivery sold for $735. For an additional $35 it was equipped with two extra seats to convert this to a Depot Hack. Body builder is unknown.

A 1920 Ford chassis fitted with a Model 803 York Suburban body. It features full back seats which are covered in tan leather. Wood framed windshield with plate glass and roll-up side curtains were standard. The body is finished in natural wood.

had a Suburban or Country Club model. Some builders also called them Estate Cars.

York Body Corp. of York, Pa., said of its DeLuxe Model 803 Suburban Body, "It's natty and classy". York built bodies primarily for the Model T. However, its bodies did fit other chassis. The Suburban as built by York is described as follows: "This is a natural wood four-panel suburban body, trimmed in tan leather cloth with plaited spring cushions and backs. The center seat is in halves, affording ready access to the rear seat. Finish is in natural wood with a specially designed natural wood windshield with plate glass, with a close slatted top and round corner front. It is always shipped knocked down unless otherwise specified. Fenders are extra." This would indicate that most bodies were dealer assembled and installed.

Martin-Parry Body Corp., also of York, Pa., described its Suburban Body on the 1921 Dodge chassis as, "every feature of Martin-Parry workmanship that could be introduced with advantage has been unsparingly lavished upon this first Dodge body in our desire to make it a perfect vehicle which would appeal to a discriminating clientele and enable it to give lasting service."

Mifflinburg Body Co. described its No. 135L Country Club or Suburban Body for the 1922 Overland as, "the most attractive Country Club Body on the market today. The last word in style, comfort and finish. The high panels protect the occupants. The center seat is adjustable and allows easy access to the rear seat. Curtains with large lights enclose the body in bad weather. It is upholstered in imitation tan leather with curtains to match."

Then there was the J. T. Cantrell & Co. of Huntington, N. Y. They hailed their Suburban Bay as "ideal for the Southern Estate, or for the Winter Vacationist in the South. Light, sturdy and comfortable, it is designed to withstand the hardest usage over all sorts of roads. It accommodates seven passengers or, with seats removed, a surprising amount of goods and luggage."

By 1922, body builders began to advertise their wagon bodies in *Country Life* and *Fortune*. These were magazines aimed at the rich. Elaborate catalogs were printed for dealer use. Most bodies were either shipped to the dealers knocked down, or the dealer merely ordered a chassis from the factory for direct shipment to the wagon builder. With the advent of the woodie body builder and the standardization of body types, the quality of the Station Wagon body improved. The type of wood was carefully selected and the craftsmanship was of the highest quality.

The first production station wagon was introduced in 1923. It was the Star Station Wagon, built by Durant Motors. It was an open air design, as were most wagons of the day, with a low profile box. The framework was finished in natural wood while the small panels were stained walnut. There were three doors, two on the right side and one on the left. Seats were upholstered in artificial leather, with the top covered in the same material. Roll-up side curtains were furnished for bad weather. The body was mounted on a standard Star chassis.

No, this isn't a Ford armored car. It's a collapsible cab, offered by York. It was light-weight and could be carried under the arm. It weighed only 46½ lbs. It was used by dealers to drive chassis from the dealership to the body builder, or for factory pick-up of a chassis. It afforded protection against the weather.

This York body, Model 808 Suburban fitted to a Ford chassis. Features included full back seats, 3 doors, roll-up side curtains, extra guard rail for the third seat, and patented spring locks for the doors.

This is a 1920 Model T Dairy Wagon. The body is by Hercules. This example was owned by Rippys Veteran Car Museum, Denver.

A 1921 Chevrolet Light Delivery Wagon. Once again Chevrolet offered this model with the optional seats. With seats it sold for $855. As a delivery wagon, it was priced at $820.

A 1921 Renault Wagon. It is curious to note the interest in this type of vehicle was even evident in Europe. The body looks like it may well be a Cantrell. The owner could have taken his imported car to Cantrell for a custom body. Compare this body to that fitted to a Dodge chassis of the same vintage. This example is owned by K. B. Nassen of Rockville Centre, N. Y.

This Woodie is not a station wagon. It's an early attempt at a camper wagon. It is being pulled by a 1921 Essex. Photo courtesy of American Motors.

An enterprising minister from Brooklyn, N. Y. built his own woodie on a Model T chassis. Although his design was unorthodox for a wagon, it served his purpose to a "T."

Built by Cotton Body Co. of Concord, N. H., this suburban body is mounted on a Model T chassis. The Cotton bodies were easily recognizable by the cowl treatment. The cowl was covered with a leatherette fabric, as were the side panels. It was usually of an alligator type pattern. Note that this model has only the two seats instead of three. Another feature of this wagon was the optional side-mount spare.

This is a Galvin and Gilmore, Detroit, body on a 1921 Model T. The body is a combination of wood panels and metal reinforcing bars. The seating is in true jittney fashion.

A 1921 Dodge with a Park Auto Body by Martin Truck and Body Co. of York, Pa. This is one of the earliest examples of a Martin body on a Dodge.

This Ford chassis is fitted with a Depot Hack body of unusual design. The seats are arranged in jittney fashion. The owner of this example is Roaring "20s" Autos, Wall, N. J.

This is Mifflinburg's No. 130A Suburban Body mounted on a Ford Model T chassis. Note the low profile of the wagon box and the guard rail for rear seat passengers.

Another of Mifflinburg's wagon bodies. This one was called the No. 131A Country Club. It's for a ½-ton Ford chassis. Note the arm rests are part of the body framing.

This Mifflinburg Suburban body has a high profile. It was designed for the ½-ton Ford chassis. The arm rest on this body, although part of the body, are more streamlined, indicating a more DeLuxe model.

An Overland chassis with a Mifflinburg body. This one is of the high profile design.

A 1922 Model T Ford chassis fitted with a York Suburban Body No. 805. This was the largest of the York Suburban bodies, providing seating for ten passengers. The center seats were split and folded for easier access to the other seats.

A Chevrolet chassis with a Mifflinburg Suburban No. 135A Country Club body. This is a high profile box design. This was trend toward a newer design to enclose the passengers even more.

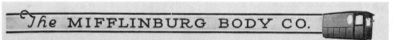

The MIFFLINBURG BODY CO.

A Chevrolet ¾-ton Delivery Wagon with extra seats in place. This was a Depot Hack conversion. Note that these seats were not split back. Access to all seats was therefore a little awkward.

The Light Delivery Wagon was offered by Chevrolet with the optional seats for conversion to Depot Hack. Note that there is also provision for side mounted spare. This unit sold for $525 as shown.

A 1922 Model T chassis with a Suburban body to Waterloo Body Corp. of Waterloo, N. Y. The box is of the low profile design. This model has an optional tool box mounted on the running board.

This distinctive body was called the "Beverly." Built by Cotton Bocy Co., it is mounted on a 1922 Maxwell. Note the optional side mounted spare. The rear seats appear to be set a little higher than the driver's seat.

The 1922 Reo Speed Wagon could be converted to a Depot Hack. The body builder is unknown. This example was owned by Ray Rickenbaugh of College Point, N. Y.

A 1922 Essex. The body builder is unknown, although it strongly resembles a Martin-Parry body. It is finished in natural wood, and has roll-up side curtains.

A Cantrell body mounted on a 1922 Dodge chassis. This same body was also available for Studebaker, Ford, and Essex. Note the arm rest for the front seat is part of the body frame and panel.

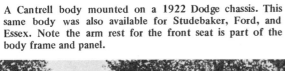

The 1922 Dodge is fitted with a Cantrell Suburban body. Note the separation of the center seats. They were fixed in this fashion to provide easy access to the rear seat.

1920 - 1923

A low profile Suburban body mounted on a Chevrolet chassis. It could have been built by Mifflinburg or Cantrell.

A 1923 Buick fitted with a high profile Martin-Parry Suburban body. Note the built up rails used for arm rests. This unit sold for $935 complete with roll-up curtains.

A Cantrell Suburban body on a 1923 Model T chassis. Note the rails and built-up panels for arm rests.

The 1923 Star. It is credited with being the first production station wagon. Framing was natural with dark stained panels. This is a three door model with two doors on the right and one on the left. Seating capacity was for seven passengers.

Another view of the Star Station Wagon. This illustrates the wagon with the seats removed, doubling as a light delivery truck. It sold for $610 fully equipped.

This is the Martin-Parry No. 168 Combination Depot and Country Club body fitted to an Overland Model Four commercial chassis.

The Martin-Parry No. 169 Fancy Baggage and Delivery Body, mounted on the Overland Model Four commercial chassis. This is essentially the same body as the No. 168, with seats removed.

This attractive and distinctive Cotton-Beverly body, by the Cotton Body Co., is mounted on an Essex chassis. By 1923, Cotton had moved its operations from Concord, N. H., to Boston, Mass. Note the alligator type of material used to cover the panels. The same material was also used on the seats.

This is a 1923 Canadian Model T with possibly a Cantrell body. Photo is courtesy of The Antique Automobile.

The Canadian Model T wagon with side curtains rolled down, ready for bad weather. Note the small windows, making visibility extremely difficult.

Note the larger windows in the side curtains on this 1924 Model T wagon. The body may well have been built by Mifflinburg.

With the improved quality of the Woodie, featur continuously changed. Greater attention was given to t ease of entrance by the passengers and the snugness side curtain fit to guard against bad weather. Four doc were added by most builders. Window openings we completely framed in most designs by 1926. A multitu of snaps were fastened to these frames, so the side curtai could be more securely held in place. Visibility throug the side curtains gradually improved. There was a defini trend toward improving passenger comfort.

Body builder ads in *Country Life* continued to be aim at the affluent. H. H. Babcock Company of Watertow N. Y., lauded its Estate Car. "The car, indispensable f Suburban Home or Country Club, is ideal for hunting a fishing parties, picnics, marketing. The governess' car, th servant's conveyance—a handy car for scores of purpose For its distinctive individuality, it has been selected the House of Morgan, of Gould, of Swift, of Hill and sco of others of America's first."

Cantrell on the other hand stressed its all weath features, as advertised in the January 1925 issue *Country Life*. "For day-in-day-out service during our har northern winters, the Cantrell Suburban Body, mount on a light car chassis, has many advantages. Equipped wi snug fitting side and rear curtains, it may be taken out the worst of weather and given, with impunity, the so of treatment that is ruinous to an expensive touring c or sedan.

A 1924 Buick chassis fitted with a Cotton body. Most Cotton bodies feature a side-mount spare. This was a three-door model—the driver entered from the right side.

A Cantrell body mounted on a 1924 Dodge chassis. Note the narrow rear door as compared to the front door. The windshield is stock metal frame. It makes the roof appear to be cantilevered.

A 1924 Franklin fitted with a one-off wagon body. The body builder is unknown. However, this was either a very advanced design for 1924, or the body was mounted on this chassis at a later date. Note the full framed front door, and the appearance that the wagon is fully enclosed—which it is. There is glass all around and the front doors have roll-up windows. These are very advanced features for 1924. This fine example is owned by Frederick F. Robinson of Danbury, Conn. Photo courtesy of Air Cooled News.

This is a rear view of Frederick F. Robinson's Franklin wagon. Note the almost boatlike slope to the rear of the body. The tailgate swings down while the tailgate window hinges upward. Photo courtesy of Air Cooled News.

A 1925 Reo Speed Wagon. This was an express body available with three extra seats, which provided seating for 10 passengers.

This Chevrolet, with a Martin-Parry body, is a four-door model. Both doors hinged in the center. Doors are full framed and full width. With the side curtains in place the wagon looks very snug, with enough room for seven passengers.

A 1925 Chevrolet with Mifflinburg Suburban Body Model No. 34. This model represents a whole new design change. The open air look was gone. Window openings were completely framed. Doors were full width and there were four of them. All-weather curtains were mounted on the inside and rode up out of sight on tracks. The whole body had a much cleaner, symmetrical appearance. Framing was natural ash, with mahogany panels.

A Chevrolet chassis with a Springfield No. 38 Suburban body. This was a less expensive model. It had four doors, a somewhat lower profile box, and roll-up side curtains. It was finished in natural wood. These models were phased out as the more closed version became more popular. This body was 66 inches long, 44 inches wide, and 56 inches high. The body alone weighed 550 pounds.

A Dodge chassis with a 1925 Cantrell Suburban body. This body was also available for Ford chassis. Note that this body still maintains the open air look, although it did have side curtains to guard against bad weather.

A 1926 Chevrolet chassis fitted with a No. 39 Suburban body by Springfield Body Co., Springfield, supplied many bodies for Chevrolets during 1925-26. This body, like the Mifflinburg body, was of the new design, with framed windows and full width doors. This was a 10-passenger body with a length of 93 inches, width of 44.5 inches, and height of 56 inches. The body alone weighed 725 pounds.

A 1926 Dodge chassis with a body by Babcock. This was an unusual design. The wood framing was covered by sheet metal, and the roof supports were steel, as was the windshield frame. There was some caning work at the belt line. It was a four-door model with a passenger capacity for nine. Roll-up side curtains were provided for bad weather driving. The center seats could be folded out of the way when not needed.

A 1926 Ford with a Mifflinburg Suburban Body No. 6. Note the similarity to the Springfield No. C34 body, and the fact that the Ford front end has been air-brushed into the picture.

Body by Babcock

A Springfield Body No. 364 mounted on a Ford chassis. Its length was 67 inches, width 44 inches, height 56 inches, panel height 22 inches, and net weight was 675 pounds. It's illustrated here with side curtains in place. These slid up on tracks into the inside of the roof when not in use.

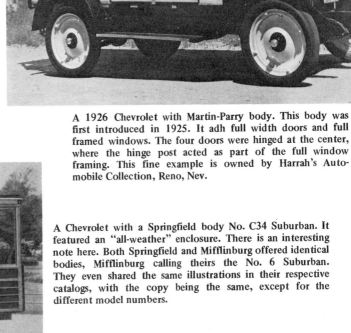

A 1926 Chevrolet with Martin-Parry body. This body was first introduced in 1925. It adh full width doors and full framed windows. The four doors were hinged at the center, where the hinge post acted as part of the full window framing. This fine example is owned by Harrah's Automobile Collection, Reno, Nev.

A Chevrolet with a Springfield body No. C34 Suburban. It featured an "all-weather" enclosure. There is an interesting note here. Both Springfield and Mifflinburg offered identical bodies, Mifflinburg calling theirs the No. 6 Suburban. They even shared the same illustrations in their respective catalogs, with the copy being the same, except for the different model numbers.

A 1926 Ford chassis fitted with an older York body. This is the open air design more prevalent in the earlier 1920s. This fine example is owned by the Henry Ford Museum/ Greenfield Village, Dearborn, Mich., and is in service as a tourist attraction, taking visitors for rides around the historic village.

A Ford chassis with the Springfield No. 364 body. It is illustrated here without the side curtains in place. Upholstery was in imitation black leather.

In 1927 more and more body builders were emphasizing passenger comfort. Mifflinburg featured its No. 634 Suburban Body with "All-Weather" enclosure. The flexible glass openings were made larger. Side curtains were installed on spring loaded rollers and concealed under the side head piece. One could quickly pull the side curtains down and snap them in place when the weather turned for the worst. There were six individually framed openings per slide plus the tail gate. A curtain was installed in each opening. Side panels were raised higher, offering the passengers more protection. The four doors were made larger, permitting easier entrance to front and rear. The woodie was losing that open air look.

Attention was also given to quality of construction and aesthetic beauty. The frame work of the Mifflinburg No. 634 was made of selected white ash, for greater durability. It was chamfered and mortised and tenoned at all joints. Panels were given a satinwood finish while the white ash frame work was finished naturally, giving the body an attractive contrasting appearance.

The Cantrell Suburban Body for 1928 featured four completely framed doors. The lower door as well as the window opening were made into a single door, the same as a closed sedan. Dodge was a big customer of Cantrell, but the body builder was also pushing Chevrolet, Buick, Cadillac, Chrysler, Franklin and Graham-Paige. Bodies for the Dodge and Chevrolet could be supplied anywhere, usually knockdown for dealer assembly, whereas bodies for the other chassis were available within driving distance of the factory.

In announcing the new Model A for 1928, Ford also decided to manufacture its own station wagon bodies. The Iron Mountain, Mich. plant, which was started in 1920 in making wooden parts for the Model T, such as floor boards, roof rails, pillars, etc., produced the station wagon parts. These parts were then shipped to the Murray Body Company in Detroit for assembly. The Ford station wagon for 1927 was made of maple harvested in the Iron Mountain area. Ford owned vast forest reserves in and around Iron Mountain.

The body of the 1927 Ford wagon featured the fu... door with window openings and door framed as one un... The doors were large for easy access and were hinged b... means of a full length piano type hinge. This was done f... strength and durability. The side curtains had large ope... ings and were snapped to the outside of the framewor... Seven individual canvas panels were used. The spare ti... was fender mounted, as were most of the spare tires... this era.

In 1929 an unusual body was offered by Springfiel... The hardwood framework of this body was covered wi... sheet metal, painted the same color as the hood and cov... The full frame doors were then edged with stainless... nickle-candium strips. The roof edge was edged with the... strips, and they were used at the belt line in a double ro... for decorative purposes. Instead of side curtains, pull-u... type windows were used. The window was made of a st... metal frame covered with canvas. Large openings were c... into the canvas and flexible glass sewn into the openin... The windows were raised by pulling them up from the... envelope type pockets. Once raised they were snappe... across the top of the framework to hold them in plac... There was a window of this type in each of the four doo... plus two in each quarter section. The tailgate curta... continued to snap-on from the outside. It was a ve... attractive wagon, but apparently not very popular as mo... of the conventional woodie type wagons were sol...

Constructed in 1927 by an unknown body builder was this interesting Chevrolet. The well-restored vehicle, owned by Loran Titus of Excelsior Springs, Mo., appears to have utilized the cowl, windshield framing and sun visor of the 1927 Chevrolet closed cars, yet is fitted with the painted radiator shell of the Chevrolet light commercial chassis. The very modern looking wagon is a 7-passenger, 4-door model, with a 2-passenger center seat and a 3-passenger rear seat.

An open air Springfield body is mounted on a 1927 Chevrolet chassis. It has a natural wood finish and is constructed of ash. It only has doors on the right side.

A 1927 Buick chassis with a suburban open air type body by either Springfield or Martin-Parry. The body is finished in natural wood. Seating capacity was for seven passengers. This three-door model was owned by Mr. Stone of Canton, Conn., when the photo was taken.

A 1927 Chevrolet with a Springfield body is shown here with side curtains in place.

A 1927 Dodge chassis fitted with the new Cantrell Suburban body. Note the enclosed look with full width and full length doors. The center seats were separated at the center for easier access to the rear seat. The rib design was also changed on this body. There was now a combination of vertical and horizontal pieces. Other manufacturers also followed this design.

A 1927 Dodge chassis being readied for shipment to a body builder to be fitted with a station wagon body. Most auto manufacturers shipped their chassis in this manner.

A 1927 Model T station wagon. This was the last year of the Model T. Note the unique side mounting of the spare. Doors were on the right side only.

A 1927 Star with a Mifflinburg body. This was the No. 634 Suburban body, with all-weather enclosure, continuing the trend toward fully enclosing the station wagon body.

A 1927 Model T chassis fitted with a Springfield body. This was Springfield's No. 6 Suburban. Note that this body is identical to the Mifflinburg No. 634. It is curious to note that in each of the respective body builder's catalog, the backgrounds for each of these body illustrations were identical. Both companies used the same printer who inadvertently did the illustrations in exactly the same manner for both catalogs, and usually air-brushed in the various chassis rather than photograph each make separately.

The New Ford Station Wagon

The new Ford Station Wagon has been designed to meet the needs of large estates, country clubs and families having summer homes in the country or by the seashore. It is particularly well suited to such use because it combines the sturdiness of a light truck with the flexibility and comfort of a passenger car.

Seating accommodations are provided for eight people, including the driver. Baggage is carried on the large tail-gate. The seats in the rear compartment, though securely anchored when in use, can be removed quickly and easily when the car is used for hauling.

In appearance, the new Ford Station Wagon reflects its sturdy construction. The body has uprights of hard maple, with ply-wood sides finished in natural grain. The sill is unusually rugged. Fenders are full-crown, heavy and capable. Seats are wide, deeply-cushioned and finished in blue-gray artificial Spanish leather. Doors are wide, carefully fitted and substantial, with full-nickeled handles in conservative scroll design. The side curtains, which can be put up easily and quickly in bad weather, are made in tan-gray to harmonize with the body finish.

The new Ford Station Wagon brings you the same alert performance, ease of control, safety, speed, power, reliability and economy that are characteristic of all the new Ford cars. Its easy-riding comfort is particularly appreciated on rough roads.

By 1928 the station wagon had taken on enough popularity to warrant its addition to the Ford line. Ford introduced a whole new car for 1928—the Model A. This late 1929 ad marked the first time a major auto manufacturer had actually advertised a Station Wagon.

The 1928 Ford Station Wagon. Its body was finished in natural wood. All-weather curtains were fastened to the outside of the framing. Doors were full width and length. They opened at the center and were hung with full length piano type hinges. Photo courtesy of Model A Restorers Club.

This promotional vehicle, a 1928 Ford chassis fitted with a Conestoga Wagon, was one man's literal translation of a "Wagon." "Go west young man." Maybe the man in the photo is Horace Greely, taking his own advice. Photo courtesy of Ford Life.

A 1928 Ford chassis. Woodies of this era came in all sizes and shapes, as witnessed by this switch yard wagon. This unusual wagon was owned by Roaring 20's Auto of Wall, N. J.

A 1928 Ford chassis fitted with a Springfield No. 5 Estate Station body. This is a very clean and attractive design. The body is constructed from steel panels inside and outside over a hardwood frame. The doors were extra wide. This design was one of the earliest having the rear door follow the line of the rear fender, a practice which later became common and is in use today. This wagon was available with two or three seats. The body was 70 inches long, 44 inches wide, 50 inches high, and weighed 800 pounds.

A Chevrolet chassis fitted with the new Martin-Parry Suburban body. Note the closed appearance of the body design. The doors were full width but not full length. Roll-up side curtains were fastened on the inside.

This awesome looking vehicle is fitted with a depot hack body of unknown origin mounted on a 1928 Fargo chassis. It could very well have been built by a local cabinet maker or a do-it-yourselfer. This type of wagon was fading fast. It looks like it might have been used by some mountain resort or lumber camp.

The year 1929 was a milestone in wagon building. It marked the first year a major auto builder began mass producing his own station wagon. The 1929 Ford wagon was built at Ford's Iron Mountain facilities in the upper peninsula of Michigan. Its components were then shipped to the Murray Body Co. of Detroit or to Baker-Rawling in Cleveland for assembly.

A 1928 Chevrolet with a Mifflinburg Suburban body. It features a new rib design of horizontal and vertical pieces, and full width half doors. The center seats were separated to provide easy access to the rear seat.

A rear view of the 1929 Ford wagon. Ford produced 5,200 of these wagons. They sold for a whopping $695, and were the second most expensive car in Ford's 1929 list, being exceeded in price only by the pretentious open front town car.

This 1929 Buick is fitted with a somewhat outdated open air type suburban body. The body builder is unknown.

A 1929 Model A Ford is fitted with a Springfield No. 2 Suburban body. Even though Ford was manufacturing its own bodies, chassis were still being ordered and shipped to other body builders.

A 1929 Dodge commercial chassis with a unique wagon body of advanced design. The wood framework is covered with sheet metal, and painted the same color as the hood and cowl. Edges and seams were covered with stainless steel strips, which also served to accent the belt line. Doors are full width and the windows are self-storing. The body builder is unknown, although it bears a strong resemblance to a variation of the Springfield No. 5 Estate Wagon.

The Mifflinburg No. 32C Suburban body is mounted on a 1929 Chevrolet chassis. Seating capacity was for 7 passengers. The dimensions of this body were identical to the Springfield Bar Harbour.

A 1929 Chevrolet chassis fitted with a Springfield Bar Harbour Suburban body. A genuine polished plate glass windshield with a hand wiper was featured. A rear vision mirror and rubber floor mat were also standard. The body was 69 inches long, 44 inches wide, and 50 inches high.

Ford continued to be the leader in station wagon building, having produced some 3,800 wagons for this year. Its wagon design was unchanged from the previous year. The wagon parts continued to be made at Ford's Iron Mountain plant and were assembled by Murray Body Co., in Detroit or by Baker-Rawling in Cleveland, Ohio. The trend toward a closed-car design continued. However, snap on side curtains were still used to weatherproof the vehicles. Bodies were made of maple and finished in natural wood. Craftsmanship improved, as the body design improved. The cost of the Ford station wagon was reduced in 1930 to $650, but still it remained the most expensive car in the Ford line-up for that year.

Using the Ford station wagon body as the basis, some interesting vehicles were created in 1930, that today we would classify as Woodies. They were mail trucks, panel delivery wagons, ambulances, etc. One such version was the Traveler Wagon: An early attempt at a camper or mobile home. It had the appearance of a station wagon, but only had two doors, instead of the usual four. The tail gate was replaced by a pair of center locking doors. The camper compartment was screened in, with all-weather roll-up canvas side curtains. It could sleep two, had storage compartments and a water tank. It made a great vehicle for hunters or fishermen.

Other auto manufacturers did not follow Ford's lead, but continued to have wagons built by independent body builders. A growing number of smaller manufacturers were shipping chassis to these independent wagon body builders as the demand for this type of vehicle increased and customers wanted their favorite car in the form of a wagon. The affluent wanted Estate Wagons on a more prestigious chassis, so a number of custom built wagons emerged. There were Packard wagons, Chrysler wagons, Cadillac wagons and a number of one-offs.

A 1930 Chevrolet chassis with Springfield Estate body No. 35. This body was of a more advanced design, but was not very popular. Plywood panels were framed in metal. The roof supports were also metal, rather than of wood. Although the engineering design was advanced, the overall appearance was of an open air look, which was slowly fading from the wagon scene.

This Dodge chassis, fitted with either a Cantrell or Mifflinburg body, features a side mounted spare. The side curtains are in place. This fine example was owned by Alden Beverly of White Plains, N. Y. It seated eight.

This 1930 Dodge is fitted with a Cantrell body. Doors were full width and fully framed. This design was typical of the trend toward a more closed look in wagons.

The Fargo Clipper Sedan was one of the early all-steel wagons. It had two front doors with sedan delivery type rear doors. Seating capacity was for seven. The total body length was 88 inches, with a 72-inch cargo area behind the driver's seat.

The Essex Depot Car body was probably done by Seaman. Finished in natural wood, it was a closed car design that was never put into production.

Fargo Clipper sedans had many uses, as shown here. This one was intended to be used as a delivery wagon, with a display of the vendor's wares in the quarter windows. The cargo area was 49 inches wide and 47½ inches high.

This Fargo was used as a mini-bus. Complete with rear canopy and roof rack, it ran between Allentown, Pa., and New York City.

A rear view of the Fargo Clipper Sedan. This type of rear door arrangement gave the best access to the rear area. The rear seat could be folded down as shown, or removed altogether for carrying parcels.

A 1930 Ford wagon. This 2-door version was built in Hawaii by a Ford distributor. These woodies were used as "Banana Wagons," to haul crops from field to market. Few survive today. This fine example is owned by Ray Mews of Honolulu.

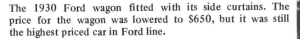

The 1930 Ford wagon fitted with its side curtains. The price for the wagon was lowered to $650, but it was still the highest priced car in Ford line.

The first Ford Sportsman. This 1930 Model A was specially designed and built for Henry Ford II, in the 1940s. It is said that this car gave inspiration to the postwar Ford and Mercury Sportsman convertibles.

A rear view of the Ford wagon with side curtains in place. Note how the curtains fit snug all around. Metal bracing on the body corners and on the tail gate helps to reinforce the body.

The 1930 Ford Station Wagon in a familiar train station setting. The side mounted spare could be ordered for either or both sides. Standard fender and wheel trim was black.

This 1930 Ford would qualify today as a bona fide Woodie. It was one of many such utility vehicles based on the wagon.

A 1930 Hupmobile Model S Station Wagon. This is a custom body with a combination of long horizontal and short vertical ribbing. It is possible that this body was built by the M. P. Moller Co. of Hagerstown, Md.

The 1930 Fargo Freighter. This was an extended version of the Clipper Sedan. Designed primarily for parcel delivery, it could be fitted with seats for bus service.

A Franklin chassis mounted with a Cantrell Suburban body. This was one of many such special bodies created by Cantrell for a prestige chassis.

A drawing of a Cantrell body on a Franklin chassis, by W. J. Josden for the Franklin Club. Only the hood and cowling were of metal, the windshield framing was of wood. This body is very similar to the bodies used on the Dodge chassis.

The popularity of the Station Wagon began to wane by 1931. The depression was taking its toll. Dodge records show only 47 chassis shipped during 1931, for use as wagons, ambulances and funeral cars. Ford was the big wagon builder again this year, but even its production had slipped badly from the previous year. Only 3,000 station wagons were built by Ford in 1931. Even the reduced price of $625 had not helped sales.

Cantrell continued to be the big supplier of wagons for Chrysler and General Motors and was doing some custom jobs for Packard, Hupp, Graham and others. Mifflinburg, Springfield, Hercules, Cotton, York and Martin-Parry were still supplying wagons, but the production was cut drastically. Most of the bodies were custom built jobs.

Then, by the end of 1931, Ford decided it would cease production of station wagon parts at the Iron Mountain plant. In mid-1931, Chevrolet purchased the Martin-Parry Body Co., and turned it into its main truck plant. No more station wagon bodies would be built here, even though station wagons continued to be classed as commercial cars and were usually based on a light truck chassis.

A Dodge chassis fitted with the new Cantrell Suburban body. It featured full frame doors and roll-up curtains that were self-storing on the inside. This new Cantrell body represented a design change. Note the combination of horizontal and vertical ribbing.

A 1931 DeSoto with a Cantrell body. This body was almost identical to the one used on the Dodge chassis. Note the variation in window size in the all-weather side curtains. It is owned by Julius Cegelski of Englishtown, N. J.

A 1931 Hupmobile. The body is possibly one built by the M. P. Moller Co. of Hagerstown, Md. This example is owned by Carl Daniels.

This 1931 Ford woodie is a unique Traveler Wagon. It was available in 1930 and 1931. It resembles a station wagon, but that's its only similarity. This wagon has two doors in the front, the rear tailgate area has doors that are full length and open in the center. The wire mesh screen is fixed with a roll-up curtain on the inside. It sleeps two and has its own water supply via a 10-gallon storage tank, which is filled thorugh the filler pipe on the roof. Photo courtesy of Model A Restorers Club.

This is another specialty Ford wagon. It is called a Special Delivery. It is the same body used for the traveler and made up of many station wagon body components.

This 1931 Ford is a homemade 2-door wagon. The overall design is typical of the era but this one appears to have glass windows. It is owned by Herman Miller of South Bend, Ind.

The 1931 Willys "6" wagon was called the DeLuxe Wagon. The builder is unknown. It is of advanced design with the appearance of an all-steel wagon and fully enclosed— although it was neither.

The 1931 Ford station wagon with side curtain fixed in place. White side wall tires were an option rarely seen in depression years.

The big news for 1932 was the announcement by one of the biggest wagon builders, that for all intents and purposes it would cease wagon production. Mifflinburg suspended production of the Standard Suburban body, confining its building to only truck bodies and some custom station wagons.

For 1932, Ford had contracted with the Mingel Co. of Louisville, Ky., to build its wagon parts. Briggs Manufacturing and Murry Corp. would continue to assemble the bodies in Detroit. Even though wagon sales were dropping, Ford still felt the need to have this type of vehicle in its line. The arrangement with Mingel continued to 1935. Perhaps Henry Ford's fondness for the out-of-doors kept the Ford wagon alive. The author believes it was this steadfastness by Ford that kept the whole wagon concept alive and ultimately made the wagon an important part of the American way of life. It certainly made Ford the leader in wagon production and sales—the undisputed "wagon master."

The 1932 Ford Model B. Body parts for this wagon were made by the Mingel Co. and assembled by either Briggs or Murry in Detroit. The body was finished in natural wood.

This 1932 Chevrolet chassis is fitted with a custom body. The wood framing is covered with sheet metal. The body builder is unknown but the design is very much like a Springfield body, and very much like a body design used on the 1929 Dodge chassis.

The 1933 Dodge chassis with a Cantrell body. The Cantrell body was available on special order, as Dodge had contracted with USB&F to do the bulk of the wagons. The Cantrell body was a combination of vertical and horizontal ribs. The framing was made of ash while the panels were of natural birch. The interiors of the USB&F and the Cantrell were identical.

The depression began to stabilize a little by 1933. Ford wagon sales rose to 2,013 units. Dodge and Plymouth contracted with the U. S. Body and Forging Co. (USB&F) to make wagon bodies in the Tell City, Ind. plant. This arrangement would last till 1941. During this period Cantrell continued to build a limited number of wagons on the Dodge chassis, but these were usually special order jobs.

The USB&F bodies were called Westchester Semi-Sedans. They featured crank-up glass windows in the front doors. This was a significant change in station wagon bodies. Canvas curtains were still being used in the rear doors and quarter windows. Interior panels of the front doors were upholstered like a sedan, while the rear doors and quarter panels were made of plywood. This, of course, was the utility area and subject to cargo loads, so the interior had to be able to take some punishment. There was little or no roof overhang. Rain gutters were added and roofs were crowned—a decided improvement over the flat roofs. Craftsmanship improved as the wagon bodies became more closed. A distinctive mark of the USB&F body was the use of a red gum wood strip at the belt line. The bodies were made of white ash framing with maple panels, all finished in natural wood. Ribbing was all horizontal.

Ford, Dodge and Plymouth continued to be the only auto manufacturers offering the station wagon as part of the total line, although all three classed the wagons as commercial vehicles and showed them in the truck catalogs.

Pictured here is the Dodge Westchester Semi-Sedan with wire wheels. The USB&F bodies were distinctive, with a red gum wood strip at the beltline. This was sort of a trademark. While the USB&F used a piano hinge for its doors, Cantrell bodies did not. Like the Cantrell bodies, the Westchester had suicide doors in front. However, the rear doors opened to the rear on the Westchester, while the Cantrell rear doors were of the suicide type. USB&F bodies were made of white ash with cottonwood panels. The floors were oak, tongue-and-grooved. The entire body was finished in clear spar varnish, inside and out. All exposed iron work was painted tan.

The front doors of the Dodge Westchester were upholstered like a sedan. Only the upholstery was done in imitation leather rather than cloth. The width of the front doors was 24 inches at the top and 32 inches at the bottom. The window was a crank up type. Full length piano hinges supported the door. The front seat was a bench type, with a full framed ridged back seat.

Dodge had contracted with the U. S. Body and Forging Co. of Tell City, Ind., to produce wagon bodies. The cars were called Westchester Semi-Sedans. Front doors had crank-up glass windows, with canvas curtains being used for the remaining openings. The example pictured has artillery wheels. All spares were side mounted.

The middle seats of the 1933 Dodge Westchester were actually bucket seats. Full wagon seating capacity was for seven passengers. The middle seats were removable or could be tilted forward. The rear seat was also removable. Side curtains were rolled up and stored inside. Note the leather door check straps. All seats were upholstered in imitation leather.

The 1933 Ford Station Wagon. The only design change for this year was in the front door. The leading frame member slanted to the front at the bottom, making the door pie-shaped. The pie-shape design was better suited to the flowing line of the front fender and hood. Ribbing was a combination of horizontal and vertical, dividing the panels into small squares. Both framing and panels were of maple. Piano hinges were used for front and rear doors, both of which opened to the front. The body was fully enclosed by means of canvas side curtains. Seating capacity was for eight adults, including the driver. The center and rear seats were removable. Total production for 1933 totaled 2,013 units. It sold for $640.

The 1933 Dodge Westchester tailgate was supported by chains. It was held level with the cargo floor, providing additional load carrying space. The size of the tailgate was 27 inches high, 48 inches long. Inside loading space from the back of the front seat to the tailgate at floor line was 75 inches. Inside width was 50 inches, inside height, floor to center roof, 47 inches.

Station wagons were put to many uses, as evidenced here by this 1933 Ford wagon. Note the solid wheels and super balloon tires, which were needed to negotiate the desert sands. The spare was uniquely mounted, being strapped to the outside of the rear door. This was done on both sides. The dual side mounts are not what a collector would call desirable.

The 1934 Dodge Westchester Semi-Sedan is dressed up in military garb. The entire car, inside and out, was painted in olive drab. The body was unchanged from the previous year. Note that while the civilian version had crank-up glass windows in the front doors, this military version used canvas side curtains all around. These curtains are rolled up and strapped to the inside top rail. Also note the iron grille guard, and tow hooks on the front bumper.

The Ford wagon was little changed for 1934. Framing continued to be made of maple or birch panels. Canvas curtains were still used to weather-proof the car. Ribbing continued to be a combination of horizontal and vertical pieces. Front doors were hinged at the rear, popularly known as suicide doors. They were also pie shaped, the bottoms being wider than the tops. This was to conform with the slant of the windshield and flow of the fender line.

Dodge and Plymouth also used suicide doors in the 1934 wagons. As a matter of fact, the Dodge, Plymouth and Ford wagons closely resembled each other.

The military became interested in station wagons and both Ford and Dodge supplied a number of wagons for the Army. These were painted olive drab and, in the case of Dodge, did not have the crank-up front door windows. Canvas curtains covered all openings.

The Cantrell wagon bodies continued with horizontal and vertical ribbing design. In some cases the framing was made of mahogany with light natural finished panels. And in the case of more expensive chassis such as Pierce-Arrow, glass windows were featured all around. Spare tires continued to be side mounted.

A rear view of the military dressed Dodge wagon. This photo shows the canvas all-weather curtains in place. Front and rear doors were both hinged at the B-post using piano hinges. The wheels are artillery type steel. The spare was mounted on the left front fender only. The wagon could have been used as a troop carrier or converted to an ambulance.

The 1934 Ford Station Wagon was unchanged from the previous year. This picture shows the wagon with its all-weather canvas curtains in place. The canvas side curtains of the Ford had large plastic windows, as compared to the Dodge. Both the front and rear doors were of the suicide type and both were hung with piano hinges. The single sidemount was placed on the right front fender.

This is a Hudson Terraplane with a Cantrell body. The same designed body was fitted to other chassis, such as Dodge. Both doors were hinged at the B-pillar, using simple sedan type hinges. The front door used a crank-up glass window, while canvas side curtains were used elsewhere. It sold for $427.

The 1934 Ford wagon was still classed as a commercial vehicle. The spare was side mounted either on the right or left side, or as an option, on both. The body was a combination of horizontal and vertical ribs forming small squares on the panels. Note the rear bumper on this example. The author is not certain whether or not this was a factory offered option. It was not standard, that much is certain.

A 1934 Pierce-Arrow fitted with a Cantrell body. At this point in time Cantrell went through a phase where it used mahogany framing with light birch panels. The body design of vertical and horizontal ribbing was indicative of Cantrell. Note that it appears that glass is used all around with crank-up windows in the front and rear doors. The spares were sidemounted on either or both sides.

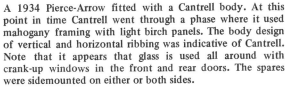

A 1934 Packard wagon. The body builder is unknown, but this may have been a custom Mifflinburg body. Note that glass windows were used all around, with the front door window probably crank-up and the rest sliders. The tailgate appears to have a fixed divided window. The photo is courtesy of the Cormorant magazine.

This is a European Packard wagon, otherwise known as a shooting break. Note that the front doors are metal while the rest of the body is wood. This was typical of European wagons. This is a rare 2-door model. It appears to have glass all around. The photo is courtesy of Patrick Van der Strict, Brussels, Belgium.

A Cantrell body fitted to a Buick chassis. Note the similarity in design to the other Cantrell bodies mounted to other makes of chassis. Both doors opened to the rear, and simple sedan type hinges were used. The spare was side-mounted on either side or both sides. It appears that glass may have been used all around in this body. If so it would have been an advanced design. The framing was mahogany with light birch panels. This wagon sold for $527 plus tax.

A Dodge chassis fitted with a Cantrell body. The body design was similar to that of the previous year. The doors were still hinged at the B-pillar, with the front door being of the suicide type. The spare was sidemounted on the right. There was still no rear bumper. Dark mahogany stained framing and light birch panels were a distinction of the Cantrell body during this period. The use of horizontal and vertical ribbing, in the fashion shown, was also a Cantrell distinction.

The Dodge military station wagon. Dodge was a large supplier of vehicles to the Army. This is a USB&F body. The wood and sheet metal are painted the same olive drab color. Doors were hinged at the B-pillar by way of piano hinges. Note that the military wagon used canvas side curtains all around. The spare is sidemounted on the driver's side on this example. It could be mounted on either side.

In 1935 Ford once again resumed production of Station Wagons at Iron Mountain. All the wood body parts were manufactured by Ford and assembled by Murry in Detroit. The Ford wagon body for this year represented a change. The suicide doors were eliminated. Both front and rear doors opened at the center post. All horizontal ribbing was used—four ribs in all. Framing was of maple, indigenous to the Iron Mountain region. Panels were of maple and/or birch. All wood was finished natural, with a coating of Ford varnish. A crank-up glass window was featured in the front doors, while canvas curtains were used for the rest of the openings.

The Ford wagon remained part of the commercial vehicle line, and its catalog elucidated, "It combines the facilities of a passenger car and a light hauling unit. It carries seven passengers comfortably. The rear seats are quickly and easily removed providing space for carrying baggage."

Dodge and Plymouth continued to offer the Westchester Semi-Sedan. It was said of the Westchester Semi-Sedan Suburban that it was adapted for: Golf Clubs, Hotels, Country Clubs, Country Estates, Suburban Schools, Transfer Lines, and Camping trips. "We can truthfully say there is nothing on the market at anywhere near this price to equal this combination in appearance, riding comfort and more-for-the-dollar-value." A brochure went on to say, "Just as the new, Deluxe Plymouth, with floating power and knee action springs, sets new standards of value, so does the Westchester Semi-Sedan Suburban body represent the greatest achievement in this style of coachcraft."

The Dodge and Plymouth differed in over-all general appearances and specifications, although both were manufactured by USB&F. The Dodge retained the suicide front doors and used its light commercial chassis with light truck front end sheet metal, whereas the Plymouth used passenger car sheet metal. The doors of the Plymouth were hinged at the front for optimum safety.

Chevrolet took a giant leap forward in 1935 and introduced the Suburban Carryall. This was an all new 8-passenger, all-steel, station wagon built on a ½-ton truck chassis. It had the general appearance of a truck. There were two doors, safety glass all around and an unusual rear door. Since most of the sheet metal for the Carryall came from the sedan delivery, the rear door was stamped like that of the sedan delivery. But where the sedan delivery door was hinged at one side, the Carryall door was split in the middle, horizontally. Half raised up, the other half let down, like the tail gate of a standard station wagon.

It is not known just how popular this advanced wagon was, but Chevrolet continues this model even today. It also dispells the popular theories that Plymouth was first with an all-steel wagon in 1949, and the subsequent notion that the Jeep was the first all-steel wagon in 1946. But it does give rise to perhaps a valid argument as to whether or not the 1929 Fargo Picket and Clipper Sedans were in fact the first all-steel station wagons.

Cantrell also referred to its bodies as Semi-Sedans when they included safety glass. The term Suburban Body thus gave way to the Semi-Sedan Suburban Body. Cantrell continued to feature dark framing with light panels.

1935

A Dodge military wagon with a USB&F Westchester body. The side curtains are fastened in place. Note the size of the plastic windows, which are small in comparison to the Ford wagon. The roof was covered with oil cloth. There was no headliner nor any insulation of any kind, making the station wagon somewaht of a challenge to drive in the dead of winter.

A rear view of the Cantrell-bodied Dodge. The canvas side curtains were rolled up and strapped to the inside roll rails when not in use. The second and third seats were removable. This provided greater cargo area. Rear bumpers were still not evident. Note the heavy outside hinges and the outside tailgate locks. These were cast pieces.

The 1935 International Model C-1 Station Wagon. The body builder is unknown. The body was of the horizontal rib design. It is not known, but it appears that the front doors had crank-up glass windows and the rest of the openings used canvas curtains. This would be in keeping with general industry practice. A single spare was sidemounted on the right.

The Plymouth Westchester Semi-Sedan, with body by USB&F. Note the tell-tale identifying red gum wood strip in the belt line, a trademark of USB&F. Both front and rear doors opened to the rear. The second and third seats were removable. The spare was sidemounted, and this one is covered with imitation leather as an option. The body looked more updated as compared with the Dodge wagon.

The 1935 Ford Station Wagon body design was new for this year. Four horizontal ribs were used instead of the combination of horizontal and vertical. The front doors had crank-up glass windows, while the rest of the openings used canvas and plastic windows. But the canvas was merely an edging or border for the very large plastic windows. The doors opened at the B-pillar and were hinged with piano hinges.

A rear view of the 1935 Plymouth wagon, showing side curtains in place. The front doors had crank-up glass windows. Plymouth doors opened to the rear while Dodge still maintained the suicide door. Note that no rear bumper was used. This was common practice.

A Chevrolet with a Cantrell body with dark mahogany framing and light panels. This body featured suicide front doors with crank-up glass windows. In order to achieve a more aerodynamic sedan design, the roof was sloped forward and tapered off at the rear.

The 1936 Chevrolet Carryall was unchanged except for hood louvers. It was once again available as a 2-door only. Chrome headlamps were an option. The Carryall was classed as a truck.

A 1936 Chevrolet version of an early camper. Mounted on the series RD 1½ ton chassis, this was a completely self-contained unit.

The year 1936 marked the entry of Hudson into the station wagon field, with its introduction of the Terraplane Station Wagon. Hudson reached peak production this year and all its models were equipped with "Duo-Automatic" safety brakes.

Dodge wagons bore passenger car sheet metal for 1936. Plymouth and Dodge shared the same Westchester USB&F bodies with safety glass windows all around. Ford wagons remained unchanged. All station wagons were still considered commercial vehicles. International Harvester continued to offer a station wagon. International never left the wagon field and today still offers the Traveler Wagon. The 1936 version was a woodie with roll-up glass door windows. The rest of the openings were covered with canvas curtains. Bodies for International Harvester were provided by M. P. Moller of Hagerstown, Md., Baker-Rawling of Cleveland, and Burket Co. of Dayton, Ohio. The 1936 wagon sold for $745.

Wagons were again put to strange uses in 1936 and some strange versions of the wagon emerged. A case in point was a Dodge-built special wagon to be used on safari. It sported 19-inch truck wheels and tires, metal storage cases over the rear fenders, a sun roof, spotlight and an animal guard in front of the radiator grill.

Derham, the custom body builder of Rosemont, Pa. custom built a station wagon for George W. Elkins of a Philadelphia suburb bearing his name. This wagon was based on the Packard 120 chassis. It was officially known as the "120-B Sport Station Wagon." Utilizing the sedan front end and rear fenders, the body was done in sheet metal over wood, finished in black, with a Derham padded roof and caning at the belt line. It also included a roof rack, which was reached by means of a ladder attached to the rear bumper at the bottom and the rack at the top. A single sedan delivery type door opened at the rear, hinged to one side.

A 1936 Dodge Westchester Semi-Sedan. The body was by USB&F. The spare was sidemounted on either the right or left fender. Front and rear doors opened to the rear. Both were hung with piano hinges. Note the use of glass all around, except the tailgate. It still had no rear bumper. The Dodge station wagon was still classed as a commercial vehicle.

A three-quarter front view of the Dodge Westchester wagon with body by USB&F. This body builder still used the red gum wood strip at the belt line to readily identify its bodies. The single windshield wiper was standard, but a second wiper was available as an option.

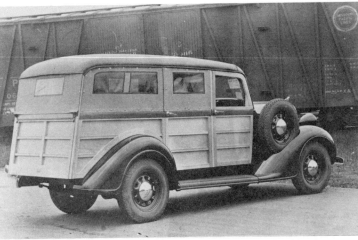

The 1936 Dodge Westchester, with canvas side fixed in place. Note how much smaller the plastic windows are in the Dodge as compared to the Ford wagons. The roof was fabric covered. The tailgate hinges were hidden while the tailgate locks were exposed. Only one tail light was standard, and it was found on the left side.

A 1936 Dodge Westchester fitted as a Safari wagon. Starting with a basic wagon body, many extras and alterations were added. Note the extra large 19-inch wheels. These were usually found on Dodge's Roadking models designed for rural and backwoods use. A military type grille guard and front bumper were used, as were dual sidemounts, a spotlight and custom fabricated tool or storage compartment over the rear wheel.

A rear view of the Dodge Safari wagon gives a detailed view of the storage compartment. Note that the front door uses simple sedan type hinges, while the rear doors are hung with piano hinges. The canvas curtains were standard wagon curtains.

The Dodge Safari wagon contained an interesting version of a sun roof. The canvas side curtains were used only on the quarter windows and tailgate. The front and rear doors had glass crank-up windows. The sliding roof panel appears to have been designed either as a camera or gun port.

Ford now offered crank-up glass windows in the front doors as standard equipment. The rest of the openings were covered with canvas curtains. Glass for these openings was optional at an additional cost of $50. This fine example is owned by Charles Bennett of Lomita, Calif. Photo courtesy of Ford V-8 Times.

The 1936 Ford all-steel wagon on a commercial light truck chassis. It was a competitor for the Chevrolet Carryall. This is a Proctor-Keefe body. It was officially called a Utility Wagon. Glass was featured all around, but only the front door glass was movable. Note the unusual rear door treatment, somewhat of an early attempt at a "door-gate."

The 1936 Oldsmobile Station Wagon with body by USB&F. Note the distinctive gum wood strip at the belt line. Crank-up glass windows were standard in the front doors, with canvas curtains for the rest of the openings. The body is very similar to the Plymouth wagon.

The International Harvester Station Wagon, 1936 version, had crank-up windows in the front doors. Bodies were supplied by M. P. Moller, Baker-Rawling and the Burket Co. of Dayton, Ohio.

A rear view of the 1936 International Harvester Station Wagon. Front doors opened to the rear, while the rear doors opened to the front. The front door used a sedan type hinge, while the rear door used a piano hinge on the C-pillar. Side curtains were mounted on the inside, except for the tailgate. The tailgate had hidden hinges. No rear bumper was used, which was common practice for the era. It also had a single stop and tail light.

An interior view of the Plymouth wagon. The front seat area looks much like a sedan, while the rear seat is very rustic. This model has the optional glass all around. The front door window is crank-up but the rear door had sliding glass.

The Plymouth Semi-Sedan with body by USB&F. The spare was fender-mounted on the right side as standard, left side as optional. The front door crank-up glass was standard, with glass all around as optional.

A 1936 Packard wagon built by the Derham Co. of Rosemont, Pa., for George W. Elkins. The body is steel over a wood frame. It featured caning at the belt line, a leather roof, roof rack and a ladder to reach it. Note the dip of the front door, which may indicate that this wagon was intended to be driven by a chauffeur. Photo courtesy of the Cormorant.

A 1936 Studebaker Dictator shooting break. This European version of the station wagon was photographed in Belgium by Patrick Van der Strict. The shooting break utilized the metal front doors of the sedan, as well as about a third of the sedan roof. The wooden body was then custom blended into the sedan's original design. It appears that this model has been subjected to some pretty sloppy bodywork around the windshield frame — obviously done long after the car was turned loose from its original builder.

The first year for a Terraplane Station Wagon was 1936. It was also the year Hudson reached its production pinnacle. All models were equipped with safety brakes. The body builder for this wagon was probably the Seaman Co. Photo courtesy of American Motors.

GMC introduced its all new 8-passenger Suburban Car. This was the same wagon Chevrolet marketed as the Carryall, only the name was changed. This policy prevails even today, as GMC and Chevrolet trucks share the same sheet metal, with only the trim being different.

Chevrolet's Carryall had a new body for 1937. The roof panel was now all-steel. Unlike the previous year, the new model resembled the passenger car line in appearance. The riding quality of the Carryall was improved through the use of shock absorbers and oversized low-pressure tires. A large number of these wagons were produced for the armed forces.

In addition to the Carryall, Chevrolet also announced a new "Woodie" Carryall. Chevrolet had contracted with Hercules to build the bodies. Cantrell still produced bodies for the passenger car chassis. Even though a major part of their production was for Chevrolet, Cantrell continued to build custom wagon bodies for other makes.

Ford began assembling its own station wagons at its Iron Mountain facility. Thus Ford became the first auto manufacturer to build and assemble its own wagons. The Ford wagon was still classed as a commercial vehicle. This year glass windows were offered as an option all around. Needless to say, more wagons were so equipped. The price of the wagon with glass all around was $775. The spare tire was moved from the front fender to the tailgate.

Dodge and Plymouth sported the same wagon bodies. They were still being supplied by USB&F, with the tell-tale red gum wood belt line strip. Safety glass was optional all around, being standard only in the front doors. All bodies were built of white ash framing and birch panels finished in natural wood.

Studebaker introduced a station wagon for the first time. The bodies were supplied by U. S. Body & Forge Co. of Buffalo, N. Y., from the Tell City, Ind. plant. These were the same Semi-Sedans used by both Dodge and Plymouth.

Packard contracted with Cantrell in 1937 to build station wagon bodies. So, for the first time Packard began offering factory built wagons as part of the line. Two wagons were offered, one on the 120 chassis and one on the new 115-C chassis. This was the company's new 110 model. The 110 wagon listed at $1,300, while the 120 went for $1,500.

The Dodge wagon body for 1937 was virtually identical to the Plymouth. This version shows the optional glass all around. The spare was still fender-mounted on the right side.

Chevrolet introduced an all new body for the Carryall this year. The 112-inch wheelbase wagon continued to be classed as a truck. A large number of these were purchased by the military.

This Dodge wagon was owned by Clark Gable, the movie superstar. Its features included dual side mounts with covers, a spotlight, dual wipers, extra front bumper guards and super balloon tires on oversized rims.

A rear view of the Clark Gable Dodge wagon. The body was by USB&F. Unlike the Cantrell body, the tailgate window was divided. Only the large section of the quarter window was movable. Note the tailgate and lift gate were supported by folding arms. The spotlight was an option, as was the spare tire cover. The rear door has a leatherette trim panel and crank-up window.

Wagons were special order for many uses. Here a Dodge wagon with USB&F Westchester body is destined for export to South America. The entire body and sheet metal were painted white. Except for the paint job, this wagon appears to be a stock domestic station wagon, again with no rear bumper.

A 1937 Dodge with a Cantrell body. This woodie was made into a sedan delivery by blocking out the quarter window. Note that Cantrell used mahogany only for the belt line member. Glass was featured in front and rear doors. Both doors opened to the rear and were hung with sedan-type hinges. The extra long overhang would indicate that this body was special ordered for the purpose it was put to, rather than a conversion of a standard wagon. The dinner bell grille guard was an option.

The Packard Six wagon was designated the 115-C. The body was by Cantrell. Front and rear doors opened at the B-pillar. Glass was featured all around, with crank-up windows in the doors and a slider in the quarters. The spare was tailgate mounted. This was not a production model, but was available on special order.

This Packard wagon is a one-off, homemade version. It was built on a 120 chassis by Robert S. Heebner in 1941. Mr. Heebner was a former Packard dealer. Note that this is a 2-door wagon made to look like a 4-door.

This unique Packard wagon was used by the Packard company as a mail car. It is a 2-door version with a paneled quarter window. The body builder is unknown. It's possible that this was a prototype.

The 1937 Ford wagon. Front and rear doors opened at the B-pillar. The spare was mounted on the outside of the tailgate. Seating capacity was for 8 passengers. Seats could be removed to increase the cargo area. While most of its competitors were featuring a one-piece windshield, Ford continued with the two-piece set-up.

Glass windows all around were optional on Ford wagons this year. The windshield and front doors had safety glass while the rest of the wagon used plate glass. Only the front door was a crank-up type window. The rear door and quarter window was a slider. The front door opened to the rear, but the rear door opened to the front. Piano hinges were used on the rear door, while sedan-type hinges were used on the front door.

This Ford wagon has optional glass windows all around. This year the spare was moved from the front fender to the tailgate. This practice would continue into the 1950's.

This 1937 Ford wagon was exported to Europe and was eventually photographed by Patrick Van der Strict of Brussels, Belgium. It carries unusual little fender parking lights, which were mandatory in England, and is equipped with right-hand drive.

This crumpled up Ford wagon was obviously owned by some governmental agency. The wood body was painted the same color as the sheet metal. The spare tire has an unusual mounting place. The custom grille work was done by the 1946 Buick convertible in the background.

A 1937 DeSoto fitted with a Cantrell body. The common practice for Cantrell during this period was to use mahogany framing with light birch panels. Glass was featured all around, with the doors having crank-up windows while the quarter window was a slider and the tailgate window fixed. The spare was sidemounted on the right front fender. Note the rear bumper and typical sedan-type tail light.

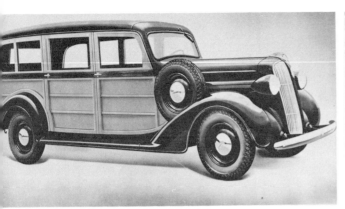

This was the year Plymouth introduced defroster vents. Wagon bodies were still being supplied by USB&F. Note that in this photo the artist mistakenly air brushed a continuation of the wood behind the spare tire. This model has the optional glass all around.

This Plymouth wagon is outfitted for some sort of expedition. Note the screened-in area, possibly to keep in or out wild animals. The body was a USB&F Westchester. There are dual sidemounts with optional metal covers. Tool boxes and roof carrier have been added.

Pontiac entered the wagon field this year with the introduction of this model. The body was by Hercules. Glass was featured all around, with safety glass in the windshield and front doors. Front and rear doors had crank-up windows, while the quarter windows were sliders. Both front and rear doors opened to the rear. Sedan-type hinges were used on all doors. Body framing was made of white ash.

The 1937 Studebaker featured airplane type shock absorbers and a Fram oil cleaning system. Wagon bodies were supplied by USB&F. Glass all around was standard.

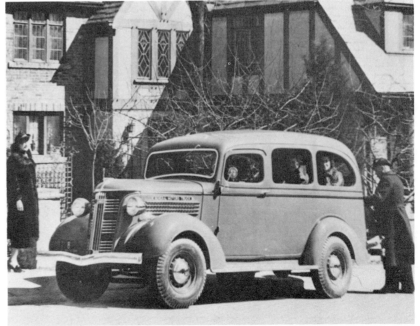

The GMC Suburban Car was unchanged from the previous year. This was a Chevrolet body with GMC name plates and trim. The name plate on the hood reads "General Motors Truck." Seating capacity was for eight. This wagon was only offered as a 2-door model.

The Chevrolet Carry-all continued unchanged for 1938 except for the nifty two tone paint jobs and the spelling of its name, now a hyphenated word. It used a 112-inch wheelbase, had a 77-inch load space, and was almost 46 inches wide. Unlike other commercial chassis, it was equipped with shock absorbers.

For 1938 Ford offered glass windows all around as standard equipment. The front doors had crank-up glass while the others were sliding. Doors opened at the center. This body was new for the year. It was built of hardwood at Ford's Iron Mountain, Mich. plant.

In 1938 Mifflinburg still turned out a custom wagon body. But these were getting fewer. Ford featured safety glass all around as standard on all station wagons. The station wagon was finally a closed car. Ford set a production record for wagons—having produced 6,000 wagons for the calendar year.

This was the first year that Dodge considered the station wagon as a passenger car. It also marked the last year for a pre-war Dodge wagon. Both Plymouth and Dodge had new bodies for 1938. They had a strong resemblance to a Cantrell design for that year. The distinctive red gum wood strip, which readily identified the USB&F body, was gone. Only Chrysler's export truck, Fargo, was available with the body that still carried the strip, and only because the body was of the earlier 1936-37 design. Dodge and Plymouth no longer called the wagon Semi-Sedans. They were simply known as station wagons. Dodge built 375 wagons in 1938, while Plymouth, which still classed the wagon as a commercial vehicle, produced 555 units. Location of the spare tire was optional, either fender or on the tailgate.

Cantrell provided Packard with wagon bodies once again. The company offered two models, the 110 and the 120. The 110, the 6-cylinder model, used a 122-inch wheelbase, while the 8-cylinder model 120 used a 127 inch wheelbase.

Chevrolet's all-steel Carryall was unchanged, except for the name, which was now hyphenated. The woodie version of the Carry-all continued to be built by Hercules. Hercules and Cantrell built the station wagon bodies for the Chevrolet passenger car line.

Studebaker, for the second year in a row, offered a wagon with a body by USB&F. The spare was fender mounted on the right side. Glass was available all around. The body design was a little unusual in that the header above the windshield was wider than on other wagons.

This Packard is fitted with a custom body by Mifflinburg. Framing was ash while the panels were mahogany. Both front and rear doors opened to the rear. Doors were hung on sedan-type hinges. Glass was used all around. The doors had crank-up windows while sliders were used in the quarter windows. The tailgate used fixed glass. The length of the body and the narrow doors provided the two quarter windows. The seating, however, was not increased, but a substantial amount of extra luggage space was provided.

Studebaker continued to use the USB&F body. Glass was standard all around. The spare, unlike many of its competitors, was fender-mounted. The Studebaker wagon was distinctive with its high windshield header section or high forehead, if you will. The welled right front fender was also used on the Studebaker's coupe-pickup in this era.

A 1938 Dodge wagon such as this was used by villains in Republic Pictures serials "Captain America." It appeared specifically in Chapter 14. This fine example was owned by Roaring 20's Autos of Wall, N. J.

The Dodge Westchester Semi-Sedan continued to use a USB&F body, but the overall design was new. The distinctive red gum wood belt line strip was gone, door ribs were spread further apart, and the spare was moved to the tailgate. Glass all around was optional. Front and rear doors used crank-up windows. while the quarter windows were sliders. Framing was white ash with birch panels. A total of 375 units were built. This also marked the last year for a production Dodge wagon until 1949.

This view of the Dodge shows its luggage carrying capacity. With the placement of the tail lights at the beltline, the only place left for the license plate holder was on the roof.

A rear view of the Dodge wagon shows that Dodge placed its tail lights at the beltline, while Plymouth put them at the bottom of the rear fender line. Like the Plymouth, the spare was moved from the front fender to the tailgate. No rear bumper was used. The license plate was roof-mounted above the rear window.

Only Chrysler's export truck Fargo continued to use the USB&F body with the red gum wood strip. This was a body of earlier design, built in 1936-37. It still used canvas side curtains, except for the front doors, and a fender-mounted spare.

Plymouth's all new Westchester wagon for 1938. The bodies were still supplied by USB&F, but the distinctive red gum wood strip was gone. Note the one piece windshield. The wipers have now been moved to the base of the windshield.

The 1938 Plymouth wagon with standard canvas curtains in place. The divider strip in the quarter windows was a wire stiffener which was sewn into the canvas. The Plymouth wagon body was the same body used by Dodge. The spare was moved to the tailgate, but it still had no rear bumper. A crank-up glass window was standard in the front door.

A rear view of the Plymouth wagon. This example has optional glass in the rear doors and quarter windows. The front door glass was standard. The quarter window and rear door window were both sliders. A canvas cover was still used for the tailgate. A single tail light was standard, but a second light could be ordered. However, there still was no rear bumper.

This example of the Plymouth wagon shows optional glass all around, including the tailgate. Both front and rear doors opened to the rear. The rear doors were hung on piano hinges and the front doors on sedan-type hinges. Tailgate hinges were hidden and the tailgate lock was operated by a single "T" handle on the outside.

THE STATION WAGON

The Pontiac station wagon for 1938 was unchanged. Glass was featured all around. The spare was mounted on the tailgate. Both doors opened to the rear, and were hung on sedan-type hinges. The body was built by Hercules. Framing was ash with birch panels.

The big news this year was the introduction of Chevrolet's first production wagon. For the first time, Chevrolet offered a wagon as part of its regular line. The wagons were classed as commercial vehicles, but were advertised as part of the passenger car line. Two new models were offered for 1939. The Master DeLuxe and the Master "85". They sold for $883 and $848 respectively. At least three body builders supplied wagon bodies to Chevrolet this year — Cantrell, Hercules and Ionia Manufacturing of Ionia, Mich. Apparently Chevrolet must have anticipated selling a large volume of wagons; henceforth the three suppliers.

Pontiac and Oldsmobile also offered production wagons, using the same body as Chevrolet. While the Chevrolet spare was side-mounted, Pontiac and Olds offered optional spare mounting. All bodies were fully enclosed and weatherstripped, approximating the sedan as closely as possible.

U. S. Body & Forge was now supplying bodies for the Willys station wagon. Cantrell for the last year built Packard wagons. Again two model Packards were offered. A total of 500 were built. The Cantrell Packard wagon for 1939 was a bit unusual in that it was built of mahogany framing and maple panels. This was the only year such a Packard wagon was offered.

Ford offered two wagons for 1939 — the Standard, which sold for $840, and the DeLuxe, which sold for $920. Production at Iron Mountain rose to 7,500 units. Once again Ford was the Wagon Master, King of the Woodies.

Dodge had no wagon for this year. Only one prototype was built and it never saw production. It was a most attractive wagon. Plymouth had another new body this year. It was probably built at Chrysler's newly acquired Pekin Wood Products Co. at Helena, Ark., and assembled at the Lynch Road assembly plant in Detroit. Plymouth was the last wagon manufacturer to offer canvas side curtains. There was probably some demand for them in warmer climates. Plymouth was now the second auto maker to build and assemble its own wagon, Ford being the first. The location of the spare on the Plymouth wagon was once again optional. Framing was of white ash with non-contrasting panels of birch.

This 1939 Chevrolet wagon was the first factory offered wagon by Chevrolet. The units were classed as commercial vehicles and at least three body builders supplied these wagons. This is an Ionia body.

This Chevrolet wagon has a Hercules body. Note that Hercules used only one horizontal rib, whereas Cantrell and Ionia used two. Glass all around was standard. The spare was fender-mounted on the right side on all Chevrolet wood wagons.

Chevrolet continued to offer the all-steel Suburban Carry-all. It was again unchanged. Seating capacity was for 9 passengers. Only the 2-door model was available. Glass was featured all around, with crank-up windows in the front doors. The rear bumper was standard. The chassis for this wagon was the ½-ton commercial light truck chassis. A similar wagon with identical body was offered by GMC.

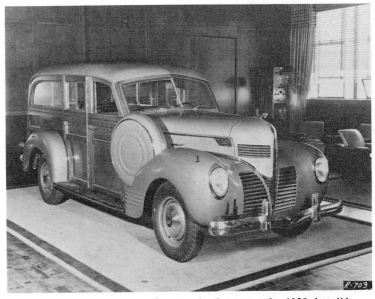

Dodge did not offer a production wagon for 1939, but did build this prototype. The wood body was by USB&F. It made a very attractive wagon, with its metal covered side-mounted spare, and looked even better with dual side-mounts. Both doors opened to the rear. Seating capacity was for 8 passengers.

Glass windows all around was a feature of this Dodge prototype wagon. The tail light was mounted on the wood body frame. The rear door and quarter windows were sliders and the front door had crank-up windows. This prototype also included a rear bumper, which was a standard feature of the Plymouth wagon. As a matter of fact this body and that one used by Plymouth were identical. Note that the rear door is a little narrower than the front door.

An inside view of the Dodge prototype wagon. The dash was wood grained. Note the floor-mounted starter above the gas pedal. The sun visor looks padded. Among the other interesting features are the open wood ribbing without headliner and the visible metal plate braces and angle irons.

Ford used the same body as in the previous year. Two models were offered—the Standard and the DeLuxe. This is the DeLuxe, with optional white wall tires. This fine example belongs to William B. MacGreger Jr. of Medfield, Mass.

This is a 1939 Ford all-steel Utility Wagon with a body by Proctor-Keefe. It was classed as a truck. Three seats were fitted in this model to accommodate up to nine passengers. The spare was sidemounted, but not in the front fender. Only this two-door model was offered. The back doors opened like a sedan delivery instead of the conventional wagon tail/liftgate.

The 1939 Ford Standard Station Wagon. Ford offered two wagons this year, the Standard and the DeLuxe. Both were 4-door 8-passenger models. Front and rear doors opened at the B-pillar. The windshield and front door glass was safety while the other glass was plate. Rear doors and quarter windows were sliders. The Standard wagons sold for $840.

Packard built a total of 500 wagons in 1939. They were offered in two series, the 110 and 120. Cantrell continued to be the factory supplier. Pictured here is a mahogany frame and birch panel body which was a typical Cantrell offering. Glass was featured all around. The quarter windows were sliders, while the front and rear doors had crank-up windows. Photo courtesy of The Cormorant.

The spare on the Plymouth wagon was once again moved to the front fender, and a rear bumper was added. But Plymouth failed to make glass all around as standard. Side curtains, as shown here, were still available, but by now were not very popular. The license plate bracket and light were hinged so the plate would be somewhat visible when the tailgate was lowered.

Plymouth for 1939 had a new body. A single, thicker, horizontal rib was used, much like on the Ford body. The rear end of the body had a convex shape, with the bottom of the tailgate curving under. It appeared a little more streamlined.

With the introduction of its 1939 wagon, Pontiac lowered the price by $120. There was more than one supplier of wood bodies to Pontiac. The body pictured here is by Hercules. The framing is of white ash, with mahogany panels. Both doors opened to the rear, and were hung with sedan-type hinges in the front and piano-type in the rear.

The 1939 Pontiac station wagon with a body by Hercules. Note the rear bumper has by now become somewhat standard in the industry. The spare was tailgate mounted. Metal arms supported the tail and liftgates. The Pontiac station wagon now listed at $990 F.O.B. Pontiac, Mich.

A Pontiac wagon with an Ionia body. Compare this body with the Hercules offering. The Ionia body featured two more horizontal ribs than the Hercules. The framing was ash with birch panels. This gave little to no contrast, which was a big change from the Hercules body. Although the detail difference can be noted, the overall basic features of the Pontiac wagon was the same no matter which body was used. They were all 4-door 8-passenger wagons with glass all around, a tailgate mounted spare and doors that opened to the rear.

A 1939 Studebaker with body by Peter McAvoy and Sons. Note the single horizontal rib and contrasting beltline strip, much like the USB&F body. The spare was tailgate-mounted. Glass was standard all around.

The world was changing in 1940. Hitler was waging war in Europe, Japan had invaded China. Back home the auto industry was accepting more and more defense contracts. The war machine was beginning to roll. These were truly unsettled times.

In the world of station wagons it was business as usual. And a booming year for wagons it was. Glass became standard all around in most wagons. The troublesome spare, or rather the problem of where to put it, was being moved inside. Side mounts were disappearing because of body sheet metal changes, which made them impractical. The tailgate spare had a weight problem. But even the inside spare presented a problem—one of space. The spare continues to give auto makers a problem even today, and there is still talk and speculation of doing away with it altogether.

Plymouth once again presented a new body for 1940.

This year marked Buick's entry into the station wagon market with this first factory-offered wagon. This was Buick's Model 59 Estate Wagon, available only in the Super series. Optional spotlight and road lights are featured on this fine example which is owned by Frank Hamusek of Yorba Linda, Cal.

Buick and Oldsmobile shared bodies this year. These were either supplied by Ionia or Hercules. The framing was of ash, with mahogany panels. The roof was fabric covered. Front and rear doors had crank-up windows. The quarter windows were sliders. The doors had concealed hinges. A total of 495 were built and sold for $1,242. This is another view of Frank Hamusek's fine car.

Both USB&F and Chrysler's own Pekin Wood Produc supplied the body for assembly by Plymouth. It was t first year Plymouth classed the wagon as a passeng vehicle. It was usually advertised along with the spor convertible. Plymouth was trying to convey the image the wagon as a utility and recreation vehicle. Glass around had finally become standard. The spare w moved from outside the car into a unique compartme built into the back of the front seat. This proved to be handy place to put the spare, or so it seemed. It wou remain there through 1948.

The big change in body design for Plymouth was the doors. The front door was made narrower, the cent post was moved a little forward leaving the rear door little narrower and straight. The back frame of the re door did not follow the contour of the rear fender's leadi edge. The piano hinge continued to be used on the re door and the tailgate.

Ford also had a new body for this year. The leading ed of the front window frame was rounded at the to eliminating a sharp butt joint. This same procedure w used on the upper rear quarter window. The horizont ribbing was lowered and the rib on the rear quarter pan was eliminated. The full length paino hinge continued be used on the rear door, but all doors now opened to th rear. The spare was tailgate mounted. It was a boom ye for Ford wagons — a total of 13,199 were built. This w up almost 5,700 units from the previous year. Of the tw models offered, the Standard looked like the 1939 mode while the DeLuxe looked new.

Over at General Motors, Oldsmobile and Buick intr duced factory wagons. Ionia continued to be the b supplier of wagon bodies to GM, along with Hercules an Cantrell. Cantrell supplied only Chevrolet bodies. Ion and Hercules supplied the bodies for assembly by Fish Body Division, while Cantrell built up the whole car. Th Buick Model 59 Estate Wagon was available only in th Super Series. A total of 495 wagons were built fo domestic consumption and six were made for export. Th Buick wagon sold for $1,242. The spare on the Buic wagon was moved inside, into a special designed compar ment that was hidden below the tailgate. The spare wa accessible without opening the tailgate.

The Buick Estate Wagon weighed 3,870 lbs. This wagon was available only in the Super Series. Whitewall tires were optional at extra cost. Note the roof top antenna. Rear fender skirts were also optional and very popular during this period.

Oldsmobile's wagon offering was available on the 70 ries. Wagon bodies of both Buick and Oldsmobile were most identical and both were supplied by Ionia. Pontiac odies on the other hand were supplied by both Ionia and ercules. The inside spare compartment however, was a uick exclusive. The Olds spare was tailgate mounted. Chevrolet wagon sales soared in 1940. A total of 2,904 its were built — 411 in the Master 85 series and 493 in the Special DeLuxe model. Of the Special DeLuxe odels, 367 of these were special ordered with double ar doors instead of the conventional tailgate. The odies were built of white ash and natural birch panels. ats were upholstered in brown leatherette or optional nuine leather. The roof was covered with a brown bberized material. Chevrolet also offered the all-steel rry-all Suburban wagon.

Packard contracted with Hercules to build its wagon odies, although some custom wagons were still built by ntrell. Two series of wagons were again available, the 0 and 120. Some 160 Series were built, but these would ve been custom wagons. A couple of these 160 wagons e in existence today.

Studebaker no longer offered a production wagon, and ould not have another wagon until 1954. Willys Overland troduced a wagon this year in the American series. It as called the Town and Country. This gives rise to all nds of speculation as to who originated the Town and ountry name plate. Chrysler's Town and Country was year away. But then there is evidence that this name ppeared on some drawings of a prototype Dodge wagon, rca 1939. Maybe Willys lifted the name. If so, it didn't em to bother Chrysler. They went ahead with it in 941 and made it synonymous with Chrysler. Anyway, olumbia had already used the name in 1901 on its two-assenger runabout (*70 Years of Chrysler*, Pg. 17).

Crosely Motors introduced a wagon this year — a two-oor model, which featured steel doors. Wood was used the rear quarter and tailgate section. The tailgate was tually two doors that opened like a sedan delivery. The oors had two small oval shaped windows. Framing and anel sections were finished natural and the roof was bric covered. With the exception of the rear doors, all indows were of the sliding type.

The Buick wagon spare tire fit snugly into a special compartment under the tailgate. The tail light and license bracket was hinged so that it would be visible when riding with the tailgate lowered.

An inside view of the Buick cargo area. Note that the cargo area is carpeted, which sets the Buick wagon in a luxury class. The spare was located in a compartment below the cargo floor and accessible from the outside. There was a single tail/stop light, which was hinged to hang level in full view when the gate was lowered. The tailgate was supported by a chain, while the liftgate was supported by folding arms.

The Chevrolet wagon was available either on the Special DeLuxe or Master 85 chassis. Bodies were supplied by Hercules, Ionia and Cantrell. This is a Cantrell body. Roof material was brown leatherette. The spare was tailgate mounted. The panels were natural finish birch plywood. Genuine leather seats were available at extra cost.

Chevrolet continued to offer the Suburban Carry-all wagon in two-door style with tailgate or sedan delivery rear doors. The rear seats were detachable when a cargo vehicle was desired.

The Crosley wagon used steel doors with wood only in the quarters and tailgate. Sliding glass was used all around. The roof was fabric covered.

The 1940 International wagon featured glass all around. This appears to be a Hercules or Cantrell body. The excellent example is owned by Neil Caswell of Milwaukee.

Ford offered two wagons this year, a DeLuxe and a Standard model. This is the Standard. The bodies of both were the same, but the front sheet metal was different. The Standard looked similar to the 1939 model. Both doors opened to the rear. The front door was hung by sedan-type hinges and the rear by a piano hinge.

The Ford DeLuxe wagon sold for $950. A record 13,199 units were built this year. Bumper wing tips, fog lights and whitewall tires are optional. This example belongs to Chuck Eichenberg of St. Petersburg, Fla.

Another view of the Ford DeLuxe wagon. This was a new body for Ford. All doors opened to the rear. The center rib was lowered and the rear quarter rib was eliminated.

Rear view of the Ford Standard model wagon. Front doors had crank-up windows while the rear doors and quarter windows had sliders. The spare was tailgate mounted. The side view mirror was mounted as part of the door hinge. The Standard sold for $875.

The Oldsmobile wagon was part of the "70" Series. It was available in Standard and DeLuxe trim. The interior made the difference between the two models. The roof was fabric covered, but this was conventional thoroughout the industry. Note the extra wide framing member over the rear fender.

A rear view of the Oldsmobile wagon. The front doors were hung with exposed sedan-type hinges. The rear doors used a piano hinge as did the tailgate. Only a single tail/stop light was featured and it was hinged. Note how the rear bumper and lower body frame member is cut out to accommodate the spare when the gate was lowered. The spare was enclosed in a metal case.

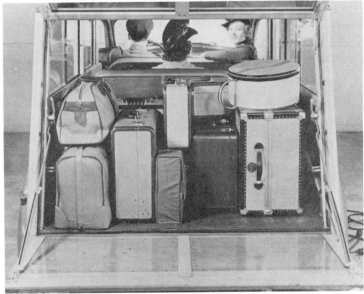

This view of the Oldsmobile clearly shows the utility of the wagon. Note how the tailgate when lowered lays level, through the use of folding arms held in place by the tension spring on the right side.

An interior view of the Oldsmobile wagon shows the narrow width of the second seat, which provided a walkway to the third seat. Note the raised platform of the cargo area, needed to clear rear axle travel.

Here is a rare one-off Packard wagon. This 1940 model was custom built by the New England Auto Body Works of New Haven, Conn., for a Mirko Paneyko. It is mounted on a 120 chassis. The cost of the wagon was $1,895. The spare was fender mounted on the right side. The present owner is Nils Skog. Photo courtesy of the Packard Club.

A Packard 110 with a Hercules body. Packard had switched from Cantrell to Hercules this year. The move was probably due to the location of the Hercules plant, which was in Evansville, Ind. Note the dark framing. This followed the Cantrell concept. The door windows were crank-up and the quarter windows were sliders. The spare was placed inside.

Note the difference in width of the doors on this Hercules bodied Packard. The dark framing and overall design strongly resembled Cantrell. Hercules, of Henderson, Ky., still builds truck bodies, mostly for General Motors.

This Packard 160 has a custom Cantrell body. Note the use of mahogany framing and light panels. This fine example is owned by Ken Price of Maize, Kansas.

Note the sleekness of the Brooks Stevens design. The all-steel roof panel was pioneered in this design, but put into production by Chrysler in 1941 with the Town and Country car. This custom Packard also has a spotlight, outside mounted air horn, and a single fog light. Photo courtesy of Brooks Stevens.

A 1940 Packard wagon with a Brooks Stevens design body. The design of the body is along the lines of the European shooting break. Photo courtesy of Brooks Stevens.

Unlike the wagons of the era, this Brooks Stevens design Packard wagon had a rounded rear end, in keeping with the flow of the fender line and proving that wagons did not have to be boxes. Photo courtesy of Brooks Stevens.

This was the first year Plymouth considered the station wagon a passenger car. It was advertised in this setting as "Plymouth's thrilling new Sportsman."

An interior view of the cargo area in the Plymouth wagon. With the second seat removed the wagon could carry as much as a sedan delivery. This is the feature that appealed to florists, hardware stores, etc. The quarter and rear door windows were sliders. The tailgate was supported by folding arms. This view also shows the spare tire compartment in the back of the front seat. The hump in the center of the cargo floor was necessary for axle travel.

Plymouth's new body for 1940 featured narrower front and rear doors. The rear door did not have a dog leg as in the previous year's models.

The rear seat area of the Plymouth wagon clearly shows the spare tire compartment behind the front seat. Note the close roof ribbing, typical of the era's wagons.

Wagons were adaptable to almost every purpose. Here is a Plymouth wagon being used as a demonstration vehicle. Note the DeLuxe grille guard option.

This Plymouth is shown with its second and third seats removed. By doing this the cargo area was greatly increased to almost the capacity of a panel delivery truck.

A detail view of the Plymouth wagon, showing the roof corner bracing, and tailgate latch. Beautiful woodwork was evident in these wagon bodies.

The roof of the Pontiac body was arched quite high, which accounted for the sharp cut of the front door window frame. Pictured here is an Ionia body.

Pontiac wagon bodies were supplied by Hercules and Ionia. The spare was fender mounted on the right side only. Pictured here is a Hercules body. The wagon cost $1,015 F.O.B. Pontiac, Mich.

The 1940 Willys wagon was called the Town and Country, which probably irks many collectors of the Chrysler car bearing the same name. The Willys body looks like a USB&F, although there is no evidence to support this.

A 1940 Studebaker Commander Station Wagon with a custom body by USB&F. Note the extreme slope of the roof, which effected the size of the front doors.

The big news in the world of woodies and wagons for '41 was the introduction in March of the Town and Country Car by Chrysler. The design of this car was a complete departure from what was considered normal for a station wagon. At a quick glance, it had the look of a station wagon and, it was a "woodie." But that's where the resemblance ended. The Town and Country Car (at introduction Chrysler carefully refrained from calling it a station wagon) followed the line of a conventional sedan. Yet it fulfilled the criterion of a wagon. It could carry up to nine passengers. It was a utility vehicle, as well as a passenger car — great for hunting and fishing and just the thing for the Beverly Hills florist. No other wagon looked so swank.

Chrysler assembled the Town and Country from component parts manufactured by its newly acquired Pekin Wood Products Division of Helena, Arkansas. The framework was made of white ash, while the panels were of Honduras mahogany. Unlike the conventional wagon, the roof of the Town and Country was all steel. It actually was the roof panel of a 7-passenger sedan. The interior was upholstered in real leather.

The Town and Country was aimed at the upper crust of the auto market. It had snob appeal. With the success of the initial introduction Chrysler finally succumbed to the masses and referred to the creation as a station wagon — the smartest "station wagon" on the road, the ads read. Now Chrysler had two wagon entries, the Plymouth and the new Town and Country. The Plymouth continued with the same basic body design of the previous year, but it was more refined. The framing pieces were made more smooth and looked massive and stronger. Framing was of white ash while the panels were mahogany. Optional fender skirts were available. The Town and

Country offered an optional roof rack, one of the first makes to do so. Other options for both cars were such items as white wall tires, outside rearview mirror, spotlight, radio and heater. This was a good year for all manufacturers, but it was the best in Chrysler history.

Ford for this year was making news of its own. This was the year it introduced the Mercury Station Wagon. The Mercury shared its body with Ford, both being manufactured at Iron Mountain. Maple was used for the framing while mahogany or gum wood was used for the panels. The body used by Ford and Mercury was a new one for this year. Ford had eliminated the exposed running board, so the bottoms of the doors were kicked out over the concealed running boards. Rear fenders were also squared, so the short horizontal rib on the rear quarter was gone. The rear door piano hinge was replaced with two sedan type hinges. The Ford and Mercury wagons were symmetrical and pleasing to the eye. Ford offered its wagon in two models — the DeLuxe and the Super DeLuxe. They sold for $1,015 and $975. The Mercury sold for $1,145.

A very significant and interesting event took place at Ford in 1941 when Henry II ordered a one-off woodie for himself. The car was designed by E. T. Gregorie. It was a modified Model A, using some station wagon wood, plus some 1935, 1940 and 1941 components. It emerged as a 4-passenger convertible, unique and said to be the inspiration for the postwar Ford and Mercury Sportsman. The car still exists and is owned by Ken Coulter of Tennessee.

Ionia continued to supply bodies to Chevrolet, along with Cantrell. It's interesting to note that at this time Ionia's official name was The Yipsilanti Furniture Co. It is a strange sight to see a body parts catalog for 1941, issued by GM, with this name printed across the cover — Yipsilanti Furniture Co., makers of "Ionia Bodies." As the auto business grew, the name simply became Ionia Manufacturing. The Cantrell body can be readily distinguished from the Ionia by the two narrow mahogany strips found in the beltline.

The Chevrolet wagon was available only as a Special DeLuxe. It sold for $995 and 2,045 units were built. Buick, Pontiac and Oldsmobile continued to offer wagons

This is the American Bantam station wagon. This was the last year of production for the company. Very few of these two-door woodie wagons were built.

American Bantam's utility wagon was an all-steel companion to the woodie wagon. The quarter windows and tailgate used snap on curtains in place of glass.

A three-quarter rear view of the American Bantam station wagon. It looks as though the front doors were fitted with crank-up glass windows, while curtains were used in the rear quarters and the tailgate.

with bodies by Ionia and Hercules. For 1941, Buick offered its wagon only as a Special. This was a departure from the previous year, when it was offered in the Super Series. Pontiac's wagon came in the Custom Torpedo Series, while Oldsmobile had its wagon as part of the "70" Series.

Packard continued to use Hercules bodies. Two models were again available, the 110 and the 120, although this year more options were offered. The buyer could now get standard or DeLuxe trim as well as a choice of engines. The DeLuxe trim featured leather for the seats, carpeted floor and chrome seat frames. A total of 600 wagons were built for 1941 by Packard.

Hudson had a wagon for 1941 in the Super Six Series. The bodies were probably supplied by Seamon Body Co. It featured glass all around, tailgate mounted spare, and chrome framed seats. The body frame and panels were made of contrasting wood, with light colored frames an[d] dark panels.

A few new custom body builders entered the marke[t] this year. Coachcraft of Los Angeles built at least on[e] known "one-off" woodie body on a Cadillac chassis. [It] was a two-door version complete with roof rack. Derha[m] of Rosemount, Pa., which built wagon bodies from tim[e] to time, this year built at least one such custom wago[n] on a Chrysler chassis. Standard Carriage Works of L[os] Angeles built a Packard wagon for famed opera sing[er] John Charles Thomas.

This was the last year of manufacturing for th[e] American Bantam Car Co. of Butler, Pa. In this last ye[ar] the company turned out two wagons, each in ve[ry] limited numbers. One was a woodie and the other a[n] all-steel body. The woodie was called a Station Wago[n] while the all-steel version was called a Utility Sedan. Bo[th] were two door models with a front end that looke[d] like a 1938 Buick.

A Special Cadillac woodie with a body by Coachcraft of California. Note the absence of horizontal ribbing. The panels were made of heavy plywood to give it more rigidity. The wagon was created for Charles Starrett, a cowboy movie star. Photo courtesy of Special Interest Auto.

Buick's wagon was available only in the Special Series. It was called the Estate Wagon. Bodies were supplied by Ionia and Hercules. It had a 121-inch wheelbase and was 209 inches overall.

The Buick wagon carried six passengers with a generous amount of cargo area. The spare continued to be carried in a compartment below the tailgate. All cushions were of Fomatex, a new type of foam rubber upholstery.

This Cadillac woodie was built by Bohman and Schwartz of California. It was built on a Series 75 limousine chassis. Doors opened at the B-pillar. Note the split rear window and added luggage rack. It was built for Harry Karl as a gift for his wife. Photo courtesy of Special Interest Auto.

The Chevrolet Special DeLuxe wagon with an Ionia body. Framing is of white ash and panels are of mahogany. The spare was tailgate mounted. The new body had five inches more floor space and three inches more interior width than the 1940 models.

A few custom bodied Cadillac wagons were built over the years. This one is a 1941 with a Cantrell body. The body looks very similar to a Chevrolet wagon. The doors open to the rear and are hung with external sedan-type hinges. The spare was probably mounted on the tailgate. The photo is courtesy of Antique Automobile.

The Chevrolet all-steel Carryall Suburban had enough room for eight passengers. The rear end opened like a conventional wagon. The spare was carried inside. It was available only as a two-door model.

This one-off Chrysler wagon was built by Derham of Rosemount, Pa. It was built on a New Yorker chassis. Note the absence of vent windows in the front doors.

The big news for this year was the introduction by Chrysler of the Town and Country station wagon. It was introduced in March of 1941 as the Town and Country Car. It was revolutionary in design. The lines followed that of a sedan, complete with steel roof panel. This was quite a departure from the conventional box. It proved that a station wagon did not have to look like a truck. This was a milestone in wagon design and concept. Pictured is the 9-passenger version. It was one of two models offered. The other was a 6-passenger version.

The Chrysler Town and Country 6-passenger model had an obvious distinction in the paneled quarter windows. The all-steel roof was borrowed from the 7-passenger sedan.

This interior view of the Chrysler Town and Country shows the rear seat in the forward position for greater luggage capacity. Carpeting was used in the rear, but a rubber floor mat was used in the front.

An interior view of the 9-passenger Chrysler Town and Country shows the jump seat in place. The rear seat was moved back on a track, 18 inches, to make room for the jump seat.

A rear view of the Town and Country. The rear bumper was the same as used for the front. The deck lid was actually two doors that opened in the center.

The rear doors of the Chrysler Town and Country are in the open position. The spare was either stored upright or flat as pictured here. The rear doors were paneled on the inside for both looks and strength.

This is an optional writing table, available in the 6 and 9-passenger Chrysler Town and Country.

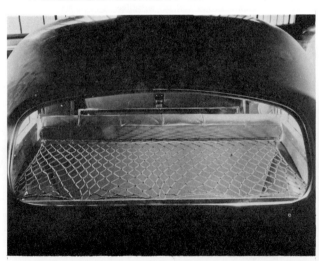

This net served as a package tray for the 9-passenger Town and Country. It was installed when the rear seat was in the forward position, and prevented packages from dropping into the luggage compartment.

Crosley continued to offer a wagon. It was a 2-door model, unchanged from the previous year. All side windows were of the sliding type. The doors were made of steel while the rear section was made of wood. It sold for $479 and probably was the lowest priced wagon on the market, excluding the American Bantam.

Ford introduced a new body this year. The bottoms of the doors were flared out to cover the running boards, and framing over the rear fenders was squared, thus eliminating the short rib on the rear quarter panel. Pictured is the DeLuxe model.

Crosley also offered a woodie panel delivery. It sold for $449. Basically, it was the station wagon with solid rear quarters and no rear seat.

Pictured here is the Super DeLuxe Ford Wagon, fitted as a Red Cross car. Note the extreme graining in the panels. This would indicate they were of gum wood. The piano hinge was no longer used for the rear doors.

This was the new Hundson wagon. Doors opened to the rear. Exposed sedan-type hinges supported the front doors and the rear doors were hung with a piano hinge. Front and rear doors had crank-up glass while the quarter windows were sliders. The spare was mounted on the tailgate. This was an 8-passenger model. The body builder is unknown.

This one of a kind woodie is a Model A Ford, built for young Henry Ford for his own use. Speculation has it that this little gem gave rise to the postwar Sportsman models. Despite the use of a Model A chassis, this vehicle was not built until 1941.

Oldsmobile offered its wagon as part of the "70" Series. Bodies were furnished by Ionia and Hercules. Pictured here is a Hercules body. Note the short horizontal rib on the quarter panel, which was not present on the Ionia body.

Another way to tell the Ionia body on the Oldsmobile is by the stainless steel beltline strip, quite evident in this photo. Hercules ended the strip at the cowl.

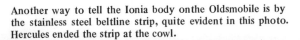

An Oldsmobile with an Ionia body in typical setting of the times. Note the absence of the short rib on the quarter panel.

The Mercury station wagon was introduced this year. Its body was shared with Ford. Only one model was offered. This fine example is owned by Will O'Neal of Hawthorne, Cal., president of the National Woodie Club.

Packard continued to have its wagon bodies supplied by Hercules. Pictured is the 120 model with DeLuxe trim. This car is owned by Hal Broda of North Hollywood, Calif.

A Packard 120, eight cylinder, with its distinctive hood ornament. The spare is mounted inside. This excellent car is owned by Bill Harris of Hyattsville, Md.

A rear view of Bill Harris' Packard 120 station wagon. The body framing is ash with mahogany panels. The spare is mounted inside. The tailgate is hung with a piano hinge. The liftgate has external locks. Note the two stop/tail lights, and the fact that both tail lights and license would be virtually hidden if the car were driven with the tailgate in a lowered position.

1941

This Packard 110 station wagon has optional fog lights. This is a six cylinder wagon. It is owned by William Kranz of Bay Village, Ohio.

This 1941 Packard Wagon was custom built by the Standard Carriage Works of Los Angeles for opera star John Charles Thomas. It is interesting that the body builder chose to follow the European shooting break design. The tailgate is actually two doors that open in the center. This car is now owned by Bill Harris of Hyattsville, Md.

The Packard 120 station wagon. This one has the optional sidemounts and an option spotlight. Front and rear doors opened to the rear and were hung with external sedan-type hinges. Both doors had crank-up windows and the quarter window was a slider. Note the mounting of the side view mirror on top of the spare tire case.

The Packard 110 model station wagon. The stark contrast in framing and panels is due to an artist's retouching of the original photograph. This was done to point up the wooden body. The rear doors were hung with only two external sedan-type hinges. The rear door was narrower than the front.

Willys continued to offer a station wagon. Bodies were probably supplied by USB&F. Note the dark beltline strip, a trademark of USB&F. Sliding glass was used in the rear doors and rear quarters. Willys was now marketing its vehicles under the name Americar. This model was available in 6-passenger form only.

The Plymouth could accommodate up to eight passengers. The rear door and quarter windows were sliders. Note how narrow the front and rear doors are. Both doors opened to the rear and used concealed hinges.

Plymouth continued with the same body introduced the year before. Framing was of white ash. Front and rear doors were narrow and box-like. Both opened to the rear.

An inside view of the Plymouth wagon. As with most wagons of the time, the roof was not covered on the inside. The Chrysler Town and Country was one of the few wagon-type vehicles with a headliner.

Plymouth was available with natural finished panels or dark stained panels. This model is pictured with optional fender skirts, which were very big in 1941.

Unlike the rest of the corporation wagons of General Motors, Pontiac used a design that had many door ribs. This may have been done to carry through the fender moulding strips. The body was of ash with mahogany panels. Both doors opened to the rear. This was an 8-passenger model.

Pontiac offered its wagon in the Custom Torpedo Series. It was priced at $1,175. Bodies were furnished by Ionia and Hercules.

1942

On December 7, 1941, the Japanese attacked the Naval base at Pearl Harbor in the Hawaiian Islands. This action plunged the U.S. into World War II. The automobile industry, already heavily committed to defense production, quickly turned its entire production might to the war effort. In terms of civilian auto production it meant no cars for the duration of the war, as 1942 auto production was short lived. By the end of February all civilian car production had ceased. Total 1942 model production was very low, but it did produce some interesting vehicles — the "Black-out Cars."

Shortly after Pearl Harbor, the government set up priorities on certain materials such as chrome, nickle, copper, steel, rubber, etc. The 1942 model car started out as the usual new car, all shiny and bright. Soon however, white wall tires gave way to black; bright chrome trim was either painted or deleted altogether. Toward the end of the production run the new cars began to look very austere, with no bright trim or what limited trim there was, painted. They became known as "Black-out" cars because of the overall dullness. Most of the cars of the last months of production were put into government pools and sold only to people who had a priority, such as doctors.

The 1942 models in general represented the third year of a three-year design cycle. The basic year began in 1940. Station wagon development stood still during this period and no new inovations were introduced. The wagon was still considered by many as a truck, to be used as a livery vehicle, on a farm, estate or resort, or as a recreation car for the rick who could afford a second car. It had not yet been discovered by the suburban housewife, probably because there was no suburbia.

Ford and Mercury continued to share the same body. Ford continued to manufacture and assemble its wagons at Iron Mountain. Two models were offered in the Ford line, the DeLuxe and Super DeLuxe. Mercury had only one model. Ford's 1942 production totaled a mere 1,222 units.

Plymouth introduced a new body this year. Window openings were enlarged. Front and rear doors were wider and the beltline frame was heavier. The rear door piano hinge was replaced by two sedan type external hinges. The beltline molding extended from the hood nose all the way to the end of the rear quarter. Door bottoms were beefed up and kicked out to cover the running boards. Glass was standard all around and the spare remained inside the car.

Chrysler continued with the successful Town and Country wagon. Refinements to the 1941 design were minor. Once again two models were offered, a 6-passenger and a 9-passenger version. There was no visible way to tell the two apart, since the paneled rear quarter window was done away with. One interesting note about Chrysler for 1942 was the reworking of a Town and Country by Coachcraft of California. This was done for a movie which starred Ray Miland and Betty Field. The standard model Town and Country had its steel top removed and replaced with a convertible top. It is rumored that this particular car was the inspiration for the postwar Town and Country convertibles, but this is doubtful.

General Motors continued to have wagon bodies supplied by Ionia, Hercules and Cantrell. Buick continued with its Special Estate Wagon, with the body being changed somewhat in the front door. This was true with all GM wagons for this year. The front door was redesigned to take the new fender sweep, which was part of the overall new GM look for 1942.

Most of the so-called independents did not offer a wagon for 1942, simply because they felt they could not afford to change a woodie body to go along with any sheet metal changes with the outlook for obvious limited production. Hudson, however, was the exception. It did have a wagon, unchanged from the previous year.

Buick continued to offer its wagon in the Special Series, with the only changes being in the front doors to accommodate the extended fender line. The station wagon was designated as Model 49. It had a wheelbase of 121 inches and was 208 inches long overall.

The Chevrolet station wagon bodies were supplied by both Cantrell and Ionia. The station wagon was part of the Special DeLuxe Series. It was an 8-passenger model. The second and third seats were removable. Safety glass was featured all around. The spare was tailgate mounted and a metal tire cover was standard. Only 1,057 were built in a short production run. All passenger car production had ceased by the end of February 1942. The Chevrolet station wagon sold for $1,095.

This custom bodied Carryall is by Mifflinburg. It was one of the last such bodies done for Chevrolet. Note that in this woodie version of the Carryall there are four doors. Cantrell also built a body for the Carryall for export. These were shipped knocked down for assembly in India.

The all-steel Chevrolet Carryall was built on a 115-inch wheelbase truck chassis. It served well as a school bus for small districts. A four-speed transmission could be ordered as an extra cost option.

The Chevy Carryall, military version, doubled as a personnel carrier and ambulance. These vehicles used the standard rear-wheel drive, and were not normally equipped with four-wheel drive.

Virtually unchanged for 1942 was the successful Chrysler Town and Country station wagon. In addition to the front end sheet metal, the biggest change was in the bottoms of the doors. These were kicked out to cover the running boards. This example is equipped with optional roof rack and spotlight. It could also be ordered with road or fog lights and rear fender skirts.

The Chrysler Town and Country station wagon. Front doors had crank-up windows and wing vents. The rear doors had slider windows. The quarter window was a two-piece assembly. One half was fixed, the other half a wing vent. All glass was of the safety laminated type. Both doors opened to the rear. The front door was hung with concealed hinges and the rear doors used exposed sedan-type hinges.

Like the Mercury/Monart wagons, these Dodges had an add-on body. These were made from government pool cars, and the markings indicate they were used by the State of New York. They may have been done by Cantrell. Interesting but not as attractive as the Mercury/Monart wagons, they obviously helped serve the vehicle problem. The dual rear wheels add an interesting note.

The clean sweep of the steel roof gave the Chrysler Town and Country wagon more of a sedan look. The unique rear doors were retained from the previous year.

The Chrysler Town and Country black-out model. This 6-passenger model was produced late in the short 1942 model run. This mint example is owned by Richard Larger of Pittsburgh, Pa.

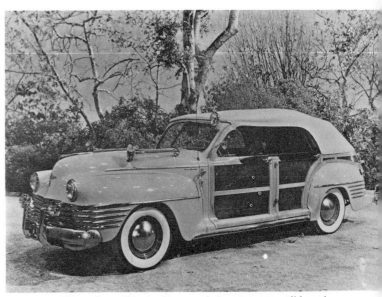

This unique Chrysler Town and Country convertible sedan was custom built by Coachcraft of California. The car was made for a movie which starred Ray Miland. It was a stock Town and Country wagon, cut down and fitted with a top. There were no windows, and the tops of the doors were covered with leather trim. Dual spotlights were awkwardly placed at the top of the windshield posts. Gaudy in appearance were the addition of air horns to the hood. Road lights and bumper grille guard were other additions straight from Chrysler's accessory catalog.

The snob appeal of this Chrysler Town and Country was complete with custom built dog trailer. Note the trailer even had a roof rack and paneling to match the tow car.

A rear view of the Ford wagon. The tailgate was hung with a piano-type hinge, and supported by folding arms. The liftgate was supported by slotted arms with locking screws. Only a single stop/tail light was standard, the second one was optional. Note the indentation in the bumper to accommodate the spare and the loose wires to the taillights.

Ford wagons continued unchanged. Two models were available – the DeLuxe and the Super DeLuxe. The panels were either light or dark, at buyer's option.

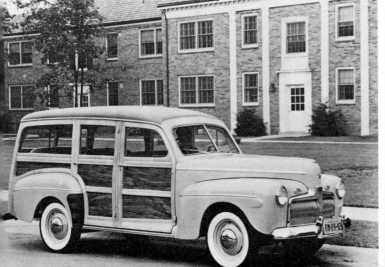

The Ford wagon with tailgate opened. Note the limited cargo space with third seat in position. The tail light and license bracket continued to be hinged so they were visible with the gate down.

This Ford wagon is equipped with optional Marmon-Harrington four wheel drive. This option was used extensively by the military, though a few such conversions did reach civilian buyers.

Only 900 of these Mercury wagons were built. Mercury continued to share its body with Ford. More than half of this year's production was exported.

The Hudson wagon was unchanged. The spare was tailgate mounted. This would be the last year for a Hudson wagon. It had a 121-inch wheelbase and a 1,000 pound load capacity. The rear and center seats were removable.

This attractive wagon is a hybrid designed by Brooks Stevens. It was built by Monart Motors on 1942 sedans and coupes from government pools. Wood was applied over the sheet metal with a wooden box hung on the back end. This increased the carrying capacity. Wood panels on the doors are actually antiqueing done over metal to simulate wood. This is one of the very few successful wagon conversions. Production count is unknown.

This is a coupe conversion of the Mercury/Monart wagon. They were built for the military, the Red Cross, and for special permit buyers. This example even had a roof rack. The design is by Brooks Stevens. The roof-mounted sirens indicate that this unit might have been fitted for ambulance use.

Oldsmobile, like the rest of the GM line changed its wagon body only slightly to accept the front fender sweep. This is a Hercules body. Compare this with the Ionia body and some major trim differences will be noted.

This is an Ionia bodied Oldsmobile. Note how the side frame member flares out at the fender sweep, eliminating the short horizontal rib. The wagon was offered as part of the B-44 series. The spare was carried under the rear floor boards.

Plymouth introduced a new wagon body this year. This body design would continue through 1948. The front doors were hung with concealed hinges while the rear doors used two external sedan hinges. Rear door and quarter windows were sliders. The second and third seats were removable. A total of 1,136 units were produced.

A rear view of the Plymouth wagon. Body framing was much more beefier. The spare was mounted inside. Only one tail light was standard. It was a hinged unit.

Pontiac offered its wagon as part of the Streamliner series. Front doors were changed to accept the new fender sweep. The rear seat would interchange with the center seat to provide 6-passenger capacity in addition to the normal 3, 5 or 8-passenger capacities. As did most other manufacturers, Pontiac continued to delete the headliner in its wagons.

The 1942 Plymouth body represented a change in design. Front and rear doors were wider, with the rear door kicking over the rear fender. Front doors had crank-up windows while sliding glass was used in the rear doors and quarters. Framing was of white ash with mahogany panels.

This 1942 Buick Wagon ultimately found itself doing duty in Africa. Photo courtesy of Olyslager Auto Library. Note the side and roof racks.

A 1940 Chevrolet wagon used by the armed forces in Australia. Photo courtesy of Olyslager Auto Library. Except for its military paint, it appears to be a relatively civilian vehicle.

A 1941 Ford dressed in camouflage paint did duty for the Air Corps in Great Britain. Photo courtesy of Olyslager Auto Library.

During the war years of 1943-45 all auto makers were engaged in the production of war materials. There was no passenger car production. Chevrolet manufactured tanks, personnel carriers, and trucks. Buick manufactured tanks, airplane engines, and shell casings. Pontiac and Oldsmobile produced similar materials.

Chrysler built airplane engines, tanks, radar units, anti-aircraft guns, sea mules and the Sperry Gyro-Compass. Dodge built trucks and personnel carriers. Plymouth produced ammunition and shell casings by the millions of tons.

Ford and Willys were prime suppliers of the "Jeep." Ford also produced amphibious "Jeeps," known as GPA's. At the Iron Mountain facilities, Ford produced gliders, made of pine and balsa wood covered with canvas. Not too long ago someone discovered one of these gliders in the Hershey, Pa. area still packed in its crate and never used. At Willow Run, Ford also assembled bombers.

Packard produced aircraft engines. Nash made propellers, cargo trailers, binocular cases and flying boat sub-assemblies. Studebaker turned out inflatable lifeboats, aircraft parts, range finders and various sub-assemblies.

Most of the government pool of 1942 model cars found its way into the military. Wagons were chopped, channeled, modified, painted grey, olive drab, camouflaged and stenciled with white stars, unit numbers, and serial numbers. Gas cans, extra spares, shovels, picks, racks, and the like were hung on them. They were a bunch of strange, sad looking creatures. On the civilian side, a few sedans and coupes were converted into station wagons, with the Mercury/Monart. being the most successful and best designed. The Mercury hybrids were designed by Brooks Stevens and built by Monart Motors, a large Lincoln-Mercury distributor. The wagons were made to fill a need required by the Red Cross and similar agencies. The idea was to take a few cars from the government pool, coupes and 2 and 4-door sedans and make wagons out of them. This was accomplished by cutting away the backs and adding a wood station wagon box, a vinyl covered roof and some wood framing over the remaining sheet metal. Matter of fact, the design was even more pleasing than the stock production unit. It's unknown just how many of these wagons were built or if any exist today.

In 1945, with the war decidedly out of favor, government regulations concerning civilian car production eased. Auto makers began working on postwar designs. Some very interesting ideas were coming off the drawing boards, such as personal luxury woodies. They were built like a wagon but they sure didn't look like a wagon. The Chrysler Town and Country convertible, roadster, and hardtop and Mercury Sportsman convertibles sure weren't station wagons. As a matter of fact, they gave a whole new image to the postwar car. The personal luxury unit would become more popular with each succeeding year, right up to the Mark IVs, Grand Prixs, and Eldorados of today.

Here's a 1941 Ford wagon that is reminiscent of the 1942 Chrysler Town and Country wagon that was customized for a Hollywood movie. Could this be a 41 Ford Sportsman? Photo courtesy of Olyslager Auto Library. Designed strictly for utility, this car was used by the British Army in North Africa.

This 1941 Ford wagon, with a chopped top, was used in Africa. Photo courtesy of Olyslager Auto Library. The fold-down windshield was definitely not a factory option.

An early artist's sketch of a proposed postwar design for Ford. The sketch is dated May, 1943. Photo courtesy of Seventy-One Society. The car is not too unlike Ford's Model A conversion of a few years earlier.

A postwar Ford design for a convertible station wagon probably expanded on some of those war time conversions.

The attractive Brooks Stevens-designed Mercury/Monart wagon. It was actually a modified four-door sedan with very nice rear end treatment.

At war's end, the rush was on to manufacture civilian cars. The public was car hungry—starved for those shiny new postwar models. All auto makers were scrambling to get back into the civilian car business.

Chrysler, although the last of the big three to get back into civilian car production, was the most ambitious when it came to woodies. They came up with a whole line of woodies, called the Town and Country models. This new line of cars was based on the success of the pre-war wagons of the same name. The name, however, was the only thing that was similar. The postwar line up called for a Convertible, a Roadster, a 2-door Hardtop, a Brougham and a 4-door Sedan. Unfortunately, when full production finally got underway in October of 1946, only the Convertible and the 4-door Sedan were actually produced. But they did manage to build seven of those Hardtops, qualifying Chrysler for the first produced two-door hardtop after the war.

Plymouth offered the same pre-war design wagon. Early wagons were finished in non-contrasting panels, while later ones had the dark mahogany finish. Dodge did not offer a wagon and none were planned. Dodge would not bring out a wagon until 1949. However, a few Cantrell bodies were built on the Dodge light truck chassis. DeSoto likewise did not offer a wagon, although a woodie sedan was considered.

Ford, the first of the big three to go into postwar production, produced its first cars in 1945. Full station wagon production began three months after the war had ended. Ford and Mercury once again shared the same body. These were unchanged from 1942.

Shortly after assuming the presidency, Henry Ford II instructed that a car be built to compete with the Town and Country. And so the Ford and Mercury Sportsman convertibles were born. A stock Ford convertible was brought to Iron Mountain where the sheet metal was cut away. A metal superstructure was substituted and wood was applied over this frame. No real engineering went into the Sportsman. Wood was applied over the superstructure in such a manner as to give it strength. The first prototype Sportsman was built in October, 1945, a full year ahead of actual Chrysler production. The Sportsman was offered only as a convertible by both Ford and Mercury. The Ford version was offered in 1946, 47 and 48, the Mercury only in 1946.

It's interesting to note that during the first three postwar years of 1946-48, Chrysler built its Town and Country unchanged. Ford also built its station wagon models unchanged during these same three years, but the Sportsman in its limited production, underwent three different changes during this time period. Three different bodies were produced—the type "A," the type "B," and the type "C". They all pretty much looked the same at first glance, but on closer examination the differences are quite noticeable. Simply put, the "A" body had longer horizontal pieces, the "C" body had longer vertical pieces while the "B" body was a combination of both.

Buick moved its wagon up to the Super series for 1946. Bodies were supplied by Ionia, 798 units were built, and the price was $2,594. The Buick body was new for the year, conforming to the new postwar sheet metal of the Super line. Oldsmobile offered its wagon as part of the "66" Series. It was available as either a standard or DeLuxe. The DeLuxe version featured genuine leather upholstery. The Pontiac wagon was part of the Streamline series. Both the Olds and Pontiac bodies were unchanged from 1942.

The Chevrolet wagon for 1946 was available only in the newly created Fleetmaster series. Bodies continued to be supplied by Ionia and Cantrell. Only 804 wagons were built in 1946. There was no change in the pre-war design. Chevrolet also assembled woodie wagons in Bombay, India on the 125-inch and 115-inch wheelbase ½-ton truck chassis.

Willys Overland entered the postwar station wagon market with a new all-steel Brooks Stevens design wagon. Willys had copyrighted the Jeep name of World War II fame and began the manufacture of the Jeep for civilian use. Willys retained the military look for the front end but Mr. Stevens created the all-steel wagon body with the look of a woodie. This basic design would last for many years to come, and is somewhat retained today by American Motors. The Jeep was a 2-door wagon. However, a 4-door version was made for the railroads for use as a rail car.

Crosley Motors, which entered the auto field prior to World War II, built a prototype woodie wagon for 1946.

The Buick Model 59 Super Estate Wagon. The postwar Buick wagon had the look of more steel than wood. The spare was still kept in a special compartment below the tailgate. Ionia was the big supplier of Buick wagon bodies.

This one-off Cadillac wagon was commissioned by cowboy star Gene Autry. It was built by Bohman and Schwartz of California. Although it was not a conventional wagon, more like an airport type limousine, it is an interesting woodie. There were three doors on each side, all opening to the rear. The front door used concealed hinges, the other doors used exposed sedan-type hinges. The quarter windows were fixed. The doors had crank-up windows. It was built on an ambulance chassis.

ut did not get into full wagon production until 1948.
ash Motors, on the other hand, entered the postwar
market with a woodie sedan, instead of a wagon. It was
ot unlike the Town and Country Sedan, which raised a
ew hairs at Chrysler. It was not as popular as the Town
nd Country and only a limited number were produced.
ittle is known about its construction, but it is a safe bet
hat the frame work was made of white ash while the
anels were of mahogany. Studebaker did not have a
agon for 1946, but they did built two prototypes —
ne a woodie and one of plastic, in a 4-door and 2-door
espectively.

There were some interesting limited number and one-
ffs built in 1946. One such wagon was built by Derham of
osemount, Pa. It was a 2-door model built on a Dodge
hassis, using much of the Dodge stock sheet metal.
emember, Dodge did not have a production wagon
his year. Another one-off was a Cadillac wagon com-
issioned by cowboy star Gene Autry and built by
ohman and Schwartz of California. This was a woodie
agon with six doors and a roof rack.
Woodies became very popular during the early postwar
ears, especially the Town and Country and Sportsman
models, so it was inevitable that someone would come up
ith the idea of upgrading a pre-war car to look like one
f these snazzy looking new wood body jobs. The
ellpod Co. of New York offered a kit to the do-it-
ourselfer, of thin wood framing and woodgrain Di-Noc,
o apply over the sheet metal doors and rear quarters of
ny car, to give it the look of a Sportsman or Town and
ountry. The subsequent popularity of these kits is
nknown. They were, however, available for a few years.

Bodies for the 1946 Chevrolet wagon were supplied by
Ionia and Cantrell. Framing was of white ash with mahogany
panels. The Chevrolet wagon this year appeared only in the
new Fleetmaster Series.

This Chevrolet Carry-All wagon was made of Teakwood
framing with masonite panels. It was a 9-passenger model.
Safety glass was featured in the windshield with plate glass
in all the other windows. The car was built on the
125-inch wheelbase truck chassis. It was assembled in
Bombay, India, and was not available in the U.S.

This wood bodied Chevrolet Carryall was assembled in
India from parts supplied by Cantrell. Two models were
offered, one on a 115-inch wheelbase, the other on a
125-inch wheelbase. Framing was white ash with mahogany
panels. The front doors used exposed hinges and the rear
doors used a piano hinge. The spare was tailgate mounted.

The Chrysler Town and Country convertible was built on
the New Yorker chassis and powered by an 8-cylinder
engine. Whitewall tires were not available, so white plastic
wheel rings were standard. These were used to simulate the
whitewall tire in both 1942 and 1946. Dual spotlights were
also standard.

The Town and Country sedan was built on the shorter
Windsor chassis and powered by a 6-cylinder engine. Steel
luggage rack and dual spotlights were standard. The Town
and Country was built of a solid white ash framing with
ply-metal panels covered with mahogany veneer. The car
almost looked nautical, especially with the large deck lid
hinges, which reminded one of a yacht's mooring hardware.

Chrysler built 100 of these Town and Country sedans on the longer New Yorker chassis. The wheelbase was 127½ inches. The production run was for only one month. It began in December 1946 and ended in January 1947. The roof rack, dual spotlights, and fluid-drive transmission were standard. The front door hinges were concealed and the rear door used chrome plated exposed hinges. The skid strips on the roof were made of white ash. Whitewall tires were not available immediately after the war, so Chrysler offered white plastic wheel rings as standard equipment.

Only seven of these Town and Country two-door hardtops were built. This one was built for then Chrysler President David Wallace. He was credited with creating the Town and Country models. While the car was still in the company executive pool, a simulated alligator vinyl roof was added, along with a key starter. Seats were also upholstered in the same vinyl material. The car is currently owned by Allan Bridle of Hinckley, Ohio. The whitewall tires were added in 1949.

A rear view of one of the seven Chrysler Town and Country hardtops that were built in 1946. The roof panel and rear window were from a standard coupe.

The Chrysler Town and Country Brougham. This was one of five models Chrysler proposed to offer in the Town and Country line. It was to be built on the 121-inch Windsor chassis and powered by a 6-cylinder engine. Production never materialized, only a prototype was ever built. It was fully functional and after a stint in the executive motor pool, was eventually sold. It would present ultimate find today.

The proposed Chrysler Town and Country Roadster. None were ever built. This model was based on the business coupe. It would have been mounted on a Windsor chassis. It is not known of the top would have been manually or hydraulically operated. It was designed to carry a maximum of three people. However, had it gone into production, auxiliary seats probably would have been available for the rear compartment area. Sadly, the car never even reached the prototype stage.

An inside view of the Chrysler Town and Country Brougham. It was upholstered in leather and saran. Inside door panels and rear quarter panels were mahogany plywood. Garnish moulding and window trim was made of ornamental wood. The headliner was vinyl with ash strips. The rear quarter window treatment was unique, as door-type window and wing vent were used.

An inside view of the Town and Country sedan. Seats were upholstered in saran and leather and door panels were plywood mahogany panels. Note the wood headliner strips. A great deal of quality hand craftsmanship went into the Town and Country, which ultimately accounted for its demise.

An inside view of the Town and Country convertible upholstered in optional full leather. The standard interior called for leather and bedford cord. On this model, the door panels were finished in the upholstery material.

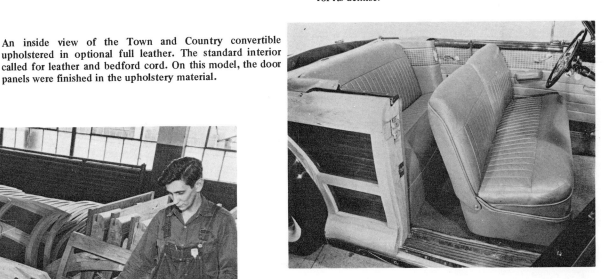

This kind of hand craftsmanship ultimately pushed up the cost of the Town and Country. Here a quarter panel is being formed and fitted by hand.

The quarter panel and deck lid assembly of the Chrysler Town and Country convertible was the first step in body assembly. After these parts were assembled and aligned they were fitted to the floor plan. Note the tremendous amount of hand labor involved.

The Town and Country sedan metal components were also hand fitted before wood assemblies were installed. Here the roof section is being guided into place in preparation for welding.

The Town and Country convertible body drop. Completed bodies were fitted to the cowl and chassis assembly as the final step in the production chain.

Town and Country component parts were all sealed before assembly. Note the lack of a mask on the sprayer – a scene that no longer would be allowed with today's industrial health standards.

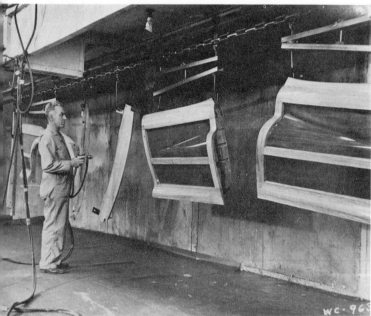

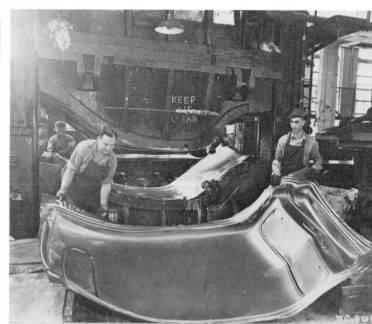

These are roof panels for the Town and Country sedan, as they come from the presses. Note that these presses were hand fed. After this step, the panels were sent to a shearing operation for finishing.

Hand tailored convertible tops are being fitted to the Town and Country convertible. This was the last body assembly step. After this point the completed bodies were fitted to the chassis.

1946

For the body parts, mahogany veneer was first glued to metal panels, then these panels were pressed into shape. They were then stained and varnished before being installed as part of the Town and Country.

Town and Country convertibles being assembled. This was the second step in body assembly. The quarter panels are being fitted to the floor pan and cowl section. The next step was the hanging of the doors.

The Town and Country sedan body drop. After this point, the bodies were completed, including the upholstery.

An inside view of the Town and Country door gives some indication as to the quality of the construction that went into these parts.

A prototype Crosley station wagon. Note the small rear window, and the dashboard mounted rear view mirror. Sliding glass was used in all side windows.

Dodge did not offer a station wagon this year. This rather strange looking one-off was built by Derham of Rosemount, Pa. This looks like a custom modification of a club coupe. The quarter windows were sliders. The back window was fixed. Note the roof rack. Photo courtesy of Lynn Zettlemoyer.

Although DeSoto did not make a wagon in 1946, a prototype woodie sedan was built. It is not known whether this body was ever mounted on a chassis.

The DeSoto Suburban was considered a "Utility Sedan." It comprised some of the features of a wagon but retained the basic sedan body. The interior was upholstered in durable vinyl. Seats were movable to increase the cargo area.

The Bellpod Co. of New York put out kits to convert pre-war cars into one of those snazzy looking postwar luxury jobs. An old Ford could look like a Sportsman, an old Chrysler like one of those new Town and Country cars.

The Ford Sportsman convertible for 1946. The Sportsman was only offered in this model. It was handsome and appealed to those who could not afford the high price tag of the Town and Country. The maple and mahogany framing was fitted over a metal skeleton superstructure. The Sportsman sold for $1,985 and was the most expensive car in Ford's line this year.

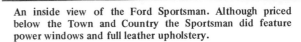

An inside view of the Ford Sportsman. Although priced below the Town and Country the Sportsman did feature power windows and full leather upholstery.

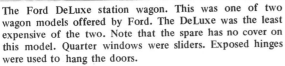

The Ford DeLuxe station wagon. This was one of two wagon models offered by Ford. The DeLuxe was the least expensive of the two. Note that the spare has no cover on this model. Quarter windows were sliders. Exposed hinges were used to hang the doors.

This is the Ford Super DeLuxe wagon. With all seats in place there wasn't much room for cargo. Note that the tailgate did not lay flat, making loading and unloading awkward. Folding, heavy wire arms were used to support the tailgate.

This Ford Super DeLuxe wagon, used south of the border as a taxi, reportedly carried fourteen passengers. This must have been some kind of a record and certainly a tribute to Ford suspension. Note that while the area behind the third seat was no caverness space, it could still carry a live hog, and did in this photo. Photo courtesy of Ford Life.

A rear view of the Ford Super DeLuxe station wagon. The liftgate was supported by slotted arms with locking screws. The front doors were supported by concealed hinges. Both the liftgate and tailgate used piano-type hinges. Only one taillight was standard. The right-hand one was an accessory.

Only one wagon model was offered by Mercury. The body was the same as that of the Ford. This was basically a 4-door, 8-passenger wagon. Doors opened to the rear. The spare was tailgate mounted and enclosed in a metal case. The Mercury wagon sold for $1,788.

The Mercury Sportsman convertible was only produced for six months in 1946, the only year it was offered. Only a very few were built. The author is fortunate in owning one of these examples. It is now undergoing full restoration.

Nash did not build a station wagon this year. Instead it offered a woodie sedan. Only a limited number were built, and only a couple are known to exist today. They are very rare.

The Oldsmobile standard station wagon. The wood bodies were supplied by Ionia and Hercules. The quarter windows were sliders, which was common practice. The rear door is more narrow than the front. Concealed hinges were used for the front doors, exposed hinges for the rear. Oldsmobile, like the other GW divisions, attempted to integrate more sheet metal in the wagons, as evidenced by the front fenders. The rear end was more slanted to give it a more streamlined appearance. The overall wagon design blended well with the rest of the car line.

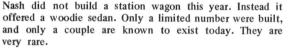

The Oldsmobile "66" DeLuxe station wagon. Some of its premium appointments included real leather seats. It was rated at ½-ton load capacity.

The Plymouth wagon for 1946 was offered two ways —
one with contrasting panels and one as shown here, with
natural panels. The body design was unchanged from pre-war
models. Sliding glass was used in the rear doors and quarter
windows. The spare was mounted inside. The roof was still
fabric covered, despite Chrysler having introduced the Town
and Country with a steel roof panel.

An inside view of the Plymouth wagon shows the spare tire
compartment in the back of the front seat. The tailgate
folded level for easier loading. The body continued to be
paneled on the inside.

This Plymouth Special DeLuxe station wagon was dark
stained mahogany panels. Framing was of white ash and
the spare was mounted inside. The dark panels became
available later in the production run.

A view of the Plymouth tailgate. All hinges were hidden
and of the piano type. The glass was fixed. A single stop/
tail light was standard. It was also hinged. The rear bumper
was free of bumper guards. This enabled the gate to be
lowered flat and level.

The Pontiac station wagon was part of the Streamliner
series. This is an Ionia body. Three horizontal ribs were used
on the doors and tailgate. The spare was mounted inside.
The roof was still fabric covered. Like a conventional sedan,
the front doors used concealed hinges and the rear doors
exposed hinges.

Studebaker did not have a station wagon this year. However, two models were planned. The one pictured here is the woodie version. Doors opened at the B-pillar. Sliding glass was used in the rear doors and quarter windows. This prototype was photographed extensively and used in many sales folders and presentations, but it never went into production. Photo courtesy of Don Scheuring of Parma, Ohio.

Studebaker did not have a wagon this year, but at least two models were planned and prototypes were built. This is a plastic bodied 2-door version. The white section is plastic. Photo courtesy of Car Classics.

The Willys wagon for 1946 was an all-steel Brooks Stevens design. Pictured here is a prototype, photo courtesy of Brooks Stevens. It is very similar to the production version.

A rear view of the Willys wagon. Note the level tailgate for easy loading. The spare mounting has been pushed up against the side wall to increase the load area.

The all-steel Willys wagon was a combination of the military version jeep and a wagon box. The Brooks Stevens design was unique, in that the panels simulated a woodie which is what the competition was offering. It gave the best of both worlds — the easy maintenance of steel, with the attractiveness of wood. Note the tireless spare rim mounted just behind the right rear quarter window.

This Willys 4-door wagon was specially built for railroads as a rail car. It transported rail inspectors and maintenance crews. A 4-door wagon was not available to the public.

Auto production continued at its peak, turning out ose warmed over 1942 models as fast as assembly lines owed. There was talk about new models, but the Big ree were in a race to catch up with demand. Kaiser-azer introduced a new car, but had no wagon. idebaker had new models, but no wagon. And so it went. Ford continued unchanged with its wagon, as a DeLuxe d Super DeLuxe. It also continued with the Sportsman nvertible. Mercury again offered only one model wagon, ng the same body as Ford. The Mercury Sportsman was scontinued after a brief six months production in 1946. Chevrolet wagons were again available in the Fleet-ster series. Bodies were still being supplied by Ionia d Cantrell. The Chevrolet wagon was unchanged. Buick fered a wagon in the Super series and for the first time in e Roadmaster series. The body was the same for both odels. The Roadmaster sold for $3,249, while the Super ld for $2,805. A total of 2,331 Buick wagons were ilt this year.

Oldsmobile continued with its wagon in the "66" ries. It was unchanged from the previous year. Pontiac ntinued unchanged in the Streamliner series. Bodies for th makes were supplied by Ionia.

Chrysler's production of the Town and Country settled two models, the 6-cylinder 4-door sedan and the cylinder convertible. The sedan was based on the indsor chassis and the convertible on the longer New orker chassis. The only real wagon offered by Chrysler rp. was the Plymouth. It was unchanged from the evious year. Bodies for the Town and Country and the ymouth wagon were supplied by Chrysler's Pekin Wood oducts Division in Arkansas. Chrysler and Ford were the ly two manufacturers to build and assemble their vn woodie wagons.

The Buick Model 59 Super Estate wagon. This model remained unchanged from the previous year. Buick integrated more sheet metal into its wagons than any other GM offering. This was largely due to the Buick fender configuration. The front fenders had more sweep than the other GM divisions. Ionia supplied the woodie bodies. The Buick Super wagon sold for $2,805. A total of 2,849 were produced.

The new Buick model 79 Roadmaster Estate wagon. This model was newly introduced this year. The body was supplied by Ionia and was the same as the Super series body.

A rear view of the Chevrolet Fleetmaster wagon. Note the two taillights and the bumper cut-out. This example is owned by Bob Lentz who works for Chevrolet at the Parma, Ohio plant.

The Chevrolet Fleetmaster wagon was unchanged for 1946. Bodies were supplied by both Cantrell and Ionia. The only real significant change to any of the lines was in the grille. This year the grille had bolder horizontal bars that extended into the front fenders. The roof was fabric covered and the spare was mounted on the tailgate. Chevrolet offered the wagon only in the Fleetmaster series. It sold for $1,893 and 4,912 units were built.

The Chrysler Town and Country 4-door sedan was one of two models offered by Chrysler this year. The steel roof rack and dual spotlights were offered as standard equipment for the early part of this year.

This Chrysler Town and Country convertible has a custom camping trailer. The convertible was based on the New Yorker chassis and was powered by an 8-cylinder engine.

Mid-way in the model year Chrysler changed from a steel roof rack to a wooden one. Mahogany veneer panels also gave way to Di-Noc and spotlights became optional, as were the bumper-mounted fog lights.

This inside view of the Chrysler Town and Country convertible shows the optional full leather upholstery. Standard interior of the Town and Country convertible was a combination of leather bolsters and pleated bedford cord. This was a special order interior in white leather. Note the matching white piping on the carpeting.

Who could forget Marie "The Body" McDonald, posed here with her Town and Country convertible. The Town and Country was a favorite of the movie colony.

1947

Chrysler introduced the Traveler this year. This was a utility sedan very much like the DeSoto Suburban. It blended many features of the station wagon into a sedan configuration. The roof rack was the same one used on the Town and Country sedan. A canvas cover was included with the car, to be used in covering luggage placed within the roof rack.

Schwartz and Bohman body builders of California continued to build one-off Cadillac wagons. This 6-door version was built for a movie studio to carry actors to location.

DeSoto continued to offer its popular utility sedan, the Suburban. It is shown here in a typical 1947 setting. In the background is the famed DC-3.

Crosley advertised a wagon in 1947, but it did not go into production until 1948. The station wagon and panel delivery were the same car except for the quarter window. Note the unique sports-utility — a convertible pick-up.

Ford offered two wagons for 1947, the DeLuxe and the Super DeLuxe. The bodies were unchanged. Ford manufactured and assembled these bodies at the Iron Mountain, Mich. plant. The wood — maple and ash — was harvested from Ford-owned forest land in the nearby upper Michigan peninsula. The Super DeLuxe version sold for $1,975.

The Ford Sportsman for 1947. This is a "B" body, with a combination of long vertical and long horizontal framing pieces. The front end trim reflects the only real changes for this year.

There was only a single offering from Mercury. The wagon was unchanged from the previous year. The wood body was shared with Ford. With the exception of the Mercury sheet metal and a slightly longer wheelbase, the car was identical to the Ford. The price tag was higher at $2,207.

The Oldsmobile wagon was unchanged and bore a strong resemblance to Pontiac and Chevrolet. The bodies were furnished by Ionia and Hercules. Note how the rear door was narrower than the front door. The spare was tailgate mounted.

The Plymouth station wagon for 1947 was identical to the 1946 model, right down to the white plastic wheel rings. Whitewall tires were still unavailable. The wide, smooth contoured framing, first introduced in 1942, gave the wagon an appearance of great strength. Plymouth wagons of this period were very attractive.

The Willys all-steel wagon was unchanged. The spare was stored inside vertically against the right quarter. Willys attempted to give its wagons world-wide appeal by advertising it with exotic backgrounds.

A rear view of the Plymouth wagon. The spare was still mounted inside. Because the tailgate folded down level, it was not possible to use bumper guards on the rear bumper. Compare this with the Ford wagon.

The Pontiac Streamliner station wagon was unchanged and bore a strong family resemblance to the Oldsmobile and Chevrolet. Only the Buick wagon stood apart in the GM line-up of wagons. Pontiac made real changes only in the grille and the deletion of chrome strips from the fenders. The wood bodies were supplied by Ionia and Hercules.

upply was beginning to catch up with demand. The
Three however, continued with the same old warmed
r 1942 designs, but hinted strongly that new postwar
igns were most assuredly in the wings. The really new
gs were coming from the so-called independent auto
kers.

ackard introduced a totally new design for 1948,
ich included a new station wagon. It was called the
tion Sedan. Its design followed the basic 4-door sedan.
r all practical purposes it was the 4-door sedan with
od applied. It was the first wagon to be built in a
kard assembly plant. The wheelbase was 120 inches
l it was powered by a 130 horsepower, 8-cylinder
ine.

Nash continued with its woodie sedan, but this would
the last year for that model. Total three-year pro-
ction amount to a mere 1,000 units. Willys again
ered the Jeep station wagon. It was unchanged from
previous two years. This year the company built
h simulated caning, instead of the fake wood panels.
nternational Harvester offered a woodie wagon on its
it truck chassis. It was a 2-door model. Crosley finally
its wagon into production. Like the Jeep, it was
steel with fake wood panels. It was beginning to be a
n of the times. Wood was on the way out. But the look
wood was still popular and would continue to be
pular.

After the war a number of new auto companies were
med. Armed with dreams of grandeur and a dream car
the drawing board, these companies vied for their
re of the ripe market. Some built prototypes and some
ually got into limited production. But in the end all
ly failed. One such entry was the Bobbi-Kar, which
er became the Keller. As the Bobbi-Kar, a station wagon
1 an Urban Sedan (both woodies) were planned. Only a
gon prototype was built. Later when this same car
s re-named the Keller, a few more wagons were built.

The Bobbi-Kar wagon. This was a prototype that never
went into production. The company was later reorganized
and the car was re-named the Keller. A few more wagons
were built under this name.

The Bobbi-Kar Urban Sedan. This proposed woodie sedan
never was built. The company went out of business before
any production was started.

The Buick Roadmaster Estate Wagon. This was the second
year for this model. It was unchanged. Whitewalls were now
being offered as options.

The Buick Super Estate wagon was one of two wagons
offered by Buick this year. The bodies were furnished by
Ionia. The Buick wagon, like the other GM lines, and for
that matter just about every other manufacturer, was
unchanged. Quarter windows were fixed. The spare was
stored inside in a compartment below the cargo floor. It was
accessible through a door located just below the tailgate.
The Super wagon sold for $3,124 and 7,018 were built.
This was a substantial jump from the previous year.

The Chevrolet Fleetmaster wagon. Bodies were still being supplied by Ionia and Cantrell. The design was unchanged from the previous year. Construction continued to be ash pillars, mahogany panels, and a reinforced leatherette top with a ribbed wood ceiling.

The Fleetmaster Station Wagon, Model 2109, reached a record production of 10,171 this year, despite the fact that it was the only Chevrolet priced over $2,000 — with a base price of $2,013. The 3,405-pound car used a body of ash framing with mahogany panels and a leatherette top. However, the windshield posts and underbody were of steel. The rear mounted spare was equipped with a cover and lock.

All of the GM Divisions offered wagons again unchang from the previous year. An interesting controversial n concerning Chevrolet emerged in 1948. This was t matter of the Country Club model — a woodie claim by many to be a product of Chevrolet and Fisher Bod Both strongly deny the model. The Country Club w usually an Aerosedan with a woodie treatment to the do and quarter panels. Actually, neither Chevrolet or Fish Body had anything to do with the Country Club ca The woodie kits were dealer installed. Robert Peterson Monument, Col. was an original owner of one of th kits. He states that in 1948 he bought a Fleetmas convertible and had his dealer install the kit for unde hundred dollars. This was in Oklahoma City. He reca that there were posters advertising the kits but literature as such was available. The kits did dress up t car very nicely. But to find one today is very ra

A footnote to another of the GM Divisions was a n body design for Oldsmobile. The new body design w introduced to two of the Oldsmobile lines, the "76" a "88." They called this new design "Futuramic," A wag was offered in both series. Although they were wo bodied wagons, most of the car was sheet metal, includi the roof panel.

Ford and Mercury shared the same body again, u changed, but for the last time. The Ford Sportsman w offered again although none were produced in 1948. hold-over 1947 cars were sold as 1948s. The only way tell a 1948 Sportsman is by its serial number. Tho beginning with 899A are the 1948s.

The Chrysler Town and Country convertible and sed also were unchanged. Plymouth also offered its wag unchanged for 1948. DeSoto produced the Suburb utility sedan. Chrysler also offered the Traveler. Both we similar cars, but were only substitutes for wagons.

Bob Peterson of Monument, Col. remembers having his local delaer install a Country Club kit on his newly purchased Fleetmaster convertible. The photo of his car was taken in 1949. Note the Packard swan and eyebrows over the headlights, both very popular in those days.

The Chevrolet Country Club kit. The kits were usually installed on the Aero Sedan. In spite of popular thinking, these were not factory built woodies. This fine example is owned by Kim Norback of California.

The Chevrolet Carryall Suburban wagon. Its design was unchanged. There was room for eight passengers. It was available only as a 2-door model, using basic sheet metal of the ½-ton panel truck.

The Chrysler Town and Country Convertible, for the third year in a row, remained basically unchanged. Chrysler would continue to produce it through February 1949. However, all units produced after December 31, 1948 were titled as 1949 models. Whitewall tires were once again available options. The spotlights and rear fender stone shields were also options. Pictured here was the author's car, which is now owned by Jack Wilkkum of Valley City, Ohio.

This inside view of the Town and Country convertible shows an optional full-leather interior. The standard interior was leather bolsters and pleated bedford cord on the seats, with pleated leather and flat bedford cord on the door and quarter trim panels. The dash on this model is unusual in that it is made of marbleized plastic. Dashboards were usually of solid plastic.

The Chrysler Town and Country sedan also was unchanged. Whitewalls were again in vogue. The steel roof rack was replaced with a wooden one. Spotlights were options. This fine example is owned by Milton Smazik of Brookfield, Ill.

The DeSoto Suburban usually came in 2-tone paint combinations. The luggage rack and vinyl upholstery were standard equipment. The rear seat folded down to provide access into the trunk. This also made it possible to carry long pieces of cargo.

The Chrysler Town and Country continued to remain popular with the Hollywood set. Pictured here with his special built Town and Country is famed cowboy star Leo Carrillo. The hood with steer head was used only for public appearances. A stock hood was otherwise mounted. The car was painted to match the star's Palomino pony. This car is now on display at Harrah's Auto Museum in Reno, Nevada.

The Crosley wagon finally went into production this year. The little 2-door, 5-passenger wagon met some popularity and remained in production for a few years. Pictured here is a load of these wagons on their way to dealers' showrooms. The photo also dramatizes their small size. The convertible parked on the street is a 1946 Mercury while the truck hauler is a 1948 Chevrolet. Photo courtesy of Action Era Magazine.

The Ford Sportsman for 1948 was actually a 1947 model. None were built in 1948, but those that were left over became the 1948 models. The only way to tell a 1948 model is by its serial number.

The 1948 Ford wagon was unchanged from 1947. Whitewall tires once again were offered as an option. This excellent example is owned by Dr. Thomas Garrett of High Point, N. C.

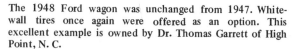

Another view of Dr. Garrett's 1948 Ford wagon. Note the rare roof rack. The roof rack was offered by Ford, but not many Fords were equipped with it. Also note the optional spotlight and fog lights.

GMC Division offered a station wagon similar to the Chevy Carryall. Only the name was changed. Most likely the body was by Cantrell. This fine example was owned by Floyd Persons of Poultney, Vt. It used the ¾-ton light truck chassis.

The International Harvester woodie was a 2-door wagon. Seating capacity was for eight passengers. The body builder is unknown. It was mounted on a ½-ton chassis. The door window was a crank-up type while the other windows were sliders, except the tailgate window, which was fixed. Note that the wipers are mounted above the windshield. This was a carryover from pre-war practice. This fine example is owned by Henry Shirley. Photo courtesy of Action Era Magazine.

The Medical Department of the Lincoln-Mercury Division of Ford Motor Company converted this 1948 Mercury Station Wagon, Model 79, into a full ambulance. The vehicle contained stretcher and attendant space, oxygen, and other emergency items. This was the last year that Mercury would use a fully wooden body on its wagon. In regular form, the wagon weighed 3,571 pounds and cost $2,207.

The Mercury wagon once again shared its body with the Ford wagon. It was unchanged. Only one model Mercury wagon was offered. It had seating capacity for eight passengers.

This was the last year for the Nash woodie sedan. The total 3-year production amounted to a mere 1,000 units, making this a very rare collector car today.

The Keller Station Wagon. It was originally called the Bobbi-Kar, but subsequently renamed when the company was reorganized. Only a few of these wagons were built.

The 1948 Oldsmobile Futuramic "76" and "88" Station Wagon. Oldsmobile introduced this new body design this year as a preview of 1949. Two wagons were offered in this design. Very little wood was used with this envelope body design. The roof panel was steel.

This 1948 Oldsmobile wagon wears an optional sun visor. The sun visor was a very popular item among all makes of cars. This was the predecessor to the sun shade windshields.

A rear view of the Oldsmobile Futuramic wagon. Most of the wood was confined to the tailgate area. The spare was carried inside. Rods under the taillights pushed these units into a visible position when the tailgate was lowered.

A rear view of the Oldsmobile Model "66" wagon. The quarter windows were sliders. The spare was mounted inside. The single tail light was hinged. The tailgate was hung with a piano-type hinge while the liftgate used external hinges. Note the use of a standard sedan-type bumper. The roof was still fabric covered.

An inside view of the Packard station sedan. It was upholstered in vinyl, and carried six passengers, with ample cargo area.

Packard introduced its first postwar wagon this year. The Station Sedan, as it was called, was a 4-door, 6-passenger model. The station sedan was a derivative of the 4-door sedan. Sheet metal was cut out of the door and wood added. Wood was overlaid on window frames. The roof panel was extended and a wagon box was added. Basically the overall design followed that of a sedan, pretty much as did the 1941 Chrysler Town and Country. The Cormorany hood ornament and rear fender skirts were options, as were the whitewall tires and side view mirror.

The Plymouth wagon for 1948 was a carbon copy of the 1946 and 1947 models. While other car makers were offering crank-up windows in their rear doors, Plymouth hung onto the sliders. The second and third seats were removable. Even though whitewall tires were available, Plymouth still featured the white wheel rings.

The Plymouth Sampan Bus. This hybrid wagon was and is prevalent in Hawaii. There are 12 in operation in and around the city of Hilo. They are very much like the Philipino Jittney, which is based on the Jeep.

The grille and minor trim changes were the only visible difference in the 1948 Pontiac. The wagon bodies were unchanged. They were supplied by Ionia and Hercules. The roof panel was still fabric covered. Front and rear doors had crank-up windows. The spare was mounted inside.

The do-it-yourselfers were still at work. This hybrid woodie is a combination of Pontiac, Dodge, and a few other makes. The spare is a unique treatment, as is the trunk compartment. This car was photographed at the Ford-Mercury Show in Dearborn.

The Willys Jeep wagon got a facelift this year. Simulated caning at the beltline was featured, instead of the fake woodie panels.

A milestone year in station wagon history occurred in 1949. The year marked a turning point. Station wagons were becoming very popular. Americans were making the trek to suburbia. The trend was to move away from the central city. This, coupled with the baby boom, gave rise to the popularity of the wagon. Its utility and versatility were recognized as desirable qualities by those who lived in suburbia, but worked in the central city. Now the wagon was used to haul people to the train station, to catch the 8:20, instead of hauling them away to some hotel.

A great many changes took place in the station wagon this year. The Big Three auto makers finally introduced new postwar designs and with these came new station wagon designs. More sheet metal and less wood was prevalent this year. And more all-steel wagons were introduced.

Ford introduced a new wagon to go along with its new postwar design. For the first time Ford offered two-door wagon. It was the only model available. The ro panel was all-steel, so for the first time Ford wagons ha a headliner. The rest of the body was wood, with the spa still mounted on the tailgate. Mercury shared the san body but the doors were contoured differently to matc Mercury's new postwar design. Ford implemented th use of Micro-Waves to achieve these contours. Son consideration was given to offering a Sportsman mod this year, but the idea never got past the building of single prototype. Ford reached record production wi 39,477 wagon units.

This was the last year for a Chrysler Town and Count convertible. A 2-door hardtop, the Newport, was promise but only a prototype was built. Wood in the Town an Country was no longer structural, as more steel su framing was used. Early models featured Di-Noc pane These later gave way to painted panels.

Chrysler reintroduced a wagon this year. It was 4-door, wood body wagon with all-steel roof and tailgat The spare was uniquely mounted in the tailgate in compartment that was stamped into the tailgate met The spare was then covered by a metal door. It could removed without opening the tailgate.

DeSoto introduced a production wagon for the fir time. And Dodge reintroduced a wagon this year. Chrysl DeSoto and Dodge all shared the same wagon bod DeSoto also continued with its Suburban model an brought out a companion car called the Carry-All. Th Carry-All was a Suburban with a shorter wheelbase an no roof rack.

Plymouth had two wagons this year — a Special DeLux and a DeLuxe. The Special DeLuxe was a woodie wit the same basic lines as the other corporate offerings. Th DeLuxe was an all new, all-steel 2-door model.

Chevrolet entered 1949 with a new wood body for i new postwar wagon. This body was first introduced b Oldsmobile in 1948 on the Futuramic Series wagon Now Chevrolet, Oldsmobile and Pontiac all shared th same body. These were supplied by Ionia. Shortly aft production for the new model year began, all three G Divisions switched to an all-steel wagon, using simulate wood decals. The basic design of the steel wagons was different from the wood version. This would be the la year for a Chevrolet woodie except for some wood bodi made by Cantrell for the Chevrolet truck chassis. Old mobile and Pontiac also offered their last woodies th

Buick, along with the other GM Divisions, introduced new sheet metal this year. Although this wagon looks like it is all-steel, about over third of it is wood. The greatest area of wood is in the tailgate. This is the Roadmaster Estate wagon. The only Buick style to have a production figure under 1,000 was the Roadmaster Estate Wagon, of which only 653 were built. At $3,734 and 4,490 pounds, it was Buick's most expensive and heaviest model. Dynaflow was standard in all Roadmasters, optional on Supers this year.

With the new body styling, the Super Estate Wagon, Model 59, did not have much room left for the wooden body. The roof was now all-steel, and the only large expanse of wood was on the tailgate. Rear windows were still of the sliding type, and the quarter windows were fixed in place. The car cost $3,178, weighed 4,100 pounds, and had a run of only 1,847.

This Cadillac woodie sedan was built for Mexico's President Miguel Aleman. Maurice Schwartz of California did the body work. It was mounted on a stretched Series 62 chassis. Photo courtesy of Special Interest Autos.

ear. Buick, on the other hand, continued to produce a
oodie wagon thru 1953.

Packard's Station Sedan was once again available, un-
hanged. Willys and Crosley both continued to offer
l-steel wagons with simulated wood. Kaiser-Frazer in-
oduced the Kaiser Traveler and Frazer Vagabond. These,
owever, were not wagons. They were utility sedans.
he designs were similar to the DeSoto Carry-All.

One of the last of the postwar wagon babies made its
ebut in 1949. The Playboy was introduced this year.
ut alas, only a prototype was built. It was a 2-door
oodie wagon, with a capacity for seating four adults.
he design was clean and well done, reminiscent of the
ter Rambler wagons.

Chevrolet's new postwar woodie wagon had bodies furnished
by Ionia. The new envelope design and steel roof panel left
very little wood. The upper rear door hinge was exposed
while the lower hinge was concealed. The inside of the
wagon was finished like a sedan, only the upholstery was
vinyl instead of cloth. With the introduction of the steel
roof panel, the Chevrolet wagon now had a headliner.

Shortly after the 1949 models were introduced, Chevrolet
announced this all-steel wagon. It looked like the woodie,
but the wood was simulated. This was the last year for the
Chevy woodie.

Cantrell continued to manufacture bodies for the Chevrolet
Carryall chassis. This would be Chevrolet's last real woodie
wagon. It was built through 1955 on the ½-ton truck
chassis. The body was 118 inches long, offering 86½ inches
of load length and 63½ inches of width.

Guy Barnette & Co. of Memphis specialized in converting the
standard station wagon into ambulances such as this attractive
unit. The model features DeLuxe chrome stone guards,
special rocker panel trim, and wide whitewalls. The Barnette
company also produced a similar model fitted for use as a
funeral hearse.

A rear view of the Chevrolet DeLuxe station wagon. Most of
the wood was found in the tailgate area. The spare was
moved inside below the cargo floor. The single tail light
was hinged and swung down when the tailgate was lowered.
Sedan rear bumpers continued to be used. This was the last
year for the Chevrolet wood wagon. It sold for $2,267.
Only 3,342 were produced.

National Body Co. of Knightston, Ind., supplied these
hearse bodies for the Chevrolet chassis, using a cut-frame
extension to lengthen the wheelbase. The company built
hearse, ambulance, and flower car bodies, using the standard
station wagon as a base. All units were built to order, after a
Chevrolet dealer sent both the order and vehicle to National
for the conversion.

This was the last year for the Chrysler Town and Country convertible. The luxury woodie had met with continued sales resistance. The high initial cost and subsequent difficult maintenance were the leading causes for its demise. But it was the last literally handcrafted American production car. For the buyer that wanted that kind of quality in a convertible, then this was the last chance, and 1,000 buyers could not resist, for that was the total production. The first 300 produced featured di-noc panels. These were later dropped in favor of painted panels.

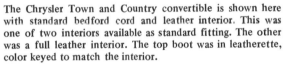

The Chrysler Town and Country convertible is shown here with standard bedford cord and leather interior. This was one of two interiors available as standard fitting. The other was a full leather interior. The top boot was in leatherette, color keyed to match the interior.

A rear view of the Chrysler Town and Country convertible. Loading and unloading luggage was difficult, although the trunk itself was huge.

Later Chrysler Town and Country models featured painted panels. Framing was of white ash, over a steel skeleton. This example was photographed in the assembly lot of Chrysler's Jefferson Ave. plant in Detroit.

An all-leather interior was one of the choices in the Chrysler Town and Country convertible. The door trim was in matching material.

The Chrysler Town and Country Newport 2-door hardtop was proposed and was featured in sales catalogs, but it was never put into production. Only this one prototype was built. More than likely production bugs could not be worked out in time, so the model was held over till 1950.

1949

A rear view of the Chrysler Town and Country hardtop prototype. The rear window was referred to as the clearbac window. Visibility was vastly improved.

A trunk view of the Town and Country Newport prototype. Unlike the convertible model, the Newport trunk opened down to the gravel pan. This made access easier. The trunk compartment was fully carpeted. The inside of the deck lid was fiber lined, as were the side panels.

Chrysler re-introduced a station wagon to its line this year. But it was not called a Town and Country. Instead it was designated the Royal. Framing was of white ash with di-noc simulated wood panels on the outside and real mahogany panels on the inside. The body parts were manufactured by Pekin Wood Products of Helena, Ark., a Chrysler subsidiary. The wagons were assembled in Detroit at the Jefferson Ave. Plant. The rear doors had sliding glass because the door design made the use of crank-up windows impossible.

Close-up view of the Chrysler Royal wagon. The unique tire compartment was built into the tailgate, but the tire could be removed from the outside, as the lid of this compartment was hinged like a door. Note that the liftgate was hung with three hinges. These were butt hinges which were partially exposed. Tail lights were mounted right on the wood framing. The single stop light was mounted in the center of the tailgate. It was not hinged.

The Chrysler Royal wagon had an all-steel top and unique spare tire carrier. All Chrysler Corporation wagons looked alike, even down to the spare tire compartment. The tailgate was hung with two heavy external hinges. Like a conventional sedan, the front doors used concealed hinges and the rear doors external hinges.

The special spare compartment of the Chrysler wagon in its open position shows how the spare was easily accessible without opening the tailgate.

The Chrysler Royal wagon interior was upholstered in a new vinyl called Tolex. It had an alligator skin texture. Doors were paneled in wood and rubber mats were used on the floor.

This is a steel skeleton of the Chrysler Town and Country convertible. The white ash framing was bolted to this sub-framing.

Metal panels are here being installed into the rear quarter section of the Town and Country. An excessive amount of hand labor was required to construct these bodies.

Deck lid framing of the Town and Country convertible is being hand sanded. This is the type of hand craftsmanship that built quality into this prestigious car, and also resulted in its subsequent demise.

Rear quarter framing for the Town and Country is getting its first varnish seal coat. Current industrial health standards would today require the sprayer to wear a mask.

A Town and Country door is being sprayed with an undercoater. This served as a sound deadener and sealer.

Metal panels are being fitted into Town and Country doors. Note the number of jigs required to hold the door framing in place. Production line techniques were impossible on these bodies.

The inner steel box of the Town and Country door is positioned after sealing. The steel box carried the window regulator and lock mechanism. It, too, had to be hand fitted.

The Town and Country steel skeleton and cowl section is receiving its finished coat of color paint. At this point, no wood has yet been applied to the frame. Doors and panels would later be color matched to the skeletons.

Town and Country doors are here being inspected before being released from the jigs that held them in place during assembly.

This inspector is checking tolerances on the Town and Country rear quarters. Wood pieces received a very rigid inspection.

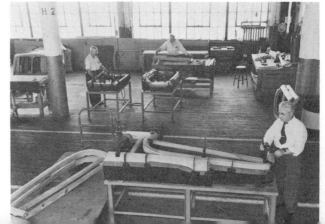

This Town and Country skeleton, fitted in a body jig, is now ready to receive its wood framing. A quarter panel is here being readied for attachment.

The wood framing is being fastened to the steel skeleton in this part of the Town and Country assembly process. Note the large amount of specialized tooling necessary for this rather limited production style.

A finished Town and Country body is being lifted from the body jig. The doors and trunk deck are still to be fitted.

The Crosley wagon for 1949 was virtually unchanged from the previous year. It was a 2-door, 5-passenger model, all-steel with simulated wood panels. The front door had a crank-up window, while the side window was a slider. Seats were upholstered in simulated leather. Note the Kaiser-type hood ornament. This fine example is owned by Bob Hickman of Pittsburgh, Pa.

A Town and Country body is receiving its final coat of varnish. Because the panels were painted, extensive masking was necessary to prevent varnish overspraying.

A finished Town and Country body is being lowered through an opening in the floor for the final body drop. At this stage, the body is complete.

Another new model introduced by DeSoto this year was the Carry-All. It too was a utility sedan. It incorporated some of the features of a station wagon into a sedan. The rear seat folded forward to provide a station wagon type cargo area through the trunk. Skid strips were also provided. Folded back in position, the Carry-All became an ordinary 4-door family sedan. This appealed to those who needed two types of vehicles but could only afford only.

The station wagon was a new introduction by DeSoto this year. The body for this wagon was shared with Chrysler. The wide front door required the rear door to kick over the rear fender, preventing the use of crank-up windows in the rear doors. The quarter windows were fixed, so the only opening windows were found in the doors. The DeSoto wagon could seat eight passengers. The two rear seats were removable.

DeSoto continued to offer the Suburban, which was a utility sedan. It was built on the long wheelbase taxi and limousine chassis, and with the use of jump seats could accommodate up to eight passengers. The roof rack was standard. It is very curious that the roof rack was standard on the Suburban but not on the station wagon.

For the first time since 1938, Dodge re-introduced a station wagon model. Only a single version was offered, a 4-door, 8-passenger wagon. The body design was identical to all the other Chrysler division wagons. The wood bodies were provided by USB&F. The roof was all-steel. The rear door and front door had movable windows; all the other glass was fixed.

The Dodge wagon, like its corporate counterparts, featured a steel roof and a unique spare compartment in the tailgate.

In addition to the Chevrolet Carryall, Cantrell also built woodie bodies for the Dodge ½-ton truck chassis. This example is owned by Al Behn of Maple Park, Ill.

Ford discontinued its 4-door wagon in favor of the 2-door. The new body design featured an all-steel roof and tailgate, sliding glass in the quarter windows and seating for eight passengers. The spare was still tailgate mounted. Ford's new wagon is pictured here at the Iron Mountain, Mich. plant. The wagon bodies were built and assembled here.

The all new Ford wagon featured an all-steel roof, which meant that for the first time a headliner was installed in a Ford wagon.

This stretched 4-door Ford wagon was built by Siebert of Toledo, Ohio. It featured a roof ventilator in the rear compartment. Photo courtesy of Ford Life.

A proposed 1949 Ford Sportsman. Only this prototype was built. Photo courtesy of Don Butler.

Kaiser did not offer a station wagon, but it did have a utility sedan called the Traveler. It was offered in two versions – a Standard and DeLuxe. The configuration was that of a sedan, but the back opened into a tailgate and liftgate. The cargo capacity was that of a station wagon. Loading was easy, and could be accomplished from the back end or rear door. Pictured here, loaded to capacity, is the Standard model. Photo courtesy of Richard Langworth.

The Kaiser Traveler utility sedan, unlike the DeSoto Carry-All or Chrylser Traveler, featured an entire back end that opened up. With the rear seat folded forward, the cargo area was as great as that of a station wagon. Note the skid strips. This is the DeLuxe version of the Kaiser Traveler. The rear fender skirts were standard. Photo courtesy of Richard Langworth.

1949

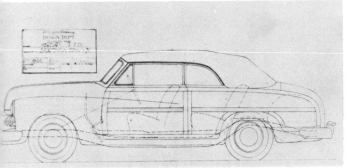

A Sportsman model was proposed for the 1949 Mercury and also for Lincoln. It would have been a soft top. Photo courtesy of Special Interest Autos. Ford concluded that construction would have been too expensive for such a limited production vehicle.

By virtue of sharing the Ford body, Mercury offered an identical 2-door, 8-passenger wagon. The Mercury wagons were also built at Iron Mountain. The rear fender skirts, shown here, were optional. The Mercury wagon sold for $2,715.

The Oldsmobile Series "76" Futuramic Station Wagon. This model wagon was first introduced in 1948. It was unchanged this year. This was the woodie version which would soon be discontinued.

A rear view of the Oldsmobile woodie wagon. The roof was all-steel. The spare was mounted inside. Swing up taillights with unique push-rods continued on the tailgate.

A rear view of the new all-steel Oldsmobile wagon. This was the Series "76." The wood look was only simulated through the use of Di-Noc film. The taillights on this model no longer used the exterior push-rods.

The Oldsmobile Series "88" wagon. The body was the same as on the "76" Series. This was the woodie model. Door panels were finished in wood inside.

The Packard station sedan was unchanged from the previous year. The hood Cormorant was optional as were the fog lights and spotlight.

A rear view of the Packard station sedan. A major part of the wood was found in the tailgate area of this all-steel wagon. Note the optional back-up light. Sedan components were used throughout, except for the roof and rear quarter section.

The newest model from Chrysler Corporation was this all-steel Plymouth wagon, a 2-door, 6-passenger model. The forward set of quarter windows were sliders, while the other set was fixed. The tailgate was two-piece and the spare was moved inside. This wagon was considered more of a workhorse than the woodie version. Total production for Plymouth wagons this year was 3,443 units.

Plymouth's wagon for 1949 resembled other wagons in the corporate family, but its body was all its own. Taillights on the body edges did away with the need for swing-down units.

Wagons were meant to be work vehicles, as depicted by this new Plymouth all-steel wagon. The flat folding tailgate was a definite advantage of working wagons. Without a spare tire attached to it, the tailgate was easier to handle. And, a solid rear bumper could be used, as depicted here.

A rear view of the Plymouth wagon with tailgate down. Note that with the third seat in place there wasn't much cargo area. This problem has never really been solved in 8-passenger wagons. Seats were still the removable type rather than the fold-down design.

A prototype of the Playboy station wagon. Its lines are very pleasing and reminiscent of the later Rambler wagons. It would seat four.

Pontiac's woodie wagon for 1949 shared its body with Chevrolet and Oldsmobile. This prime example is owned by Ross Whitehead of Tucson, Ariz.

A rear view of Ross Whitehead's beautiful Pontiac woodie wagon. This was the last year for a Pontiac woodie with real wood. The spare was mounted inside. As did Oldsmobile, the Pontiac wagons also used push-rods to insure that the taillights and license would be visible at all times.

Like its corporate brothers, Pontiac also offered an all-steel wagon. It was introduced shortly after model introduction. Note the optional fender skirts.

A rear view of the Studebaker wagon. The roof was fabric covered although it looks like steel. The body builder is unknown, but it may well be a Cantrell body, exported. The vehicle was not equipped with a rear bumper, and its taillights are mounted on the body edges, away from the tailgate. Wagons of any type were quite rare in Europe at this time, so this strange Studebaker was really an oddity, both at home and abroad.

This rare Studebaker wagon was photographed in Belgium. It is similar to the body offered by Cantrell for the Chevrolet and Dodge light truck chassis. Photo courtesy of Patrick Van der Strict, Brussels, Belgium.

Buick continued to offer a woodie wagon. This was the Roadmaster model. Although it is a true woodie wagon, most of the wood can be found only in the tailgate. This example is owned by James Kimble of Fort Wayne, Ind.

The 1950 Buick Super Estate Wagon. This was Model 59. It was a 6-passenger wagon. Bodies for both Buick wagons were the same. It used a 121.5-inch wheelbase and was 204 inches long overall. It weighed 4,115 pounds.

Chevrolet's Styline DeLuxe Station Wagon was an all-steel wagon with simulated wood. It was designated Model 2119. Perhaps because of the all-steel, virtually maintenance free body, Chevrolet sales sky-rocketed. A total of 166,995 wagons were produced this year. Another factor that probably helped boost sales was that Chevy's wagon was a 4-door model. Ford was offering only a 2-door. Price tag for this wagon was $1,994.

A rear view of the Chevrolet wagon clearly indicates that the spare was housed inside the car. Note the level tailgate and swing-down tail light and license.

At the start of the fifties the station wagon had becom firmly entrenched. It was most assuredly here to sta The big three auto makers were even expanding the wagon line to include several models.

By 1950, a few basic design principles had been s down for station wagons. What was now established wou become the rule of thumb. These principles have remaine unchanged, to date. For one thing, wood was out, ste was in. Simulated wood decals were acceptable and we usually found in the more expensive models. Next, th station wagon would, unfortunately, look like a bo Chrysler's attempt at getting away from this with th introduction of the Town and Country had failed. The was no way to get the extra cargo space without lookin like a box. However, it was decreed that the wagon mu look like a sedan below the beltline. This was a mus Next, the station wagon could be a 2-door or 4-do model. It could carry from 6 to 10 passengers. And, th rear seats must be of a design so as to fold or be remove altogether to provide a flat, unobstructed cargo floo

All of these principles had by now been established Their interpretation would vary slightly according t manufacturer. The only area in which new design concep would be tried, was and still is, the tailgate sectio And, of course, the never ending problem of what to d with the spare would exercise the talents of the designer

Buick wagons for 1950 came in two models, th Roadmaster and the Super. Both were woodies. Chevrole Oldsmobile and Pontiac all shared the same basic all-ste body with simulated wood decals. The bodies were b Fisher.

Chrysler offered a Town and Country 2-door hardto the Newport. It would be the last Town and Countr woodie. The name would subsequently be used to desi nate Chrysler wagons. Only 700 of the Town and Countr Newports were built. Chrysler also continued to offer th Royal wagon. The tailgate of the Royal was redesigne It was now all steel, and the rear window cranked dow into the tailgate. The Royal shared its body with bot Dodge and DeSoto. Plymouth continued to offer it woodie wagon unchanged from the previous year, an also had available the all-steel wagon. An interesting not for 1950: Chrysler built 99 all-steel wagons and labele them Town and Countries. They were used primarily a ambulances. But it did offer a preview of what was t come in 1951.

Ford and Mercury wagons were unchanged, still sharin the same bodies. Both were woodie wagons. Nash r introduced a wagon in March. It was the first wagon sinc 1941. This was the Model 5024 Rambler, a 2-door all-ste wagon. Packard offered its Station Sedan for the last yea Sagging sales forced its demise. There would be no mor Packard wagons until 1957. The Willys wagon was u changed, and would remain so through the 1950s.

1950

Chevrolet continued to offer the Carry-All Suburban. It was designated Model 3106. This year it could carry up to eight passengers. It was built on the ½-ton truck chassis. The rear doors were of the panel delivery type. A 3-speed column shift was standard, but a 4-speed floor shift could be ordered.

Only one Town and Country model was offered by Chrysler. It was this 2-door hardtop, designated the Newport. Like the previous year's model, the superstructure was steel with wood applied, somewhat like the Ford Sportsman of 1946-48. Early models carried simulated wood panels, while the later models had these panel inserts painted the same color as the front sheet metal.

An interior view of the 1950 Chrysler Town and Country Newport. By the standards of the day, it was a super luxury interior. It would, by today's standards, be considered an optional luxury interior. Real leather and nylon cord were the materials used, and the buyer was given a full range of color combinations to pick from.

Chrysler continued to offer the Royal Station Wagon for 1950. Few changes were made from the 1949 model. It had a steel roof, white ash framing and simulated wood insert panels. This was a 4-door, 6-passenger wagon based on the Windsor chassis.

Only 700 Town and Country Newports were built in this last year for the beautiful style. The rear window styling was referred to as "Clear-bac," indicating that visibility to the rear was excellent, which it was. The wrap-around rear bumper of 1949, which was indigenous to this model, was replaced with a standard sedan bumper this year.

A rear view of the Chrysler Royal wagon shows the change that was made in the tailgate. The spare was moved inside and the rear window now lowered into the tailgate.

Only 99 of these all-steel Town and Country wagons were built in 1950, and they were primarily used as ambulances. This was a preview of what was to come. After 1950, Chrysler no longer produced the Town and Country luxury car, but it kept the name and applied it to its line of all-steel station wagons.

This was the limited production all-steel Town and Country Station Wagon. It is shown here dressed up in its ambulance garb, complete with red flashing light and siren. This ambulance was produced by Chrysler and was made available through its regular dealer outlets.

An inside view of the Chrysler Royal woodie wagon. Inside panels were real mahogany plywood. Note the protective skid strips and upholstered wheel housings. By any standards, this was a beautiful cargo area.

After the absence of one year, Chrysler re-introduced the Traveler Utility Sedan. Now those who did not care for the conventional station wagon could have a real sedan with most of the wagon's features, for the Traveler incorporated many of the features of a wagon into a sedan. These included a roof rack and rear folding seat. With the rear seat folded there was cargo access clear through to the trunk. The Traveler sold for $2,580.

An inside view of the all-steel Chrysler Town and Country wagon ambulance. The interiors of both the Royal woodie and the Town and Country were identical. This photo shows just how the stretcher was installed. One of the features of the 1950 Chrysler wagon was the introduction of the disappearing tailgate window. This was one of the features which made the Chrysler wagon such a natural to ambulance conversion.

The Crosley Station Wagon. Crosley was one of the early pioneers in compact cars and all-steel station wagons. The quarter windows and door windows were of the sliding type. The wood panels were simulated. This 2-door was the only wagon model offered by Crosley. It carried 5 passengers.

A rear view of the DeSoto wagon. The man in the photo is demonstrating a new feature, the disappearing tailgate window. This feature was found on all Chrysler Corporation wagons for 1950, with the exception of the Plymouth. The disappearing window provided easier loading. It would take the rest of the industry a number of years to adopt this feature.

The DeSoto Station Wagon was available only in the Custom series. The roof was steel, the body was of white ash framing with simulated wood insert panels. Inside panels were of plywood and the seats were upholstered in "Tolex" – a new vinyl of simulated alligator material. DeSoto shared its wagon body with both Chrysler and Dodge.

The DeSoto Diplomat Custom Station Wagon was an export wagon based on the Plymouth. It was in fact a Plymouth dressed up in DeSoto trim. It was not available in the United States.

The DeSoto Diplomat Commercial Utility. Again, this was a Plymouth wagon with DeSoto trim. This two-door model was a 6-passenger wagon, the only all-steel DeSoto wagon sold in 1950. It was not available in the United States.

Dodge continued to offer two models in the station wagon line, and each was distinctly different. The standard station wagon was the Coronet with wood grain on the body sides, while the Dodge Sierra was an all-steel wagon. The attractive woodie shown here tipped the scales at 3,850 pounds and sold for $2,883 while the Sierra weighed 3,726 pounds and cost $2,503. Dodge built a total of 600 of the woodie wagons and another 100 of the Sierra type this year. Like all Coronet models, these cars rode on the 123½-inch wheelbase and were powered by a 6-cylinder engine that produced 103 horsepower at 3600 RPM from its 230 cubic inches.

In 1950 some men still dreamed of manufacturing the car of their dreams. This was the Mini Sedanette, a 3-wheel prototype built by Capt. James Martin of Rochelle Park, N.J. It never made production. Photo courtesy of Special Interest Autos.

Ford station wagons for 1950 were unchanged. All Ford models received a face lifting this year, but it wasn't much of a lift. Not wanting to tamper with success, Ford made only minor changes to the grille and dashboard. Ford offered only one type of wagon, a 2-door, 6-passenger version.

Ford offered the 4-wheel drive Ranger model to compete with the Chevrolet Carry-All Suburban. Both were based on the light truck ½-ton chassis and both were 2-door models with the same passenger capacity. Side windows, with the exception of the door, were of the sliding type. However, the Carry-All was a far more popular vehicle than the Ranger.

A rear view of the Ford wagon. Note that while the Ford wagon is a true woodie, the tailgate window section is all-steel. Ford still featured the two-piece tailgate with rear mounted spare. The tail light on the right is an option. Quarter windows were of the sliding type. This model is missing its rear hubcaps.

To demonstrate the roominess of the Ford, this family carried a boat inside. Now it looks like they are picnicking on a golf course, so it seems the boat is for water holes. And the kids probably think it's great fun. Having lost their seats, they now get to ride inside the boat while Daddy drives around looking for those water holes. Watch out for the sand traps.

In 1950, Ford Motor was considering a woodie sedan based on the Lincoln. As evidenced by this line drawing it would have been pretty neat. Rear fender sheet metal continued to form the lower back panel. The continental wheel was a nice touch. One can only speculate on whether the actual model would have been as attractive as the design exercise.

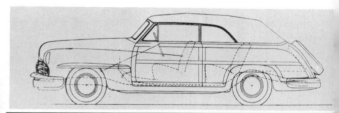

Another view of the proposed Lincoln woodie. This one with a soft top. One wonders if Ford would have called it a Sportsman? Photo courtesy of Special Interest Autos.

The Mercury Station Wagon was a 2-door, 6-passenger model. The body was identical to the Ford. The roof was steel, and a two-piece tailgate was still featured. Quarter windows were of the sliding type. The tailgate window was framed in steel. This was the only wagon Mercury offered. It was one of the sharpest wagons on the market, and carried a price tag of $2,560.

In March of 1950, the Nash Rambler Model 5024 made its bow. This was a 2-door, 6-passenger station wagon — an all-steel version decked out in two-tone paint. Nash, together with Crosley, were pioneers in compact station wagons. The Rambler had an 82 horsepower engine and gave up to 30 miles per gallon.

The top of the Oldsmobile wagon line was this "88" Series wagon. A 4-door, 6-passenger model, this too was an all-steel wagon with the wood treatment being simulated. Extra bright metal trim and standard rear fender skirts immediately identified this wagon as the luxury model.

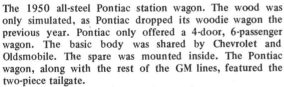

The Oldsmobile Model "76" 4-door, 6-passenger wagon was the least expensive Olds wagon. The wood was simulated, as the body was all-steel. Rear fender skirts were optional.

The 1950 all-steel Pontiac station wagon. The wood was only simulated, as Pontiac dropped its woodie wagon the previous year. Pontiac only offered a 4-door, 6-passenger wagon. The basic body was shared by Chevrolet and Oldsmobile. The spare was mounted inside. The Pontiac wagon, along with the rest of the GM lines, featured the two-piece tailgate.

Studebaker did not have a production station wagon this year. However, several of these Cantrell bodies were supplied on ½-ton Studebaker truck chassis. This version, called a Town Car, wears large balloon tires, possibly for use in the Near East desert countries, where Studebaker was still a very popular make.

The Plymouth Special DeLuxe Suburban wagon was one of three wagons offered by Plymouth this year. It was the top of the line and unchanged from 1949. The two-piece tailgate was still retained. It was the only Chrysler Corporation wagon with this feature.

A rear view of the Plymouth Special DeLuxe Suburban. The continental tire compartment was retained, while the other Chrysler Corporation wagons stored the spare tires inside. This fine example is owned by Bill Powers of Anaheim, Calif. Photo courtesy of National Woodie Club.

The Plymouth DeLuxe 2-door, 6-passenger all-steel station wagon was first introduced in 1949. Side windows were of the sliding type. The tailgate was a two-piece affair.

New for this year was this Plymouth Special Suburban model, a 2-door, 6-passenger wagon. It was the DeLuxe wagon with extra trim and luxury appointments. The center side window was of the sliding type. The spare was mounted inside. Seat cushions and backs were upholstered in tan bedford cord.

The Willys station wagon was unchanged for 1950. This basic design, introduced in 1946, remained unchanged throughout the 1950s. It was the only true postwar station wagon design, in that it was not based on a sedan design of any previous type.

Buick wagons for 1951 were unchanged. They were still bodies and the bodies were still by Ionia. Chevrolet, Pontiac and Oldsmobile all offered all-steel wagons with simulated wood applique. These bodies were by Fisher. The Chevrolet wagon sold very well as its design was very pleasing.

Chrysler introduced its new Town and Country all-steel station wagons this year in three different series — the Windsor, Saratoga and New Yorker. Dodge and DeSoto both introduced new all-steel wagons. In addition to the wagons, DeSoto also had the Suburban and Carry-All utility sedans in their line-up. Plymouth introduced a new battery of names for its three series — the Cranbrook, Cambridge, and Concord. The station wagon was in the Concord series. Two models were available, the Concord Suburban and the Concord Savoy. The Savoy was the more DeLuxe version. Both models were 2-door and all-steel.

Ford and Mercury wagons were unchanged. Both were 4-door models and were still woodies. Ironically, in this last year of the Woodie for Ford Motor Co., the bodies were made by Ionia.

Nash continued with its 2-door Rambler wagon. It was called the Custom. The body style was unchanged.

A Bently Shooting Break. This European body builder took a page out of the American wagon book. This design was not in keeping with the usual shooting break, which called for a steel front door.

Buick was now the only remaining GM Division producing a real woodie wagon. This is the Super Estate Wagon. The wood body was made of white ash and mahogany. The body was built by Ionia. The greatest area of wood remained in the tailgate section. The Super wagon sold for $3,133. A total of 2,212 were built.

The Buick Roadmaster Estate Wagon, Model 79R, was a 4-door, 6-passenger real woodie wagon. It was the only real woodie produced by General Motors. Four port holes on the front fenders identified this wagon as being the top of the line. This wagon carried a price tag of $3,780. Only 679 were built.

This Cadillac wagon was custom built for Minneapolis contractor Merril M. Madsen, by Coachcraft of Los Angeles. The designer was Philip Wright. It was built on a Model "62" chassis. The spare was mounted inside. The rear window retracted into the tailgate and was power operated.

Only one model wagon was offered by Chevrolet. It was in the DeLuxe Series. A 4-door, 9-passenger model, it was an all-steel wagon with simulated wood treatment. Chevrolet sales took a nose dive this year. After having produced 166,995 wagons the previous year, only a meager 23,586 were sold this year. The two-piece tailgate was retained and rear fender skirts were standard. The Chevrolet wagon sold for $2,191.

The Chrysler Windsor Town and Country Wagon was one of three wagons offered by Chrysler this year. Pictured is a 4-door, 6-passenger model. In addition to the disappearing tailgate window, Chrysler wagons featured a vent window in the rear passenger doors. The cost of the Windsor model was $3,083.

The Saratoga Town and Country wagon. This model was powered by the newly introduced famed Hemi V-8. It was a 4-door, 6-passenger wagon. Features included the disappearing tailgate window and rear door vent windows. The Saratoga wagon was new for this year. Only 1,967 were produced. Sandwiched between the New Yorker and the Windsor, it sold for $3,183.

Offered as a standard production until 1951 were these Windsor Town & Country ambulances. The cars used the standard wagon bodies, with interior conversions made at Chrysler's own plant on a to-order basis. A total of 153 were sold.

The interior of the new Windsor Town & Country ambulance shows how the vehicle was set up for one stretcher patient. The attendant's seat could be folded down flush with the floor, and a second stretcher, shown folded here, could be put into use. The vehicles were not well enough equipped to be considered a true ambulance, but they did provide relatively inexpensive emergency first aid transportation facilities.

The top of the Chrysler wagon line was this New Yorker Town and Country wagon, a 4-door, 6-passenger model. It topped the price scale at $4,051 and remained the highest priced production wagon in America. It enjoyed a very short production run, and only 251 were built. Chrysler did not offer the New Yorker wagon in 1952.

The DeSoto Carry-All sedan. This utility sedan was companion to the Suburban. It was a less expensive model without the roof rack. The cargo area was accessible through the trunk, up to the back of the front seat. This feature alone gave it great utility. The ribbed, heavy-duty floor provided a good, substantial platform.

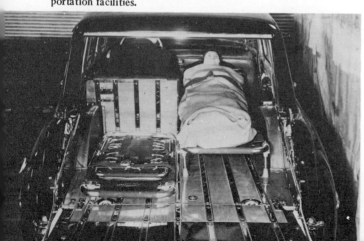

DeSoto, in addition to its station wagon, continued to offer the Suburban, a utility sedan first introduced in 1947. The Suburban incorporated features of a station wagon into a sedan. These included a roof rack and folding rear seat, which provided access into the trunk.

The DeSoto all-steel station wagon, a 4-door, 9-passenger model, was the only wagon offered by DeSoto. The body was shared with Chrysler. Like its big brother, the Town and Country, the DeSoto wagon featured a disappearing tailgate window, first introduced in 1950, and rear door vent windows. Skid strips were provided in the cargo area to prevent scuffing of the panels.

Having dropped the woodie wagon, Dodge only offered the all-steel Sierra station wagon during the 1951-1952 model run. A very attractive car, the Dodge Sierra shared basic body components with the Chrysler station wagon of the same era. In 1951 this model sold for $2,786 and tipped the scales at 3,750 pounds, but by 1952 this same car went for $2,926 and weighed 3,725 pounds. This two-year run classified the Sierra as a Coronet or D-42 Model, and like other Coronets it rode on the 123½-inch wheelbase and featured absolutely no major styling change from 1951 to 1952. Only 4,000 of these interesting wagons were built.

Only one wagon was available from Mercury, a 2-door, 8-passenger model. The body was shared with Ford. This would be the last year for a real woodie wagon for Mercury. The bodies were manufactured by Ionia. Fender skirts were optional and this wagon is shown with an optional roof antenna. This excellent example is owned by Jim Merriem of Monticello, Minn.

This was the last year for a structural wood station wagon from Ford. The woodie was unchanged from the previous two years. It was still a 2-door, 8-passenger model. The tailgate was still two-piece, with the window being framed in steel. The quarter windows were of the sliding type. Incidentally, the bodies for this wagon were produced by Ionia. Ford had closed its Iron Mountain facilities at the end of the 1950 model run. The Ford Country Squire Wagon sold for $2,255.

A rear view of the Jim Merriem Mercury wagon shows that the two-piece tailgate was retained, with spare mounted on the outside. The Ford Motor Co. wagons were the last remaining wagons that mounted the spare on the outside. Note that the rear bumper of the Mercury wagon is identical to the Ford.

Frazer did not offer a station wagon but it did produce a utility sedan called the Vagabond. This sedan was similar to the Chrysler Traveler and DeSoto Suburban. However, unlike the Chrysler and DeSoto cars, the Vagabond featured a two-piece tailgate type of rear end. With the rear seat folded, this provided excellent loading access. Skid strips were provided on the decking to prevent scuffing of the panels. Photo courtesy of Richard Langworth.

The Rambler Custom 2-door, 6-passenger wagon was one of two Rambler wagons offered by Nash this year. Side windows were of the sliding type, and the spare was mounted on the inside. Rambler enjoyed some brisk sales with this model. It had an all-steel body.

This year Plymouth introduced the Concord Savoy. It was one of two wagons offered by Plymouth this year. Only 2-door, 6-passenger wagons were available. All Plymouth wagons were all steel. The body design was virtually unchanged. Plymouth wagons were powered by six cylinder engines with manual three-speed transmissions.

Once again Pontiac shared its wagon body with Chevrolet and Oldsmobile. Only one wagon model was offered by Pontiac, this 4-door, 6-passenger version. It was an all-steel wagon with simulated wood. Rear fender skirts were standard. Two power plants were available—an economical Six and cast iron straight Eight.

Least expensive of the Plymouth wagons was the Suburban. It had the same features as its more expensive counterpart, but lacked the luxury appointments. The two-piece tailgate was retained and one set of the two quarter windows were of the sliding type.

Unchanged for 6 consecutive years was the Willys Jeep Station Wagon. It was still an all-steel wagon with simulated wood. The tailgate was still two-piece, and one set of the quarter windows were of the sliding type. The spare was mounted inside.

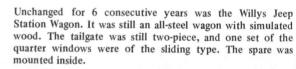

n July of 1952, Powel Crosley sold his Crosley Motors
General Tire Co. The sturdy, economical little car
n Cincinnati was two decades ahead of its time. After
gas was only 23 cents per gallon. Who cared about gas
eage. The last Crosley wagons cost $1,000 in 1951,
last year of their manufacture.

uick was still offering a woodie wagon. It was now the
y real woodie American wagon available. All of the
er GM Divisions were building the all-steel wagon
h simulated wood applique. Chevrolet, Pontiac and
smobile all shared the same wagon body, built by
er Body.

hrysler dropped the New Yorker Town and Country.
ere were now only two Chrysler wagons, the Windsor
the Saratoga. Dodge, DeSoto and Plymouth wagons
e unchanged. None of the Chrysler Corp. wagons
ried any wood, real or simulated.

ord and Mercury offered new models this year. The
gon line was expanded to three series for Ford and two
dels for Mercury. Ford continued to be a holdout in
ping the spare mounted on the outside of the tailgate.
top of the Ford and Mercury line carried simulated
od panels and real wood hang-on framing.

ash changed the name of its Rambler wagon. It was
v known as the Rambler Greenbrier. It was still a
oor, 6-passenger model, with two-tone paint, unchanged
m previous years.

Buick Roadmaster Estate Wagon Model 79B. This was the
only woodie offered by GM. A 4-door, 6-passenger model,
it was unchanged from the previous year. It cost $3,780.
Only 359 were built.

Buick Super Estate Wagon. Most of the wood was found in
the tailgate. The Super and Roadmaster shared the same
body, but the two models could be told apart at a glance
by counting those famous Buick portholes. The Roadmaster
had four. The Super was also known as the Model 59. It cost
$3,133 and was the only Super to exceed $3,000 base price.

Chevrolet's single wagon offering was all-steel with simulated
wood. Rear fender skirts were standard. This was a 4-door,
9-passenger model. It cost $2,297. A grand total of 12,756
were built.

Chevrolet continued to offer the Carry-All Suburban. This
was a two-door wagon that could seat 9 passengers. It was
offered in a choice of 12 colors and two-tone combinations.
It used a 116-inch wheelbase and carried a 4,800 lb. G.V.W.
rating. A 3-speed synchromesh transmission was standard,
a 4-speed optional.

A Chevrolet Carry-All Suburban with a woodie body by Cantrell. These were special order bodies. The same type body was used on the GMC chassis, the Dodge and Studebaker light truck chassis.

Chrysler Windsor Town and Country, ambulance conversion. The Chrysler wagon adapted well to this type of usage. A total of 153 were built by Chrysler, all on special order.

Chrysler Saratoga Town and Country wagon. The New Yorker model was dropped. This was the only wagon available with a V-8. It cost $3,950.

The Chrysler Windsor Town and Country wagon, a 4-door, 6-passenger model, was unchanged from the previous year. It cost $3,220. Only 1,967 were built in its two-year production run.

DeSoto Firedome 8 Wagon. This all-steel 4-door wagon was also available in the Custom 6 series. The body was identical with the Chrysler wagon, with the major exterior difference being in the exterior trim.

The Mercury wagon was available in the Custom Series. Add-on wood framing did not lend itself to the new Mercury body, providing instead a rather patchwork appearance. The 3-seat version cost $2,834, while the 6-passenger model cost $2,775. The car weighed about 3,800 pounds.

Ford's new body for 1952 lent itself well to the wagon treatment. This is the top of the line Country Squire. Hang-on framing was real wood, panels were decals. This year Ford returned to the four-door wagon. It sold for $2,385.

Ford Country Sedan wagon. This was Ford's first year for the all-steel wagon. The spare was also moved inside for the first time. The Country Sedan was a very attractive wagon and sold well at $2,250 base price, F.O.B. Dearborn.

Plymouth's top of the line wagon was this Concord Savoy model, a 2-door, 6-passenger wagon.

The Plymouth Concord Suburban was the less expensive wagon offered by Plymouth. It too was a 2-door, 6-passenger model, differing from the Savoy primarily in interior appointments.

The bottom of the Ford wagon line was this 2-door Ranch wagon. It was Ford's only 2-door offering. It was rather austere in comparison to the Country Sedan and Country Squire, but sold well at $2,080 to the utility-minded trade.

An inside view of the Plymouth Concord Savoy wagon shows the attractive 2-tone fabric and plastic combination used in the upholstery and paneling. The floor mats were rubber.

Nash continued to offer the Rambler Greenbrier wagon, a 2-door, 6-passenger model. Pictured here with the wagon is none other than famed golfer Sam Snead. The car was designated the Model 5224.

This was Pontiac's top of the line wagon. It shared its all-steel body with Chevrolet. The wood was simulated. Sliding rear quarter windows were used.

This was the less expensive of Pontiacs two wagon models offered in 1952. The wood was simulated. This was strictly a no nonsense work wagon, despite its relatively attractive appearance.

A fancy version of the Willys wagon could be had with simulated caning at the belt line. This made the rather military-looking wagon a bit more attractive, especially with the wide whites. Few of the fancy jobs had 4-wheel drive.

Willys offered two wagon models this year. Both looked the same as the previous year's. However, the simulated pressed steel panels were not decorated with wood-like decals, but were painted in body color. This is the 4-wheel drive version.

This was the last year for the Buick Woodie wagon, and subsequently the last year for a production American woodie wagon. An era had come to a close.

Buick once again offered a Roadmaster and Super Estate wagon. Both were 6-passenger wagons, with bodies by Ionia. The Roadmaster sold for $4,031 and 670 were built. The Super sold for $3,430 and 1,830 were built. Chevrolet, Pontiac and Oldsmobile again all shared the same basic all-steel wagon body. However, the simulated wood treatment only appeared on the DeLuxe models. The lesser models used the same sheet metal panels, but these were painted to match fenders and hood. Chevrolet introduced a one-piece curved windshield.

Dodge and DeSoto each offered two wagon models. The Dodge Sierra wagons were available in the Coronet and Meadowbrook series. Both were 2-door versions. DeSoto continued with the Firedome V-8 and introduced the Powermaster Six. Both were 4-door models. Plymouth offered two wagons, this time in two different series. The top model Savoy was in the Cranbrook series. The lesser model Suburban in the Cambridge series. Both were 2-door models.

Ford maintained the same three series. The Country Squire, with add-on woodie trim, was the top of the line. The Country Sedan, a 4-door without the woodie trim, and the 2-door Ranch wagon. Mercury offered only one wagon in the Custom series. It had simulated wood panels, 4 doors and was available as a 6 or 9-passenger model. The add-on wood framing and simulated panels had an improved appearance over the previous year.

The Buick Roadmaster Estate Wagon is shown here with accessory Skylark wire wheels. It was designated Model 79-R and sold for $4,031. Only the sportscar-like Skylark was higher priced. The wood body was manufactured by Ionia. It was made of white ash and mahogany. Only a limited number of these wagons were produced — 670 in all.

Another view of the Buick Roadmaster wagon. Those tell-tale four portholes immediately identified this model. The fine example pictured here is owned by Michael Baker of Flint, Mich. Note the optional spotlight.

This was the last year for the Buick woodie wagon. It also marked the last year for an American production Woodie wagon. Again, most of the wood was found in the tailgate.

Three portholes identified this wagon as a Buick Super Estate Wagon. This is a 4-door, 6-passenger wagon. The two-piece tailgate was still retained. This would be the last year for a Super series wagon. The wire wheel covers were optional. Only 1,830 were made and sold for $3,430.

A custom built Cadillac Station Wagon. The design was by Brook Stevens. The body was of real wood, but the body builder is unknown. The roof was steel. It had a two-piece tailgate, with two handles on the tailgate window. A basic 4-door sedan was worked up into the wagon, with the original sedan dimensions retained. Seating capacity was for nine passengers. It is assumed that either oak or white ash was used for the body.

Available only as a 4-door, 9-passenger model was the Chevrolet Townsman. This was the only year that the expensive Townsman appeared in the 210 DeLuxe series. The simulated wood treatment was confined mainly to the tailgate section. The quarter windows were of the sliding type. A total of 7,988 of these wagons were produced. They sold for $2,273.

The Chevrolet Townsman 210 DeLuxe wagon was new for this year. It was the top of the Chevrolet line of wagons. Two-tone paint and simulated wood treatment were some of its features. Fender skirts were an option. The one-piece curved windshield was introduced this year.

The Chevrolet Handyman 210 DeLuxe was a 4-door, 6-passenger model. This example featured a two-tone paint combination. And, although the metal stamping could accommodate the simulated wood treatment, this model did not carry it. The simulated wood was relegated to the top of the line. The Handyman 210 DeLuxe sold for $2,123 and 18,258 were produced.

The Chevrolet DeLuxe 210 Handyman was Chevrolet's most popular model. It did not have simulated wood. Two-tone paint was very popular and helped make this a very attractive wagon.

Available only as a 4-door, 6-passenger model was the Chevrolet 150 Special Handyman. This was Chevy's least expensive wagon. It usually sold in one solid color, although two-tone paint combinations were available. For the first time, Chevrolet featured folding rear seats. The quarter windows in this model were fixed. The Special Handyman sold for $2,010 with 22,408 being produced.

Once again Chevrolet offered the Carry-All Suburban. The all-steel wagon was based on a ½-ton truck chassis. This year a two-piece tailgate was featured. It had a seating capacity for up to nine passengers. The Carry-All was available in single solid colors or two-tone combinations.

Chrysler restored the New Yorker Town and Country to its line-up. This one is pictured with optional wire wheel covers, spotlight, and trailer hitch. Chrysler wagons also featured a crank-down rear window.

One of two wagons offered by DeSoto this year was this Powermaster Six all-steel station wagon. It was a 4-door, 6-passenger model, powered by a thrifty 6-cylinder engine. It featured, in addition to a disappearing tailgate window, a curved one-piece windshield. The spare was mounted in a compartment beneath the cargo floor, as it had been since 1950.

The DeSoto Fire Dome V-8 all-steel station wagon. This body was shared with Chrysler, and carried the same features including a disappearing tailgate window and vent windows in the rear doors.

The least expensive of the 1953 Dodge station wagons was the Meadowbrook Suburban for six passengers. Only available with the 230 cubic inch Six, the Suburban, like its Coronet relative the Sierra, rode on a wheelbase of 114 inches. This car sold for $2,201 and weighed 3,190 pounds. Dodge station wagons this year offered a full 68½-inches of usable cargo space when the rear seat was folded down, 44 inches when this seat was up, and 91¼ inches with the seat folded down and utilizing the bottom half of the tailgate for a loading surface. The compartment had a maximum width of 49¼ inches.

The most utilitarian model in the Coronet Series was the Sierra station wagon offered with a V-8 engine only. A 2-door wagon, this vehicle rode on a wheelbase of 114 inches like all 1953 Dodge wagons. In its Coronet V-8 trim this vehicle sold for $2,528 and tipped the scales at 3,425 pounds. Unlike some of today's large wagons, the 1953 Dodge Sierra would only seat six passengers and had a 2-piece tailgate at the rear.

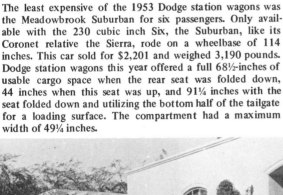

This was the DeSoto Diplomat-Custom Special Commercial Utility wagon. It was an export wagon based on the Plymouth body and chassis. Only the trim was DeSoto.

The Ford Country Squire was part of the new Crestline series. It was a 4-door, 9-passenger model that sold for $2,410. The hang-on framing was still made of wood. Some may argue that this qualified it as a real woodie. Probably if the Chevrolet Country Club models of the late forties can be considered as woodies, then this is in fact a woodie.

Unchanged from the previous year was the Ford Country Sedan. It was now a part of the Customline series. Pictured is a 4-door, 6-passenger model. The two-tone paint was an option. 1953 marked Ford's Golden Anniversary. All Ford wagons sold well, as they always did. The Country Sedan was priced at $2,270.

This is a rear view of the Ford Ranch Wagon. The Ranch Wagon was part of the low priced Mainline series. It was the only 2-door Ford wagon. The two-piece tailgate was retained and quarter windows were of the sliding type.

The bottom of the Ford wagon line-up was this Ranch Wagon, part of the Mainline series. It was available with a Six or V-8 engine. It only came as a 2-door, 6-passenger model, priced at $2,095.

Kaiser did not have a station wagon, but it did offer the Traveler. The Traveler was a utility sedan, like the DeSoto Suburban and Chrysler Traveler. It was a basic 4-door sedan that combined some of the features of a station wagon. Some of these features included a tail and lift gate, folding rear seat and skid strips. Unlike the DeSoto and Chrysler models, the Kaiser had a luxury interior, upholstered in rich cloth as pictured here. Photo courtesy of Richard Langworth.

1953

New this year was the Nash Rambler Custom Station Wagon. Nash advertised its Rambler line as "Compact Cars," a term that would become so prevalent in the 1970s.

Still the only producer of compact station wagons was Nash, with its Rambler wagons. These were 2-door, 6-passenger models, neat little packages, reminiscent of the Playboy prototype wagon of a few years earlier. The tailgate was of the two-piece type, conventional in the industry. Only one set of quarter windows were sliders; the rear set was fixed. The spare was mounted inside, and the Rambler featured a one-piece curved windshield.

Pontiac, like Oldsmobile, still shared the wagon bodies with Chevrolet. The Pontiac was unchanged from the previous year. It was a 4-door, 9-passenger model. The wood treatment was simulated by a photo transfer process. The fender skirts were standard. Pontiac wagons sold in the $2,500 range.

Plymouth offered two wagons this year. Both were 2-door, 6-passenger models. The Cranbrook Savoy, pictured here, was the top of the line. The two-piece tailgate was retained. Only one set of quarter windows were sliders.

This year Mercury moved its wagon up to the more luxurious Monterey series. This was a 4-door, 8-passenger wagon. The two-piece tailgate was retained, and quarter windows were fixed. Still featured was real wood hang-on framing and simulated wood decal panels. This was the only wagon offered by Mercury. It sold for $2,826.

The Cambridge Suburban was the least expensive Plymouth wagon. It had the same features as the Savoy, but less of the luxury trim. The Cambridge was usually sold with single paint colors, but two-tone combinations were available. The one-piece curved windshield was a feature that was new this year.

New for this year was the Buick Century Estate Wagon, a 4-door all-steel, 6-passenger model. The two-piece tailgate was retained. Rear doors had vent windows. The quarter windows were fixed. Buick featured the wrap around windshield this year. The wire wheels are options, usually found on the Skylark. The Century sold for $3,470 and 1,563 were built.

A rear view of the all new, all-steel Buick Special Estate wagon. The spare was located in a compartment under the cargo floor. This was conventional for the industry. The three portholes once again identified the series. The Special sold for $3,163. A total of 1,650 were produced.

Buick introduced an all-steel wagon this year. From no on any and all woodies produced were special order ca or of limited production. Cantrell still made such woodi on truck chassis for Chevrolet, GMC, Dodge and Stud baker. New for this year was the Buick Century Esta Wagon and the Special Estate Wagon. Neither had a hi of wood, not even the simulated kind.

Chevrolet made a bit of a wagon splash when it intr duced the Nomad, a showcar based on the new Corvet sportscar. This sporty 2-door wagon, with a rather d tinctive roof design, toured the country as part of t GM Autorama. Public acceptance was so great that t wagon design was subsequently adapted to a producti wagon, though not on the Corvette chassis.

All Chrylser Corp. divisions offered wagons in 2-do and 4-door models, either as 6 or 9-passenger. None these wagons featured any wood, real or simulated. Fo continued with three series and four models of wagor It would be the last year for real wood framing for Fo and Mercury. Mercury continued with a single wago offering.

Nash introduced a 4-door wagon, the Cross Country. distinction was a dip in the roof panel, which lat became sort of a Rambler trademark. A roof rack w standard equipment on this model.

Packard did not have a production wagon, but it d collaborate with the Henney Co. to produce a few all-ste wagons. These were 4-door models with two quart windows and a roof rack. The number produced is u known. The design was very similar to that of t Packard-Henney funeral cars and ambulances of the e

The most popular Chevrolet wagon for 1954 was this Handyman model in the 210 DeLuxe series. It sold for $2,133 and 27,175 were made. This was a 4-door, 6-passenger wagon. The two-tone paint combination was optional. Although the sheet metal was stamped for it, this model did not feature the simulated wood.

Graduating from the 210 DeLuxe Series to the Bel Air Series was the Townsman Wagon, Model 2419. This year the wood grain trim consisted of only a small belt band. The 9-passenger model was Chevrolet's least popular model, and only 8,156 were built. It cost $2,283 and weighed 3,540 pounds.

A rear view of the Chevy Handyman wagon. The quarter windows were fixed. The spare had been carried inside for many years now, so the dip in the bumper merely accommodated the license tag. Rear fender skirts were optional. This year's wagon showed very little change from the previous year.

1954

Chevy wagons still retained the two-piece tailgate. The carrying capacity of the Chevy wagon was on par with its competition, but that was nothing really spectacular. It was, however, adequate. Note that Chevrolet backup lights were built into the tail light lense.

There were two models of the Chevrolet Carry-All Suburban. This was the Model 3106. It featured panel delivery type rear doors. The Model 3116 featured a tail/liftgate. Both models were based on the ½-ton light truck chassis. This was the same chassis for which Cantrell built woodie bodies.

Least expensive of the Chevrolet line up of wagons was this Handyman model in the 150 Special series. The body was identical to the other Chevy wagons, and some of its features were the same. This was a 4-door, 6-passenger wagon. It was usually sold in a single paint color, although two-tone combinations were available. The Handyman wagon sold for $2,020.

. The Chevrolet nomad

Because the Windsor Series was no longer in production, the 6-cylinder Town & Country wagon now had to move to the Windsor DeLuxe Series. Not a popular model, it had a production run of only 650. It cost $3,321 and weighed 3,955 pounds. It used the standard 125.5-inch wheelbase chassis, and was built in 6-passenger form only. Chrysler had a strange place for its name plates this year — the rear fenders. It appeared to be an afterthought.

A sensation at the GM Autorama auto shows this year was the Nomad, a unique station wagon based on the new Corvette sports car. The response that Chevrolet received about this wagon prompted it into offering a production version of the Nomad for the following model year. However, the real Nomad would be based on standard Chevrolet design, not on the unique and interesting Corvette.

One of two wagon models offered by Chrysler this year was the New Yorker Town and Country. It was available only as a 4-door, 6-passenger model. Features included a disappearing tailgate window and rear door vent windows. The quarter windows were fixed. The series identification script was moved to, of all places, the trailing edge of the rear fender. The New Yorker wagon sold for $4,024. Only 1,100 were built.

The DeSoto all-steel Firedome Station Wagon was one of two wagons offered by DeSoto. The Firedome was powered by a Hemi V-8. DeSotos shared their wagon bodies with Chrysler and offered the same features. DeSoto wagons were priced from $300 to $500 below the Chrysler counterparts.

Of the two wagons offered by DeSoto, the Powermaster was the least expensive. It was powered by an economical 6-cylinder engine. Features included an optional automatic transmission. The Powermaster was a 4-door, 6-passenger model.

DeSoto continued to export the Diplomat wagon. Shown here is the Diplomat Custom Special Commercial Utility. It was a 2-door, 6-passenger wagon based on the Plymouth. None were sold in the continental United States.

Called the Sierra, Dodge's 4-door station wagon was also offered with the customer's choice of either the V-8 or the Six. The Sierra was available as either a 2 or a 3-seat wagon seating six or eight passengers. In 6-cylinder form, the Sierra 2-seat wagon weighed 3,430 pounds and cost $2,719. The 3-seat version with the Six went for $2,790 and tipped the scales at 3,435 pounds. With the V-8, the 3-seat version cost $3,031 and weighed 3,660 pounds while the 2-seat version weighed 3,605 pounds and sold for $2,960. All Dodge station wagons rode on the 119-inch wheelbase.

Beginning to offer station wagons on the 119-inch wheelbase, Dodge this year offered both 4 and 2-door body styles. The least expensive of the Dodge station wagons was the 2-door Suburban equipped with a 6-cylinder engine. In this form this vehicle cost $2,229 and weighed 3,185 pounds. The Suburban was also available with the 230 cubic inch Six and in this form cost $2,517 and tipped the scales at 3,400 pounds. The Suburban 2-door had one folding rear seat. The rear cargo area measured 45½ inches in length. When lowered, the Suburban offered a full 70¾ inches of cargo area behind the driver's seat.

At the top of the Ford wagon line, and unchanged, was the Country Squire, a 4-door, 8-passenger model. This was the last year for real wood hang-on framing. Ford Motor Co. remained the only manufacturer to feature the woodie treatment.

The Ford Country Squire 4-door, 8-passenger wagon. The two-piece tailgate was retained. Rear doors had vent windows, which was conventional for the industry. Quarter windows were of the sliding type. This model with its woodie treatment was very attractive. It sold for $2,415.

The Ford middle of the line wagon was this Country Sedan, available as a 4-door, 6 or 8-passenger model. The two-tone paint combination was optional. The Country Sedan was found in the Crestline series. It sold for $2,280.

Ford's low priced wagon received some body side trim, and two-tone paint, which improved its appearance considerably. Ford still retained the two-piece tailgate.

The Ranch wagon was part of Ford's Customline series. Pictured here, it was the least expensive Ford wagon, selling for $2,110. The two-tone paint was optional. Quarter windows were sliders. The tailgate was two-piece. Ranch wagons were available with Six or V-8 engines.

Mercury continued to offer a single wagon. It was the Monterey, a 4-door, 6 or 8-passenger model. This was the last year for hang-on wood framing. Quarter windows were sliders. The tailgate was two-piece. The Monterey Station Wagon sold for $2,776.

The Nash Rambler Cross Country was a 4-door, 6-passenger wagon with a distinctive dip in the roof panel. The roof rack was standard.

Plymouth's low priced wagon was also found in a new series called the Plaza. This wagon had the same body features of the Belvedere but none of the frills. Only one set of quarter windows were sliders. The tailgate was two-piece. The spare was found in a compartment below the cargo floor.

Plymouth renamed its top of the line wagon this year. Belvedere Suburban was the new prestige Plymouth wagon. A 2-door, 6-passenger model, it had a tailgate which was still two-piece. Only one set of quarter windows were sliders. The Belvedere interior featured a combination of pleated vinyl and basket weave vinyl. Plymouth wagons had the best looking interiors in the low priced field.

PONTIAC

The Pontiac Chieftain DeLuxe Station Wagon was the top of the line. Rear fender skirts were optional. The wood trim was simulated and only at the belt line. This was a 4-door, 9-passenger model.

This Super Station Wagon was a result of collaboration between Packard and the Henney Company. Only a few were made on special order. The four doors opened at the center. It had a unique double quarter window and the roof rack was standard. This was a 6-passenger model. The body design was very similar to the Packard-Henney funeral cars and ambulances that enjoyed a high degree of popularity in this era.

New for 1955 was the introduction of Chevrolet's
Nomad station wagon. This was a 2-door sport wagon
used on the successful GM Autorama showcar. However,
instead of using Corvette components, stock Chevy sheet
metal was used. Pontiac, by virtue of sharing wagon bodies
with Chevrolet, had a similar wagon called the Safari. In
addition to the Nomad, Chevy offered four other wagon
models. Pontiac, in addition to the Safari, offered a
4-door model, the Chieftain. Neither Buick nor Olds had
such a sport wagon.

Chrysler continued to offer two wagons, the New
Yorker and Windsor Town and Country. DeSoto had a
wagon available only in the Firedome series. Dodge offered
wagons in the Royal and Coronet series. There were 2-
door and 4-door models, as well as 6 and 9-passenger
versions. Plymouth finally came around and met its
competition with a 4-door wagon. But there were still
only two models in Plymouth's line-up.

Ford switched from real wood veneer framing to fiberglass. Their simulated woodie, the Country Squire, was
now truly simulated. Ford offered a total of four wagon
models. Mercury offered two wagons, the Monterey, with
simulated wood, and the Custom. Both were 4-door
models.

With all the wagon activity that was going on, the
number of models being offered and the number of units
being built, finally prompted Hudson to reintroduce a
wagon. It was a version of the 4-door Rambler wagon,
called the Cross Country. This also prompted Studebaker
to return to the wagon field with a new 2-door model.
The Hudson re-entry was short lived though, being produced only in 1955 and 1956. Studebaker, however,
continued to produce wagons until its demise in 1964.

At the top of the Buick wagon line was this Century Estate
Wagon, Model 69. It was a 4-door, 6-passenger model.
The wheelbase was 123 inches and the power plant was a
236 horsepower V-8. The Century had the distinctive four
portholes, which immediately classed it in the luxury series.
The two-piece tailgate was retained, and the rear doors had
vent windows. This was conventional for the industry.
The Century wagon sold for $3,175.

The Buick Special all-steel Estate Wagon, Model 49, had a
wheelbase of 122 inches and was powered by a 188
horsepower V-8. Whitewall tires were optional. The Special
sold for $2,974.

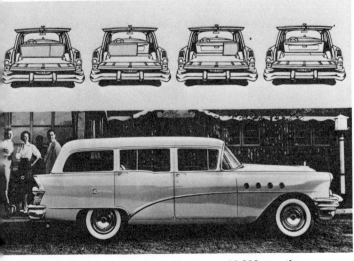

The only Century with a base price above $3,000 was the
Estate Wagon, Model 69, which cost $3,175. It weighed
3,995 pounds. The car this year used an interesting optional
3-passenger rear seat that could be folded down to 2-pass-
enger size, or 1-passenger size, or completely down to make
one continuous cargo floor. Buick built 4,234 Century
wagons.

This Cadillac station wagon has a body built by Hess and
Eisenhardt of Rosmoyne, Ohio. It featured simulated wood
sides. This example is owned by Jacob Orrs.

General Motors show car. The Nomad was such an attraction success that a production Chevrolet Nomad was introduced this year. However, standard Chevrolet sheet metal was used instead of the fiberglass Corvette parts.

Newly introduced this year was this Chevrolet Nomad wagon. It was modified from the 1954 GM show car. Its unique features were slanting roof pillars, hardtop type doors, and full wheel cut outs in the rear fenders. This fine example is owned by Steve Garrett, Noblesville, Ind. It features the accessory GM wire wheel covers, seldom seen on Chevrolets.

This distinctive rear end treatment marked the Chevrolet Nomad. Also distinctive was the ribbed roof panel and the wrap-around quarter windows. The innovated quarter windows did away with blind spots in backing up. Full wheel cut outs were another distinctive feature. Unlike its sister wagons, the Nomad had a disappearing tailgate window. The Nomad weighed 3,270 pounds, and sold for $2,571. A total of 8,286 were produced this first year.

An inside view of the Nomad wagon. The spare was mounted in a compartment in the rear floor, at the tailgate. Like the outside, the inside had distinctive trim.

A view of the cargo area of the Chevrolet Bel Air Beauville 4-door wagon. With the rear seat folded, the cargo capacity was 87 cubic feet. It was one of the largest in the industry. Note the use of wrap-around rear windows for better back-up visibility.

This is the Chevrolet Bel Air Beauville 4-door wagon. Some 24,313 were produced. The price tag of this top of the line wagon was $2,361. A Six or V-8 power plant was available.

Newly introduced this year was the Chevrolet "One-Fifty" Handyman. This 2-door wagon was the bottom of the Chevrolet wagon line and proved to be very popular, as 17,936 were built. It cost $2,129 and weighed 3,260 pounds.

The Chevrolet "Two-Ten" Handyman. This 2-door, 6-passenger wagon was part of the 210 Series. It had a two-piece tailgate and fixed quarter windows. The 210 Series was now the lower middle class. The Handyman wagon carried a price tag of $2,178. This model proved to be popular and a total of 28,918 were built.

Chevrolet continued to offer the Suburban Carry-All. It was based on the ½-ton truck chassis and was part of the 3100 Series.

This was the woodie version of the Chevrolet Suburban Carry-All. The body was built by Cantrell and was available as a special order unit. The roof was fabric covered. Framing was of white ash with mahogany panels. The chassis was a ½-ton light truck. This fine example is owned by Pat Woods, Holyoke, Mass. Similar bodies were built for Dodge, GMC, and Studebaker trucks.

This was the Chrysler Windsor DeLuxe Town and Country wagon. Powerflite transmission was optional. The cost of this wagon was $3,332. A total of 1,983 were built. It was only available as a 4-door, 6-passenger model.

The Chrysler New Yorker Town and Country wagon. This model was found in the New Yorker DeLuxe Series. It was a 4-door, 6-passenger model only. Features included a self-storing tailgate window which was operated from the outside by means of a crank handle. Note that the tailgate hinges are mounted externally. Chrysler was the only wagon to have this distinction. The New Yorker model sold for $4,209, again making it the highest priced production wagon. Only 1,036 were built.

The DeSoto Firedome station wagon. DeSoto wagons shared the same body with Chrysler wagons. THis 4-door model carried 6 passengers in utmost luxury. It was upholstered in gray vinyl and houndstooth check.

This is the DeSoto export wagon, the Diplomat. It again was based on the Plymouth body and chassis with DeSoto trim. It was available as a Six or V-8, outside the U.S.

Available as either a 2 or a 3-seat wagon, the Royal Sierra was the top wagon offering from Dodge in 1955. The Royal Sierra Custom was added in mid-year and was their tops. It had Lancer styling and chrome rear fins. The 2-seat version sold for $2,659 and weighed 3,655 pounds while the 3-seat wagon sold for $2,761 and tipped the scales at 3,730 pounds. All Royal Sierra wagons were of the 4-door type. Bumper guards and wings seen on this car were optional at extra cost.

Called a Suburban station wagon, the Coronet station wagons were offered with either 2 or 4 doors and in either 2 or 3-seat versions. These cars were also available with the customer's choice of a V-8 or a Six. In its 3-seat version, this car cost $2,668 and weighed 3,695 pounds. The 2-seat version weighed 3,590 pounds and cost $2,566.

Pictured here is the Dodge Coronet Suburban wagon, a 4-door, 6-passenger model. It was available as a Six or with a V-8. This model carried a price tag of $2,463 and weighed 3,480 pounds.

The Dodge Coronet 2-door wagon was the least expensive Dodge wagon. It cost $2,452. It was available as a 6-cylinder or V-8. Note that while Chryslers and DeSotos had self-storing tailgate windows, the Dodge did not.

Top of the Ford wagon line was this Country Squire model, a 4-door, 8-passenger wagon. Ford's top of the line wagons still sported the woodie treatment, but this year the framing was made of fiberglass. The panels were decals of simulated deck planking. This gave the wagon a nautical look.

Another distinctive feature of the Ford Country Squire was two-tone paint. The quarter windows were sliders. The two-piece tail/liftgate was retained. The Country Squire without options sold for $2,495, topping Chevy's comparable Bel Air model by $134. But it was $76 less than the Nomad.

This was the Ford Country Sedan. This middle of the line wagon was available as a 8-passenger or a 6-passenger model, with two engine options, a Y-block V-8 or I-block Six. The Country Sedan sold for $2,380.

A new version of the Ford Ranch wagon was this Custom Ranch Wagon. This DeLuxe version was achieved by the addition of a chrome strip and interior trim. The 2-door, 6-passenger model was available with either a 6-cylinder or V-8 engine. Two-tone paint combinations were available, but this model usually sold in a single color. The price tag was $2,210.

This Australian Hybrid was built by Hugh Stanton after World War II. It is based on a 1939 Ford truck chassis, using 1933 and 1939 sheet metal. It has three doors, besides the tailgate, and a battery mounted on the right side running board. The dashboard is made of solid walnut. Present owner is Carol Down of Auckland, New Zealand.

The Ford Ranch Wagon was the least expensive Ford station wagon. It was available only as a 2-door, 6-passenger model powered by Ford's 223 cubic inch Big Six. The price tag for this wagon was $2,145.

A Cadillac wagon conversion by Hess and Eisenhardt of suburban Cincinnati. Note the absence of rear fender skirts. The wagon conversion was similar to the building of an ambulance. This was one of a fleet of 12 wagons built for the Broadmoor Hotel of Colorado Springs, Colo. A special feature was plexiglass panels in the roof for passenger viewing of the mountain scenery. They were referred to as the Cadillac Sky View fleet. This 12-passenger wagon was powered by a 250 HP V-8. Photo courtesy of Hess and Eisenhardt.

This ½-ton GMC truck chassis is fitted with a Cantrell woodie body. This model was similar to the Chevrolet Carry-All. It was available only on special order. This was a 4-door, 10-passenger wagon. The rear door and quarter windows were sliders. The tailgate was two-piece. Cantrell also made the same type body for the Dodge and Studebaker ½-ton truck chassis.

The Mercury Custom was the lesser of two station wagons offered by Mercury this year. The body was the same as the Monterey without the simulated wood. The cost of this wagon was $2,686.

At the top of the Mercury wagon line was this Monterey wagon, a 4-door, 8-passenger model. The quarter windows were sliders and the tailgate was two-piece. The framing for the simulated wood treatment was made of fiberglass and the panels were decals. The two-tone paint was standard. The Monterey sold for $2,844.

This is a 1955 Popular, another Australian hybrid. It is powered by a 72 cubic inch, 30 horsepower, 4-cylinder engine. The wheelbase is 90 inches. It is built on a British Anglia light truck chassis. Current owner is Lou Henry, Christchurch, New Zealand.

Another view of the Australian 1955 Popular. The body is made of silver ash and marine plywood. The body was built using an English Ford Sales catalog as a guide.

The Hudson Rambler, Model 5518-2. This was the first year for this model, and marked the reintroduction of a Hudson wagon, the first since 1941. It was short lived, though, since it was discontinued at the end of the 1956 model year.

The 1955 Rambler, Model 5514-1. This 2-door, 6-passenger model was the most popular in the American Motors line-up. The tailgate was two-piece and the quarter windows were sliders. It was powered by an economical 6-cylinder engine.

The Plymouth Plaza Suburban was a 2-door, 6-passenger wagon. This was Plymouth's low priced wagon. One set of quarter windows were sliders. The tailgate was two-piece. This model was available with either a 6-cylinder or V-8 engine. Other options included power brakes and power steering.

The top of two wagons offered by Plymouth was this Belvedere 4-door Suburban. Optional equipment included an automatic transmission for the first time, plus a choice of a 6-cylinder or V-8 engine. The wheelbase was 115 inches.

Studebaker reintroduced a wagon this year in the form of this 2-door version called the Commander Conestoga. It was a 6-passenger model powered by Studebaker's dependable 6-cylinder engine. This unit has been fitted as an emergency vehicle, complete with siren, red flasher, and 2-way radio, by its volunteer fireman owner.

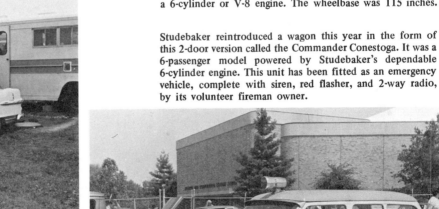

The Pontiac Safari wagon was the counterpart to the Chevrolet Nomad. General specifications were almost identical. Today the Safari is the rarer of the two specialized wagons. Note the wire wheel covers that were offered as options on all GM cars this year.

The Buick Special Estate wagon at $2,775 was a bargain in luxury wagons. The Special was a 4-door, 6-passenger wagon. The quarter windows were fixed and the tailgate was two-piece. The length of the body with the tailgate up was 206.7 inches. For its class this was a relatively short wagon. All Chrysler Corporation wagons, including Plymouth, exceeded 208 inches. The Buick wagons had the greatest ground clearance at 8.5 inches. This exceeded even the Willys Jeep wagon. The Special was a very popular wagon, and a substantial 13,770 units were built.

A rear view of the Buick Special Estate wagon. Again, the tell-tale portholes readily identified the various model Buicks. The Special had three; the Century had four.

Just as the Special wagon took a tremendous jump in sales, so too did the Century version, Model 69. Buick built 8,160 this year. Priced at $3,256 and weighing 4,080 pounds, it was the heaviest and most expensive model in the Century Series. Cargo space with the tailgate and rear seat raised was 44.7 inches, with the rear seat lowered it was 77.8 inches.

Chrysler continued to expand its line-up of Idea Car Joining the auto show circuit this year was a wagon calle the Plainsman. It had "Rocket Ship" styling. This 2-doo wagon had a sport roof and unique rear facing third sea The whole idea of a showcar wagon seemed to b prompted by the success of Chevy's Nomad. Howeve unlike Chevrolet, Chrysler did not incorporate the overa design of the Plainsman into a production wagon. Onl some of its features were later adapted.

The Nomad proved to be the least popular of Chevrole wagons, and remained the most expensive. Only 7,88 were built. The favorite of the Chevy wagons was th 210 Series Townsman, with a whopping 113,656 bein built.

Ford offered a total of six wagon models for 195 Again, only the Country Squire featured simulated woo Safety features were introduced, but proved not to b very popular. Standard on all Fords were seat belts, dee dish steering wheel, and padded dash, plus a wide range o options which included: air conditioning, electric cloc signal seeking radio, rear fender skirts, spot light, pow steering, brakes, windows and four-way seat. In additio to these, there was a unique vinyl cover for baggage. Th cover was snapped in place over the cargo area, just belo the window line.

Rambler introduced a new wagon design this yea called the Hardtop Wagon. It was a 4-door pillarless wago that, but for the quarter window, resembled a 4-do hardtop. Studebaker expanded its wagon line to thre models. They were all 2-door, 6-passenger versions. Th top of the line was the Pinehurst. Some very striking tw tone paint color combinations were offered.

A Hess and Eisenhardt custom Cadillac Station Wagon. The woodie treatment is simulated. The large quarter windows gave good visibility but no ventilation, as they were fixed. The tailgate was two-piece. Seating capacity was for six passengers. This example is owned by Jacob Orrs.

The Chevrolet Nomad Station Wagon was part of the Bel Air Series. Its lines were unchanged from the previous year. It was the top of the Chevy wagon line, but not very popular in its day. Only 7,886 units were built. Note the wire wheel hub caps and optional bumper overriders. The price tag for this sporty wagon was $2,707. The excellent example pictured here is owned by Bob Anderson of Houtzdale, Pa.

A rear view of the classy Chevy Nomad wagon. Although the basic Nomad lines were unchanged above the belt line, there was one noticeable change below. The rear wheel cut out was now tear drop shaped. The quarter windows remained curved and the tailgate window was self-storing in the gate. Note the distinctive tailgate strips. Bob Anderson is the wagon owner.

The Chevrolet Bel Air Beauville was the top Chevy 4-door wagon. It offered a choice of 6 or 9-passenger style, and 6-cylinder or V-8 engine. The 9-passenger sold for $2,581 and a limited 13,279 were built.

Chevy's Bel Air Beauville wagon was a prestige model but met with limited sales response. After all, a Buick wagon sold for $2,775. This compared to the $2,581 price tag of the Chevrolet.

This was Chevrolet's new Two-Ten Beauville. It was a 9-passenger, 4-door wagon which sold for $2,447. Total production was 17,988 – not much better than the Bel Air version.

The lowest priced Chevrolet wagon in the Two-Ten Series was this Handyman model, available only as a 2-door, 6-passenger model. It sold for $2,314. A total of 22,038 were produced.

The most popular of the Chevrolet wagons was this Two-Ten Townsman. The curved quarter window was fixed, and the two-piece tailgate was retained. The Townsman was available only as a 4-door, 6-passenger model. It sold for $2,362 and no less than 113,656 were built.

Lowest priced of all Chevy wagons was the One-Fifty Handyman, a 2-door, 6-passenger model. It sold for $2,270, weighed 3,289 pounds, and total production was 13,487.

The Chrysler Windsor Town and Country wagon was available as a 6-passenger model only. The price tag was a hefty $3,598 — $342 more than the Buick Century wagon. Only 2,700 were built. Note that while the fender fin blended well with the other Chrysler models, it was merely stuck on the wagon.

This New Yorker Town and Country wagon was the heaviest and most expensive model in the series. It weighed 4,460 pounds and cost $4,523. The wheelbase was 126 inches, with an overall length of 221.2 inches. A total of 1,070 were built. This was the most expensive production American wagon for 1956.

The DeSoto Firedome Station Wagon was unchanged, except for a facelift. The body was shared with Chrysler. Special features included a crank-down tailgate window. The wheelbase was 126 inches. It was powered by DeSoto's Hemi V-8.

The limousine hearse pictured here was built on the Chrysler New Yorker Town and Country chassis, using many of the wagon parts. Note the higher roof and the elimination of the vent window in the rear door. This vehicle was built by Chrysler and available through its dealers on special order.

Ford's top of the wagon line continued to be the Country Squire. It was the only Ford wagon with simulated wood trim. Available as an 8-passenger model, with a choice of 6-cylinder or Thunderbird V-8, it sold for $2,635 in basic form, without accessories.

Technically classified within the Coronet V-8 Series or the D-63-1 model line, the large Sierra station wagons were offered in either 2 or 3-seat versions. Both forms were supplied with the V-8 engine only. As a 2-seat, 6-passenger wagon, this vehicle tipped the scales at 3,600 pounds and sold for $2,716. The 3-seat version, looking the same, carried a price tag of $2,822 and weighed 3,715 pounds. Basically the body was that of the 1955 station wagon with new interiors, exterior trim and small chrome fins added to the rear fenders.

The Ford Country Sedan 8-passenger wagon was the most popular in the low priced field. It was available with a 6-cylinder or Thunderbird V-8. It sold for $2,500 — about $53 more than Chevy's Two-Ten Beauville.

Once again Dodge offered a complete line of station wagons in both 2 and 4-door body styles and 2 and 3-seat versions. The least expensive of these was the Series D-62 Coronet Suburban. This car, equipped with a 6-cylinder engine, cost $2,491 and weighed 3,250 pounds. The same car was offered in the Coronet V-8 or the D-63-1 Series. In this form the Suburban cost $2,599 and tipped the scales at 3,065 pounds. A total of 2,025 were constructed.

The Ford 6-passenger, 4-door Country Sedan was available in a multitude of two-tone color combinations. Quarter windows were sliders and the tailgate was two-piece. It offered a choice of power plants — either an economical Six or the Thunderbird V-8, though few were economy minded in 1956, with gas at about 20 cents per gallon.

New from Ford this year was the Parklane wagon. This 2-door wagon was available as a 6-passenger model only. It was the companion to the popular Country Sedan. It sold for $2,530 and was meant to compete with the Chevy Nomad. A unique feature of this wagon was the special vinyl luggage cover, which snapped over the cargo area below the window line, like a tonneau cover. The rear seat also had the sporty dip in the back center, with a chrome V-8 emblem inserted.

The Custom Ranch wagon was an upgraded version of Ford's low priced Ranch Wagon. It sold for $2,350, and was available only as a 2-door, 6-passenger model.

The lowest priced wagon in the Ford line-up was this 2-door, 6-passenger Ranch Wagon. Standard were many safety features which were found on all Ford cars for 1956, such as seat belts, padded dash and deep dish steering wheel.

Mercury's lowest priced station wagon was the Custom Commuter Wagon, available as either a six or eight passenger car. In the more popular eight-passenger form, it cost $2,819 and weighed 3,860 pounds. The six-passenger style cost $2,722.

The Monterey Station Wagon continued to be the top of the line workhorse. At $2,977, it was the most expensive Mercury this year. It was available in 8-passenger form only. It tipped the scales at 3,885 pounds.

The Rambler Model 5618-2 was known as the Rambler Cross Country wagon. Cargo capacity was increased by 33% this year. One of its features was a crank-down tailgate window. Roof racks were standard on Rambler wagons.

The Rambler Model 5613-2 introduced for the first time in station wagons a hardtop look. This pillarless wagon prompted General Motors to adopt it into their 1957 model wagons.

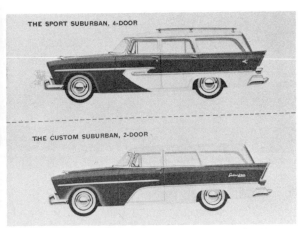

THE SPORT SUBURBAN, 4-DOOR

THE CUSTOM SUBURBAN, 2-DOOR

PLYMOUTH CUSTOM SUBURBAN, 4-DOOR

The top of the Plymouth wagon line was the Sport Suburban, pictured here with the next in line Custom Suburban 2-door. Both models were available with Power-Flow 6-cylinder or Hy-Fire V-8 engines. Other options included push-button PowerFlite transmission, power steering, power brakes, power seats and power windows.

The Plymouth Custom Suburban 4-door, 6-passenger wagon. This was the longest wagon in its field, a full 208.6 inches. And, it had the least amount of ground clearance, 5.6 inches. The smart two-tone paint combinations were standard. Quarter windows were fixed and the tailgate was two-piece. The Plymouth Custom Suburban carried a price tag of $2,575.

Joining the Chrysler family of "Idea Cars" this year was this Plainsman wagon. It measured 208 inches, bumper to bumper; was 60 inches high and 79.4 inches wide. It was powered by a special Chrysler V-8 engine and had all the power options.

A rear view of the Plainsman Wagon, Chrysler's newest Idea Car. Oddly, the rear fender design would later be adopted by the 1957 Lincoln. The unique roof was probably prompted by the Chevy Nomad.

The unique rear facing third seat of the Plainsman was later adopted to production wagons of the Chrysler Corporation. The Plainsman was upholstered with genuine cowhide.

The Pontiac Chieftain wagon was one of three models offered by Pontiac this year. Options included a choice of 205 HP or 227 HP V-8 engines and Strato-Flight Hydra-Matic transmission. This was a 4-door 6-passenger model.

This Brooks Stevens station wagon design was introduced at the 1956 New York International Auto Show. It was named the Scimitar. The wagon was developed for the Olin Aluminum Company. Photo courtesy of Harrah's Auto Collection.

The Scimitar wagon, designed by Brooks Stevens, was built by Reuter of Stuttgart, Germany, on a Chrysler New Yorker chassis. It was shown at the Geneva and New York auto show this year. Photo courtesy of Brooks Stevens.

One of the unique designs of the Scimitar wagon was this sliding rear roof, later redesigned by Brooks Stevens for Studebaker. Photo courtesy of Brooks Stevens.

The Studebaker Pinehurst wagon was the top of the wagon line of three wagons offered by Studebaker in 1956. This 2-door, 6-passenger wagon had a cargo capacity of 65 cubic feet. It was powered by a 190 HP V-8.

The Parkview wagon was Studebaker's middle priced wagon. A 2-door, 6-passenger wagon, it was powered by Studebaker's 170 HP Sweepstakes 259 V-8 engine. It was upholstered in waterproof vinyl.

Lowest priced of the three wagons offered by Studebaker was this 2-door, 6-passenger model named the Pelham. It was powered by Studebaker's Sweepstakes 185 HP Six. Some of its features included self-energizing and self-centering brakes.

Buick followed Rambler's lead and introduced the Century wagon as a pillarless model. This styling was also available in the Special. The lines were not unlike that of 4-door hardtop. Body side moulding accent strip and special two-tone paint added to the already sporty look. The rear section of the roof panel featured skid strips but no roof rack. The Oldsmobile Fiesta wagon, by virtue of sharing the same body as Buick, also featured a pillarless wagon.

This was the last year for the sporty Chevrolet Nomad and Pontiac Safari. Both were sales disappointments, though today they are sought after and very collectable cars.

Ford continued to offer one of the biggest line-up of wagon models. A total of five models were available, but this was one less than the year before. The Parklane was discontinued. Mercury expanded its wagon line to three models. The top of the line Colony Park had pillarless hardtop styling and simulated wood trim.

American Motors, formed thorugh the merger of Nash and Hudson, officially dropped the Nash name from its Rambler models. Packard re-introduced a single wagon model. It was the first wagon since 1950 — a 4-door, passenger version with standard roof rack. By virtue of merger, Packard shared the Studebaker wagon body. Studebaker further expanded its wagon line to five models. One of the newest additions was the Scotsman. This was 2-door, 6-passenger model stripped of all frills, with no bright metal trim, except for the bumpers. It looked like 1942 "Blackout" car, and was strictly a workhorse with nothing fancy. The name alone implied economy.

The Chevrolet Nomad station wagon remained a most attractive wagon, but sales were poor. Only 6,103 were built. The Nomad was a 2-door, 6-passenger wagon powered by a 283 cubic inch V-8 engine.

The Chevrolet Bel Air Townsman 4-door, 6-passenger wagon sold for $2,765. A total of 27,375 were built.

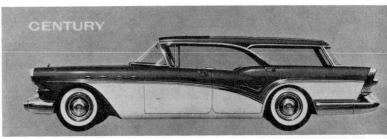

The Buick Century Estate Wagon featured pillarless styling introduced by Rambler the year before. The Century was one of two wagons offered by Buick this year, and the only model to have this styling. It cost $3,706, and 10,186 were sold.

A decorative touch but very useful when a luggage rack was installed, were these skid strips. They were a feature of the Buick Century Estate Wagon.

The Buick Special Estate Wagon had conventional 4-door styling. It was available as a 6-passenger or 9-passenger model. The Special was also available as the Riviera Estate Wagon, pillarless, in 6-passenger form. The Special Model 49 sold for $3,047, while the Riviera Estate Model 49-D sold for $3,167.

This was the last year for Chevrolet's Nomad sport wagon. Styling sbove the belt line was once again unchanged. It sold for $2,857 and was Chevrolet's most expensive model.

The Chevrolet Townsman 4-door wagon was moved up from the 210 Series to the Bel Air Series this year. There were only two wagons in the Bel Air Series this year, the Nomad and the Townsman. The Beauville which was in this series the year before, was moved down to the 210 Series.

The only 9-passenger wagon produced by Chevrolet this year was the Beauville in the middle price 210 Series. It was powered by a V-8 engine and sold for $2,663. A total of 21,083 were built.

The Chevrolet "Two-Ten" Townsman 4-door, 6-passenger wagon was Chevrolet's most popular wagon, with 127,803 being produced. It sold for $2,556.

A rear view of the "Two-Ten" Townsman. Cargo capacity was 87 cubic feet. Note that Chevrolet still used a 2-piece tailgate.

This was Chevrolet's "Two-Ten" Handyman, a 2-door, 6-passenger wagon. It had an interior of washable vinyl. This model weighed 3,402 pounds. It sold for $2,502 and 17,528 were built.

The lowest priced Chevrolet wagon was this "One-Fifty" Handyman, a 2-door, 6-passenger model that sold for $2,407 – almost $100 less than the "Two-Ten" version. A total of 14,740 were built.

Unchanged, except for the grille was the Chevrolet Suburban Carry-All. This 9-passenger wagon was based on the ½-ton truck chassis. It was designated Model 3106.

The Chrysler New Yorker Town and Country wagon was available as a 6-passenger, 4-door model. Only 1,391 were built. They sold for $4,746. Chrysler wagons remained the most expensive in the industry.

In comparison to the New Yorker model, this Windsor Town and Country wagon was rather austere. Chrysler built 2,035 of these wagons which commanded a price tag of $3,153. One of the features of the Town and Country wagon was the crank-down tailgate window.

DeSoto offered two wagons in the FireFlite Series. Both were 4-door models. This was the Explorer, which featured a rear facing third seat. The Shopper, the other model, was a 6-passenger version with no third seat.

Called the "Professional," this ambulance conversion was offered by Chrysler on either the New Yorker or the Windsor Town & Country wagon. Shown here in Windsor form, the car could be converted from a private passenger car to an ambulance within five minutes. The conversion was a Chrysler production unit, and could be ordered through any Chrysler dealer.

DeSoto's export wagon was the Diplomat. It was still based on the Plymouth body and chassis. This is the Custom Suburban 4-door, 6-passenger model.

In the FireSweep Series, DeSoto offered two models — the Explorer, 9-passenger, and the 6-passenger Shopper.

The Dodge Custom Sierra Station Wagon was available only as a 4-door, in 6 or 9-passenger models. In overall model standing, it ranked with the Custom Royal. This year Dodge introduced a crank-down tailgate window. The 6-passenger model sold for $3,087, while the 9-passenger went for $3,215.

Entering as a medium priced station wagon was the Sierra Series, offering two 4-door versions, both two and three seat, and a low cost 2-door wagon. The Sierra 4-door 2-seat wagon cost $2,946 and weighed 3,930 pounds while the 3-seat version went for $3,073 and weighed 4,015 pounds. All of the 1957 Dodges with three seats featured a rear-facing third seat called a "spectator" seat. This was a new feature for a station wagon.

The lowest priced station wagon available in the Dodge range was the 2-door Suburban. This vehicle seated six passengers on its two seats and was not available with a third seat. These low cost wagons sold for $2,861 and weighed 3,830 pounds. Even though this was the cheapest of the Dodge wagons, it still had all of the style found on the other 1957 Dodges.

The Ford Country Squire was the top of the Ford wagon line. It was a 4-door, 9-passenger wagon, featuring simulated wood trim. It was available as a six-cylinder or V-8. It sold for $2,785, only $20 more than Chevy's Townsman Bel Air model, and $172 less than the Nomad.

Dodge introduced the Town Wagon, based on the D-100 ½-ton truck chassis. It was to compete with the Chevy Carry-All. There was seating for up to eight passengers. As a 6-passenger wagon it gave about 90 cubic feet of cargo area. The wheelbase was 108 inches. With the two rear seats removed, maximum payload was 1,575 pounds. The front seat was also divided, and the one-passenger section on the far right could be removed for extra cargo space.

A rear view of the Ford Country Squire. Ford still maintained the two-piece tailgate. Wheelbase was 116 inches, and overall length was 203.5 inches.

The 9-passenger Ford Country Sedan was Ford's best selling wagon for 1957. With rear seats folded flat, the cargo floor was 106.5 inches long, with tailgate. The tailgate lowered to a level position only 24 inches from the ground. The Country Sedan sold for $2,650, which was $94 more than Chevy's best selling "Two-Ten" Townsman.

The 6-passenger Ford Country Sedan. With rear seat in the upright position, it gave 70.8 inches of cargo floor area. This model sold for $2,550. Note the annodized side trim.

Ford's newest wagon model was this Del Rio Ranch Wagon. This model replaced the Parklane. The 6-passenger, 2-door wagon did not inherit the fancy interior of the Parklane, but it did have the sporty appearance. The Del Rio was priced at an even $2,500. This compares to Chevrolet's "Two-Ten" Handyman model, which sold for $2,502.

Here is the 6-passenger Country Sedan with standard Ford side trim. The annodized trim was apparently an option on this model or a later addition of standard trim.

At the bottom of the Ford wagon line was this 2-door, 6-passenger Ranch Wagon. It sold for $2,405, which was $2 under Chevy's lowest priced wagon.

A rear view of the Ford Ranch Wagon economy model. The two-tone paint spruced up the otherwise plain looking wagon. Standard power plant for the Ranch Wagon was a 144 horsepower Mileage Maker Six. But the 212 horsepower Thunderbird 292 V-8 could be ordered.

Over in England, Ford was producing this Cortina Fordham Estate wagon as a 4-door, 6-passenger model. The roof rack was standard. It was about the size of the small Rambler wagon.

This year, Mercury made its wagons a series of their own, although the five models could be compared with the existing car series by reason of price and fittings. Most regal of the wagons was the Colony Park, which utilized a type of hardtop styling in that there were no center door pillars. It cost $3,677.

The lowest priced wagons were the Commuters. The Commuter 4-Door was available in three-seat version for $3,070 and in two-seat for $2,973. It weighed 4,195 pounds. Lowest priced Mercury wagon was the Commuter 2-Door, which sold for $2,903. The 4,115-pound vehicle was available as a six-passenger model only.

A rear view of the Olds Fiesta wagon. Note the two-tone roof with chrome skid strips, but no roof rack. Like the other GM wagons Olds still maintained the two-piece tailgate.

This is the Oldsmobile Fiesta Super 88 wagon. This body was shared with Buick. Pillarless styling was new this year. The wagon was a real standout, as was the skater admiring it.

This was the Oldsmobile Super 88 Wagon. It did not have the pillarless styling. Nevertheless, it was still a very attractive wagon.

The newly reintroduced Packard Clipper Wagon. This was Packard's re-entry into the wagon market. The new wagon was a 4-door, 6-passenger model. It shared its body with Studebaker. The owner of this wagon is Bill Harris.

A rear view of Bill Harris' Packard wagon. The roof rack was standard. The tailgate was a 2-piece affair. Note the rear fender styling is very much like the Chrysler Plainsman "Idea Car" wagon of 1956.

Plymouth introduced a new body design this year for its entire line. There were a total of five wagons this year. The top of the line was the Sport Suburban, a 4-door 9-passenger model with a unique rear facing third seat. It was hailed as the biggest wagon in the low priced field.

Pictured here are Plymouth's Sport Suburban and Custom Suburban wagons. The Custom Suburban was a 2-door, 6-passenger model. All Plymouths featured Torsion Air ride this year, and were available with either 6-cylinder or V-8 engines.

The Plymouth Custom Suburban 4-door, 9-passenger wagon. It was also available as a 6-passenger model. The Custom Suburban was the middle priced Plymouth wagon. It is shown here in striking two-tone paint. An electric rear window was standard on all 9-passenger wagons, optional on the 6-passenger models.

Plymouth wagons were also adaptable to law enforcement use. Pictured here is the Custom Suburban 4-door, 9-passenger, with the unique rear facing third seat.

The Plymouth Custom Suburban 2-door, 6-passenger model. Plymouth wagons could be had with either a 6-cylinder or V-8 engine.

Shown here with the Custom Suburban 4-door model is Plymouth's low priced wagon, the DeLuxe Suburban. All Plymouth wagons featured a disappearing rear window that lowered into the tailgate.

The Rambler Model 5718-1 was a 4-door, 6-passenger model. The roof rack was standard. American Motors stopped using the Nash name in connection with Rambler this year.

The Rambler Model 5723-2 was a 4-door, 6-passenger pillarless wagon. It featured a roof rack, disappearing rear window and simulated wood siding. Only Ford Motor Co. and American Motors had any wagon models with simulated wood trim.

The top of the Studebaker line of wagons was this Provincial V-8 4-door, 6-passenger wagon. The roof rack was standard. Twin traction drive was optional.

The Studebaker Parkview V-8 2-door, 6-passenger wagon. Sister to this model was the Pelham Six 2-door wagon. Studebaker had very striking two-tone paint combinations which lent themselves well to the wagon design. An interesting option was an inflatable air mattress custom tailored to fit the rear compartment.

This was the first year for Studebaker's Champion Scotsman Station Wagon. It resembled a 1942 "Blackout" car, and was a basic, no nonsense utility car. The two-piece tailgate was maintained by all Studebaker wagons. The cargo area was nearly eight feet long by five feet wide with the rear seat folded.

n October of 1958 the last of the great Woodie
anufacturers succumbed to pressures of the times.
antrell was purchased by a window manufacturer. The
woodie wagons turned out by Cantrell were based on
Chevrolet, Dodge, GMC and Studebaker ½-ton light
ck chassis.

Buick renamed its wagons this year. They were all called
ate Wagons, but each model carried its own distinctive
me. The top of the line was the Century Caballero.
aballero was a name once used by Kaiser-Frazer for a
cial trimmed sedan. The Buick Caballero was a 4-door,
assenger model, as was the Special Riviera. Both were
the pillarless design. On the other hand, Buick's low
ced Special had pillars.

Chevrolet dropped the sporty 2-door Nomad, but con-
ued to use the name on a 4-door, 9-passenger model in
Bel Air Series. All Chrysler Corporation wagons
ntinued to feature a rear facing third seat and a
appearing tailgate window. The rear facing seat never
catch on with competitive makes.

Big news from Ford was its new entry into the mid-price
rket — the Edsel. A total of five wagons were offered
Edsel. The top of the line featured simulated wood
ling. This was in keeping with the rest of the Ford
isions. A unique feature of the Edsel was the placement
the auto-trans selector in the hub of the steering wheel.
ontiac, like Chevrolet, dropped its sporty 2-door wagon,
Safari. And, like Chevrolet, Pontiac retained the Safari
me to designate a 4-door, 6-passenger model in the
r Chief Series. But unlike Chevy, Pontiac would
ntinue to use the Safari name on their wagons through
76.

The Buick Century Caballero Estate Wagon, Model 69,
was a 4-door, 6-passenger wagon. This pillarless model was
the top of the Buick line. Buick, like the other GM cars,
suffered in styling this year, and were drowning in chrome.
Price tag on this Century was $3,831.

Special Model 49D, 4-door 6-passenger Riviera Estate Wagon

Special Model 49, 4-door 6-passenger Estate Wagon

The Buick Special Riviera Estate Wagon, Model 49D, and the
Special Model 49. The Riviera was the pillarless wagon and
occupied the middle price range at $3,261. The pillarless
Special was the low priced Buick wagon at $3,145.

This year Buick imported its German cousin, the Opel.
This is the Opel Rekord Caravan, a 5-passenger wagon. The
2-door model offered a roof rack as standard equipment
and sold for $2,400.

Chevrolet discontinued the sporty Nomad wagon with the
1957 model. The name was applied to a basic 4-door model
in 1958. The 4-door Nomad was in the Bel Air Series. It sold
for $2,835 and was the top of the line.

The Chevrolet Brookwood was new this year. This was the
middle range wagon. It was available as a 4-door, 6-passenger
or 9-passenger, at a cost of $2,574 and $2,785 respectively.
Chevy still maintained the two-piece tailgate.

The only Chevy 2-door wagon this year was found in the new Yoeman Series. The Nomad name, which was previously applied to a sporty 2-door wagon, was now used to designate this Bel Air Series 4-door wagon.

The Chevrolet Yeoman 2-door wagon was the lowest priced Chevrolet wagon at $2,520. It was a 6-passenger unit, available with a thrifty 6-cylinder engine or a snappy V-8.

The Chevrolet Suburban Carry-All was a 9-passenger model with sedan delivery type rear doors. It was available in solid colors or sporty two-tones. As a cargo vehicle, it had a payload of 1,150 pounds. The rear seats were removable, but could not be folded down.

The Chrysler Windsor Town and Country wagon, for the first time, was available as a 6-passenger or 9-passenger model. A disappearing tailgate window was still one of its features. Only 862 were built and sold for $3,616 in the 6-passenger version, while 791 were produced in the 9-passenger model at $3,803.

The new New Yorker Town & Country wagon was offered in 6 and 9-passenger form, with the third seat in the 9-passenger models being rearward facing. Chrysler referred to this as an "Observation Seat." The 6-passenger model cost $4,868 and had a run of 775, while the 9-passenger version cost $5,083 and had a run of only 428. Both weighed about 4,445 pounds. The wagons used the 126-inch wheelbase chassis, but were 219.9 inches in overall length.

In addition to producing plain wagons, Chrysler continued to offer its ambulance conversions in both the Windsor and New Yorker Series. The cars were available on special order through Chrysler dealers, but there is no record of how many were built. This is the New Yorker version.

DeSoto offered four wagons in two series for 1958. This was the FireFlite 4-door Explorer, the top of the line. Like other Chrysler Corporation wagons, DeSotos featured rear facing third seats and disappearing tailgate windows. This model had a price tag topping $4,800.

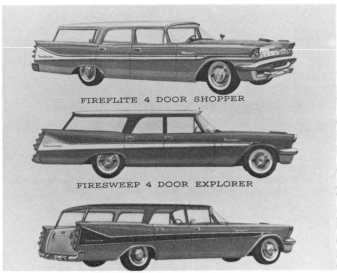

FIREFLITE 4 DOOR SHOPPER

FIRESWEEP 4 DOOR EXPLORER

Here are three of the four wagons offered by DeSoto this year. The Firesweep Shopper was the bottom of the line. It was a 6-passenger model, powered by a Hemi V-8, and carrying a price tag of $3,535.

DeSoto export wagons, which were Plymouths dressed up in DeSoto trim, included this Diplomat-Custom Sport Suburban. It was the higher priced of the two models available.

The only 2-door wagon offered by DeSoto in 1958 was this export model, the Diplomat Commercial Utility. It was a Plymouth dressed up in DeSoto trim. This was a stripped down, no frills wagon, not available in the continental U.S.

Dodge did not offer the 6-cylinder engine in any of the 1958 station wagon models. All came with the Ram Fire 350 cubic inch power plant. This was the same engine that was considered standard equipment for the Custom Royal. Topping the model range for the wagon line was the 4-door Custom Sierra offered in either 2 or 3-seat versions.

Available only with two seats and two doors was Dodge's least expensive station wagon, the Suburban. This car was a full 6-passenger wagon. All Dodge station wagons had a full 123 inches of floor length behind the front seat when the second seat was folded down. This cargo area measured 50 inches wide and 28.7 inches high. Dodge station wagons had an over-all length of 215.9 inches with a width of 78.3 inches. The spare tire was stored inside the right rear fender and covered by a small skirt. Access to this tire was from the outside.

Amblewagon of Troy, Mich. converted station wagons into economical ambulances. This 1958 Dodge Sierra station wagon well illustrates the quality of their work in this field. The rear side windows were of frosted glass and a siren was mounted on the front fender.

New from Ford Motor Co. this year was the introduction of the Edsel. Pictured here is the top of the Edsel wagon line, the 4-door, 9-passenger Bermuda. Like other top of the line Ford Motor Company wagons, it featured simulated wood.

This was the Edsel Villager 4-door, 9-passenger wagon, one of five wagon models offered by Edsel. All were powered by the Edsel E-400 V-8, rated at 303 horsepower. All Edsel wagons had ribbed vinyl floors and color-keyed all-vinyl interiors.

The Edsel 4-door, 6-passenger Villager. Two-tone paint was optional. Ford still retained the two-piece tailgate on all of its wagon lines. Some of the features offered by Edsel were self-adjusting brakes, a compass, a tachometer, and Dial-Temp air system.

The Ford Country Squire 6-passenger wagon. Again, simulated wood designated the top of the line. Dual headlights were featured this year, as was a choice of three engine options — a 265 HP 332 Interceptor V-8, a 240 HP 332 Interceptor and the Mileage Maker 145 HP Six.

A rear view of the Ford Country Squire 9-passenger wagon. Ford still retained the two-piece tailgate. The ribbed roof section was referred to as the "All-New Slipstream Roof." The ribs were there for strength as well as for styling.

A luggage rack was one of the options available on the Ford Country Sedan wagon, shown here being loaded with a trunk, to demonstrate the strength of the ribbed roof panel.

The 4-door or as Ford put it "Fordor" Ranch wagon. This was the lowest priced 4-door wagon offered by Ford. It sold for $2,570.

Ford continued to offer the sporty 2-door Del Rio wagon, available only as a 6-passenger model. Special trim and two-tone paint combinations set it apart from the lower priced Ranch Wagon. This model sold for $2,620.

Showing its versatility is the Ford Country Sedan 4-door, 6-passenger model. This was the mid-ranged Ford wagon. It sold for $2,730.

For business or pleasure was the way Ford sold its low priced Ranch wagon, shown here in the 2-door version. It carried a price tag of only $2,515, which was all of $5 cheaper than its counterpart Chevrolet.

Mercury's top of the line was the Colony Park wagon. Its design was unchanged from the previous year. Ford Motor Company was the only manufacturer to feature simulated wood on any of its wagons. The Colony Park sold for $3,201 in the 9-passenger version and for about $100 less as a 6-passenger model.

The Voyager 2-Door Wagon cost $3,535 and weighed 4,435 pounds. Among the safety features stressed on all Mercurys this year were the front-hinged hood, foot operated parking brake, and slide-type safety door locks. The wagons also had a safety lock for the second seat.

Mercury's lowest priced wagon was the Commuter 2-Door, shown here with an optional chrome luggage rack on the roof. In base form it cost $3,035 and weighed 4,400 pounds. The rear quarter windows were stationary.

The most economical wagons were the Commuters, of which this is the 4-Door version. Weighing 4,525 pounds, it was available as a nine passenger car for $3,201 or as a six passenger for $3,105.

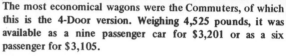

The Oldsmobile Super "88" Fiesta wagon. This was the top priced Olds wagon at $3,725. Note the two-piece tailgate with the wrap around rear window. Loading was a little cumbersome.

1958

The Oldsmobile "88" 4-door, 6-passenger wagon. Like its sister the higher priced Fiesta, it featured pillarless styling, and wrap around rear window. Note how the rear fender extends way beyond the tailgate. This added more to the sedan look.

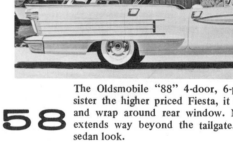

This was the last year for Packard. One model wagon was offered. It was a luxury wagon said to "Combine station wagon capacity with limousine luxury and riding ease." It was a 4-door, 6-passenger wagon, with two-piece tailgate, larger tail lights, and a somewhat overdesigned streamline styling to differentiate it from the basic Studebaker wagon upon which it was based.

The Plymouth Sport Suburban was the top of the line. It was available as a 6-passenger or 9-passenger model and featured a rear facing third seat and disappearing tailgate window. Engine options included a choice of V-8 or Six. The Plymouth wagon was the high priced of the low priced three at $3,130 for the 9-passenger Sport Suburban.

The Plymouth Custom Suburban available as a 6 or 9-passenger model. It was in the mid-range of models.

The Plymouth Custom Suburban 2-door was one of two 2-door wagons offered by Plymouth. It was available only as a 6-passenger model. One of the unique features of Plymouth wagons this year was the spare tire compartment. A unique rear fender storage area was built into the right fender. By the removal of a fender skirt type of door, the spare was accessible from the outside. This feature was available only on the 9-passenger models, which made possible a full width third seat. The 6-passenger model had its spare mounted on the inside.

Lowest priced of the Plymouth wagons was this 2-door DeLuxe Suburban, a 6-passenger model available with V-8 or 6-cylinder engine.

Pontiac's new Star Chief Custom Safari wagon. Pontiac adapted the Safari name to its entire line of wagons. The rocket ship styling was in keeping with the rest of the GM theme for 1958, as top of the line models were drenched in chrome.

The other two wagons in Pontiac's line were the Chieftain 9-passenger Safari. All Pontiac wagons were 4-door models. The 9-passenger model had sliding rear window glass.

The Studebaker Scotsman Station Wagon. Unlike today's trend, economy was not the in thing back in 1958. There was no market for a stripped down, no nonsense basic wagon, with all the utility and comfort of a dressed up model. Studebaker dropped its "Black-out" wagon at the end of the 1958 model run. The car was virtually unchanged from the 1957 offering.

The 1958 Rambler Six, Model 5818 was a 4-door, 6-passenger wagon. The luggage rack was standard. Rear fenders were re-worked into a fin on an otherwise unchanged design.

The year 1958 was a good one for Rambler. The Ambassador was the top of the line. It featured pillarless styling.

The Buick Invicta Estate Wagon for 1959 was one of two wagon models offered by Buick. Fins were at their height in 1959 and Buick's winged rear was no exception, although the design did lend itself well to the wagon models. There were no pillarless wagons this year. Both models were conventional in this respect. The Invicta was the top of the line, priced at $3,841.

Part of the new LeSabre Series was the Estate Wagon, a 4-door, 6-passenger model. It was based on a shorter wheelbase and weighed 95 pounds less than the Invicta. It cost only $3,320, a savings of more than $500.

The top of the Chevrolet wagon line once again was the 4-door Nomad of the Impala Series. New for this year was a disappearing tailgate window. The Nomad was the most expensive Chevrolet this year, with a price tag of $3,009.

Chevrolet's only 2-door wagon was the Brookwood 2-Door, of which 18,800 were built. Designated the Model 1215, it cost $2,689 and weighed 3,860 pounds. With the rear seat folded, it offered 92 cubic feet of usable load space.

Buick once again renamed its wagons. There were on two models this year, the expensive Invicta, a pillare 9-passenger model, and the lesser LeSabre, a 6-passeng version with pillars. Chevrolet wagons were considered separate series this year. They all featured "safety pla glass" all around. This offered distortion-free visibili

All Chrylser Corporation wagons were unchanged. Fo continued with six wagon models and Mercury expand its wagon line to five models. Due to sagging sales, Ed offered only two wagons this year.

Studebaker introduced the Lark. Only one wagon w available, a 2-door, 6-passenger model. Rambler increas the number of wagon models to five, and continued offer a pillarless model — a styling trend it initiated. T Custom Cross Country wagon had simulated wood. Fo was not alone this year with this feature.

Chevrolet's intermediate wagon was the 6-passenger Parkwood, Model 1635, which cost $2,867 and weighed 3,970 pounds. Also in the Parkwood line was Chevrolet's only 9-passenger wagon, called the Kingswood, Model 1645. At 4,015 pounds, the Kingswood was Chevrolet's heaviest car. It cost $2,970.

Had not wagons been considered in a separate series, the Brookwood would have fallen into the Biscayne Series. This is the Brookwood 4-Door, Model 1235, which weighed 3,955 pounds and cost $2,756. This year, all wagons shared the same basic body.

The Chrysler Windsor wagon was no longer designated a Town and Country. It was available as a 6 or 9-passenger model. It sold for $3,813 in the 9-passenger version, with only 751 being built. Chrysler wagons still featured disappearing tailgate windows and rear facing third seats.

The New Yorker Town & Country wagon continued to be available in both 6 and 9-passenger form, with the 9-passenger style being just a bit more popular. In 6-passenger version, it cost $4,907, weighed 4,295 pounds, and had a run of 444. In 9-passenger form it cost $5,122, weighed 4,360 pounds, and had a run of 564. The third seat faced backward in the 9-passenger model.

The Dodge Town Wagon, like its competitor the Chevy Carry-All, was based on the ½-ton light truck chassis. The wheelbase was 108 inches with the load length of the floor being 94-11/16 inches and the width 65¼ inches. The interior height of the cargo area was 53 inches. All this was with the seats removed. With all three seats in place it could carry up to 9 passengers.

The DeSoto Fireflite 4-door, 6-passenger Shopper. With the exception of the third seat, it had the same basic features as the Explorer. The wheelbase was 126 inches. It was powered by a 383 cubic inch V-8 rated at 410 horsepower. The Fireflite Series was designated as the Model MS3-H.

The DeSoto Fireflite 4-door, 9-passenger Explorer. DeSoto wagons again featured disappearing tailgate windows and rear facing third seats. The styling was unchanged from the previous year. But this year the top of the line Fireflite Explorer was available with the fabulous Adventurer V-8. This was a 383 cubic inch Hemi with 425 horsepower.

Dodge's most expensive car was the Custom Sierra 4-door 3-seat station wagon, roughly equivalent to the Custom Royal Series models. This car cost $3,389 and weighed 4,020 pounds. Also offered as a 2-seat wagon, the Custom Sierra went for $3,268 and weighed 3,980 pounds. All Dodge Sierras in this year were powered by a 361 cubic inch V-8 — the Custom Sierra with the 305 horsepower version and the standard Sierra with the 295 horsepower motor.

Had wagons been placed into series, the Sierra wagon would have been placed into the Royal Series. Available in two versions, 2 and 3-seat, these wagons were offered as 4-doors only. The 2-door Suburban wagon was dropped with this model line. As a 2-seat wagon this car went for $3,053 and weighed 3,940 pounds. The 3-seat version had the observation lounge rear-facing third seat and sold for $3,174 and tipped the scales at 4,015 pounds.

The DeSoto Firesweep 4-door, 9-passenger Explorer. This was DeSoto's lower priced 9-passenger wagon. It had a lot of the features of the Fireflite, such as the rear facing third seat, disappearing tailgate window, and rear bumper step plates. But it was based on a smaller 122-inch wheelbase. The engine was a 361 cubic inch 390 HP V-8.

DeSoto's export wagon, the Diplomat, continued to be based on the Plymouth. This model was the DeLuxe Custom Suburban 4-door, 9-passenger wagon. It had all the features of the domestic Plymouth Sport Suburban, but carried DeSoto trim and name plates.

The Edsel Villager 4-door, 6-passenger wagon. The two-piece tailgate was still retained. As the gate portion is somewaht smaller than the window section, this would have been a loading restriction. Visibility through the rear window was very good and the tail lights were placed high for greater safety.

Because of sagging sales, Edsel reduced the number of wagons this year to two models. Both were called the Villager. One was a 9-passenger model, which is pictured here. Edsel wagon bodies were in reality modified Ford wagons. One of the optional items was a luggage rack. There were three engine options. A 303 HP V-8, a 225 HP V-8 and a 145 HP Six.

Top of the Ford wagon line was the distinctive Country Squire with simulated wood paneling. Ford Motor Co. was the only one of the big three to feature simulated wood on its wagons. This treatment was always applied to the top of the line. This was a good year for Ford, as it took over first place from Chevrolet.

The mid-range Ford wagon was this Country Sedan, shown here in the 9-passenger version. It was also available as a 6-passenger model. Ford wagons could be ordered in various color combinations, such as this "Style Tone" combination.

Another view of the 2-door Country Sedan. This was the last year for this basic body style that began in 1957. The center side window could be rolled down. Ford boasted over 92 cubic feet of load space, with the second seat folded down. This was accomplished by increasing the body length by seven inches.

This is the Ford 2-door, 6-passenger Country Sedan, with the two-color "Style Tone" combination. Ford offered the 2-door wagon in two price ranges. This one was listed at $2,750. Whitewall tires and full wheel covers were optional.

The 2-door, 6-passenger Ford Ranch Wagon. This example is painted in two-color "Style Tone" combination, which was an extra cost option. Ford wagons had four engine options this year: a 300 HP Thunderbird 352 Special V-8; a 225 HP Thunderbird 332 Special V-8; a 200 HP Thunderbird 292 V-8 and a 145 HP Mileage Maker Six. Any one of these could be coupled with four different types of transmission – conventional drive, overdrive, Fordomatic Drive, and Cruise-O-Matic Drive, the latter two being automatic transmission.

Mercury's medium priced wagon was the 9-passenger Voyager 4-Door, costing $3,793 and weighing 4,565 pounds. All Mercurys this year featured overlapping, electric powered windshield wipers.

The Ford 4-door, 6-passenger Ranch Wagon, painted in a single color. With the tailgate lowered, the Ford wagon offered over 42 square feet of cargo area. Some of the features offered by Ford this year were 4,000 mile oil changes and "Diamond Lustre" paint finish that never needed waxing.

The top of the Mercury line was this Colony Park 4-door, 9-passenger model. This was a pillarless wagon featuring hardtop styling. Simulated wood panels indicated it was the top of the line. It carried a price tag of $3,932.

Mercury's five wagon models continued to be classed as a series unto themselves. This year, all wagons used the same basic body shell with interior and exterior modifications. One of the lower priced wagons was the 9-passenger Commuter 4-Door, priced at $3,215 and weighing 4,355 pounds. Its curved rear quarter window continued to remain stationary.

The Mercury 2-door, 6-passenger Commuter was the lowest priced Mercury wagon at $3,145. It was the only 2-door wagon on the market with pillarless hardtop styling. The commuters was one of five wagon models offered by Mercury this year.

Of apparently rather limited production was this Voyager 2-Door 6-passenger model, which was introduced but does not appear on any of the later price or specification sheets. A popular option on the wagons was to have the roof insert panel and side trim panel painted in matching tones.

The Oldsmobile Super 88 Fiesta was a 4-door, 6-passenger model which was the top of the wagon line. Oldsmobile offered wagons in two series this year — the Super 88 and the Dynamic 88. Trim and appointments were the real differences in models.

The Oldsmobile Dynamic 88 wagon. Olds styling continued to follow that of a sedan even to retaining a sedan quarter window. Pillarless design was no longer being offered. Note that full wheel covers were not standard on the Dynamic 88.

The Oldsmobile Dynamic 88 wagon in optional two-tone paint. One of the features of the Olds wagon was a disappearing tailgate window, which was power operated. Large quarter windows provided excellent visibility.

The Plymouth Sport Suburban. This was the most expensive Plymouth wagon. It was available as a 6 or 9-passenger model and was powered only by a V-8. Its 122-inch wheelbase made it one of the biggest wagons in the industry. Some of the unique features included a rear facing third seat, bumper step plates, and a spare tire compartment located inside the right rear fender well. This compartment was accessible from the outside.

The Plymouth 4-door Custom Suburban. This was a step down from the Sport Suburban, but it retained many of the same features. It was available as a 6-passenger or 9-passenger model, with optional V-8 or 6-cylinder engine. Fuel capacity for all Plymouth wagons was 22 gallons.

The Plymouth Custom Suburban was also available as a 2-door model, but only as a 6-passenger wagon, and powered only by a V-8. The feature of a disappearing tailgate window made loading of the Plymouth wagon an easy chore.

One of Plymouth's low priced wagons was this 4-door DeLuxe Suburban, 6-passenger model, available with V-8 or 6-cylinder engine. The spare was mounted inside in a lockable compartment in the rear cargo area.

The lowest priced wagon in the Plymouth line-up was this DeLuxe Suburban 2-door. It was a 6-passenger model, with optional V-8 or 6-cylinder engine. Plymouth's optional V-8 engines were the Golden Commando 395 cubic inch with 305 HP, usually found in the Sport Suburban. Then there was the Fury V-800, 318 cubic inches and 230 HP, or the Fury V-800 with Super-Pak, which boosted the horsepower to 260.

This was the year Pontiac introduced the "wide track." Pictured here is the Catalina wagon, a 4-door, 6-passenger model. One of its features was a power operated disappearing tailgate window. The tail fins were a little questionable. They appeared to be stuck on as an afterthought. Large quarter windows provided excellent visibility.

The top of the Rambler wagon line was this Ambassador, a 4-door, 6-passenger model. It featured pillarless styling and was powered by a 270 HP V-8. One of the unique features of the Rambler wagon was full reclining front seats.

The Rambler Custom Cross Country was one of four wagon model offered by Rambler this year. It featured a simulated wood accent strip. As with all Rambler wagons, the roof rack was standard. All Rambler wagons were of the Unibody construction. It was available with the Economy Six or Rebel V-8 engine.

This is the DeLuxe version of the Rambler American wagon. Note that it does not have a luggage rack, which was found on all other Rambler wagons. It is also missing a side chrome strip. Cargo capacity was 52 cubic feet. The overall length was 178.3 inches as compared to the Ambassador at 202.6 inches.

Newly introduced this year was the Studebaker Lark Station Wagon. This was a 113-inch wheelbase model, powered by an L-Head 169 cubic inch Six or Overhead Valve 259 cubic inch V-8. Horsepower for the Six was 90 while the V-8 put out 180. The Lark featured a two-piece tailgate, which was conventional for the industry. Cargo area capacity was 93 cubic feet. The turning radius for this neat compact wagon was a tight 39 feet.

The Rambler Super Cross Country wagon. One of the features of a Rambler wagon was the crank-down disappearing rear window. It provided easier loading. An optional safety feature offered on the Rambler wagon was an adjustable head rest.

The lowest priced Rambler wagon was this Rambler American model in 2-door, 6-passenger version. It was available as a Super or DeLuxe model. This is the Super, with standard luggage rack. It was powered by a 90 HP 6-cylinder engine. Wheelbase was 100 inches and the total height was 57.8 inches. Whitewall tires and two-tone paint were options.

At the start of this decade, the rules set down at the beginning of the 1950s were still holding. For one thing the wagon continued to conform to the basic lines of a sedan. This was of course with the exception of the greenhouse. The greenhouse is that portion of the car above the beltline. The rule governing the greenhouse was: that the roof panel would be as high at the tailgate as it was at the "B" pillar.

The front end sheet metal, doors and rear quarter panels followed the same lines as that of the manufacturers' current sedan model. On the inside, the second and third seats were self-storing, providing a flat, expanded cargo floor. The spare tire found its way to the inside of the wagon, where it was destined to stay. But the tailgate design was still unresolved.

Big news for 1960 was the introduction of compact car models by the big three auto makers. The compacts were an alternative to the so-called "foreign car invasion." Chevrolet debuted with its rear engined Corvair. Two models were offered, none of which was a station wagon. Ford Motor Company introduced the Ford Falcon and the Mercury Comet. Each featured two wagon models. Chrysler introduced the Plymouth Valiant, with two wagon models, a 4-door and a 2-door.

American Motors did not introduced a compact car this year. It had been producing a compact size car, the Rambler, for some time now. They also produced a sub-compact, the American. Both had wagon models. And, of course, Studebaker too had been producing the compact sized Lark. There was a single Lark wagon offered.

Buick offered two wagon models, one in the Invicta series and one in the LeSabre series. Each wagon in turn offered both 6-passenger and 9-passenger versions. Chevrolet had five wagons available, and Pontiac and Oldsmobile each offered two wagons. Chrysler had a Windsor and New Yorker wagon. Dodge had four wagons, all 4-door models, plus the newly introduced Dodge Town Wagon, a 2-door station wagon utility based on a ½-ton truck chassis. Plymouth had six wagons, one a 2-door model. This was in addition to its two new Valiant wagons.

Ford had six wagons, including the new Falcon models. Mercury produced four wagons, two of which were in the new compact series, Comet. Edsel, in its final year, offered one wagon model. It was nothing more than a face lifted Ford. The Edsel had lasted only three model years, and although it had not significantly contributed to auto history as an automobile, it has since become a study in failure.

A rear view of the 9-passenger Buick LeSabre wagon. Note the rear facing third seat, and wrap-around quarter window. Also note how the spare was awkwardly housed on the right side. The wheelbase was 123 inches with an overall length of 217.9 inches. This model sold for $3,493 and 2,222 were made. For less than $100 the extra seat was provided. Apparently this proved not to be a bargain, as more of the 6-passenger models were sold.

The Buick LeSabre, model 4435 4-door, 6-passenger wagon, was one of two LeSabre models offered this year. There were only subtle changes in basic body design. The windshield was wrap-around and the quarter windows also wrapped around. Cost of the 6-passenger model was $3,386, and 5,331 were produced.

The Invicta 9-passenger wagon. Note that the tailgate window was power operated and was stored within the tailgate. This model sold for $3,948 and 1,605 were made.

A step above the LeSabre wagon was this Invicta. This is the 6-passenger version. It had the same overall features as the LeSabre only the appointments and inside trim were different. At $3,841, it was $455 more than the LeSabre. A total of 3,471 were produced.

The Checker Superba Special Station Wagon. This was a 4-door, 6-passenger model. One of its most unique features was a power operated second seat. One touch of a button on the dash board and the seat folded down completely flat. Another touch of the button and it raised to an upright position. Checker also boasted that its cargo area was the widest of any wagon in the world. The spare was housed under the cargo floor.

A Cadillac station wagon. The body was by Hess and Eisenhardt of Cincinnati, Ohio. Note the simulated wood treatment and the two-piece quarter window. This wagon was built for Frank Porter of the Central Cadillac Company of Cleveland, Ohio. Central Cadillac was a local dealership.

The Chevrolet Parkwood 4-door, 6-passenger wagon. Note the wrap-around windshield and sedan styling. This was Chevrolet's most popular wagon. It sold for $2,854.

The rare Kingswood 4-door, 9-passenger model. It was advertised but never put into full production. Only nine were built. It carried a price tag of $2,957. The third seat was rear facing and the tailgate window was self-storing, operated manually from the outside or with a power option from inside.

The Chevrolet Brookwood 2-door, 6-passenger station wagon. The same sedan features still prevailed even in this 2-door model. This wagon appeared for the last time this year. It was Chevrolet's lowest priced model at $2,693.

Top of the Chevrolet line was this Nomad wagon. A 4-door, 6-passenger model, it featured Impala trim throughout and had a price tag of $2,996. This was Chevrolet's most expensive wagon, but it was $84 less than Ford's Country Squire. Ford, however, outsold Chevrolet in the wagon field, even with a poor body design.

The Chevrolet Carry-All was again based on the ½-ton truck chassis. It could carry up to eight passengers. Only a 2-door model was offered. Note the unusual two-tone paint treatment to the roof panel. This gave it a landau effect. The Carry-All was now being considered by families, so it was jazzed up a bit with whitewall tires and chrome trim.

The prestige wagon of the Chrysler line was this New Yorker model. It was available in 6-passenger or 9-passenger versions. The 6-passenger model cost $4,947 and the 9-passenger $4,056. Only 624 of the former and 671 of the latter were built. The Chrysler wagon remained the highest priced in the industry.

Top of the Dodge wagon line-up was the Polara Series with two offerings, a 6-passenger and a 9-passenger model. Pictured here is the 9-passenger version. It featured pillarless styling, like the Chrysler wagons, but had a roof rack, unlike the Chrysler wagons. Overall styling for Dodge this year was the look of a winged dart. The Dodge 6-passenger Polara wagon was not pillarless. For power plants Dodge offered a 383 cubic inch Ram Fire V-8. It was one of four V-8s offered. In addition to the V-8s there was a 225 cubic inch Slant Six.

The Dodge Dart Seneca 6-passenger wagon was the lowest priced Dodge wagon at $2,695 with 6-cylinder engine. This was compared to the Chevrolet Brookwood 2-door which sold for $2,693, and was Chevrolet's lowest priced wagon. Ford's lowest priced wagon was the 2-door Ranch wagon at $2,665. The Dodge was a bargain. It was big, had four doors, and a panoramic view. It was available with a 6-cylinder engine or a choice of four V-8s.

The Dodge Town Wagon D-100. Mounted on a light truck chassis, it could carry up to 1,450 lbs. of cargo, or a total of eight passengers. It featured a wrap-around windshield and delivery type rear doors.

The Chrysler Windsor station wagon was available in 6-passenger and 9-passenger form. With the introduction of this model, Chrysler reintroduced the pillarless styling to wagons. The Chrysler wagon followed the lines of a 4-door hardtop. This was the last year for the Windsor wagon. In 6-passenger form it sold for $3,678 and as a 9-passenger the cost was $3,759.

Dodge also offered two versions of the 4-door station wagon in the medium priced Pioneer Series. The 6-cylinder 2-seat wagon went for $2,787 and weighed 3,820 pounds. As a 3-seat, 9-passenger wagon the 6-cylinder Pioneer cost $2,892 and tipped the scales at 3,875 pounds. With the powerful yet economical 318 V-8, the 2-seat, 6-passenger Pioneer wagon sold for $2,906 and weighed 4,000 pounds, while the 9-passenger, 3-seat version was $3,011 and tipped the scales at 4,065 pounds.

In the Matador series Dodge had two wagon models, a 6-passenger and a 9-passenger, neither of which had pillarless styling. For this year Dodge claimed 95.8 cubic feet of closed cargo space. The Matador 6-passenger wagon sold for $3,239 and the 9-passenger for $3,354. This compared to the Polara series which carried a price tag of $3,506 for the 6-passenger model and $3,621 for the 9-passenger. This model was reworked into an ambulance by Automotive Conversion Co. of Mich. It was called an Amblewagon – a station wagon-ambulance.

The Dodge Town wagon with optional four-wheel drive. With this option it became an all-terrain vehicle for business or pleasure. It found some favor with heavy construction companies and in the oil fields.

There were no domestic wagons offered by DeSoto this year. The Marque was in trouble and rumors persisted that it would be discontinued by Chrysler. There was a DeSoto wagon available nonetheless. It was in the form of the Diplomat. The export-only model shared the Dodge body. It was really a Dodge with DeSoto trim and name plates.

Edsel's only station was the Villager, a 4-door wagon based on the Ford Country Sedan. It was available as either a six or nine-passenger car. The rooftop luggage rack was an accessory.

The Ford Country Squire 4-door, 9-passenger wagon for 1960 featured an all-new body design. This body design proved not to be very popular. Ford sales dropped, and the design was discontinued after one year. The Country Squire model sold for $3,080.

At the bottom end of the Ford wagon line-up was the Ranch Wagon. This model was available as both a 2-door and 4-door, each with a capacity of 6-passengers. The 2-door version sold for $2,665, while the 4-door sold for $2,770.

Just below the Country Squire was the Ford Country Sedan model. It was available in both a 6-passenger and a 9-passenger configuration. In the 9-passenger version it sold for $2,900.

1960

The Ford Courier was a light truck version of the Ranch Wagon, designed to replace the now discontinued sedan delivery models. It was available only as a 2-door model. All Ford wagons boasted of a 97 cu. ft. cargo area. All models offered a choice of three V-8s and one Six, plus four different types of transmissions, ranging from a manual 3-speed to a 3-speed automatic, called Cruise-o-matic.

New for this year was the introduction of the Ford Falcon compact car. There were two wagon models available, a 2-door and a 4-door. Both were 6-passenger models. Pictured here is the 2-door version. Some of its features included a crank down rear window, and a two-piece quarter window on the 2-door model gave it that sedan appearance. The wagon proved to be neat and very popular. In the 2-door version it sold for $2,225.

The Ford Falcon 4-door wagon. Note the vent window in the rear door. Among the options available was a roof rack. Ads boasted that a 4-door model was worth more at trade-in time. The 4-door model sold for $2,290 — only $65 more for those extra two doors.

The GMC version of the Chevrolet Suburban Carry-All. The 2-door wagon was mounted on a light truck chassis. It had seating capacity for 9 passengers. It is shown here with optional four-wheel drive.

The Colony Park continued to be Mercury's luxury wagon, and was the only other wagon offered this year beside the Commuter and those in the Comet line. It cost $3,837, and at 4,568 pounds, was the heaviest vehicle that Mercury produced.

Mercury offered only two wagons this year, the Colony Park and the Commuter Country Cruiser shown here. The Commuter, classed as part of the Monterey series, cost $3,127 and weighed 4,303 pounds. It used a one-piece tailgate, with roll-up window that was lowered or raised from the outside via a locking control arm. The Commuter was available with two or three seats.

Comet's most expensive model was the 4-Door Station Wagon, which cost $2,365. The six-passenger, 2,581-pound car used stationary windows in the rear quarter, but had roll-up and vent windows in the rear doors. The vulnerable, corner-mounted parking lights were similar to those used on Edsel in 1959.

Comet's economy wagon was the 2-Door version which used stationary rear windows and roll-up side windows without vents. Ford finally caught up with other auto manufacturers and began to use a one-piece tailgate, thereby doing away with the annoying upper transom. The Comet 2-Door Wagon cost $2,310 and weighed 2,548 pounds.

The Oldsmobile Super 88 Fiesta 9-passenger wagon. The third seat faced to the rear. The tailgate window was self-containing, and operated by crank on the outside or by electric motor from the inside. Note the wrap-around quarter windows.

The lower priced Dynamic 88 series offered two wagon models, a 6-passenger and a 9-passenger. The overall design of the Oldsmobile wagon followed that of a sedan. Note the extreme wrap-around of the windshield.

An American Motors Metropolitan station wagon. This neat looking little wagon never got beyond the prototype stage. There was room enough for 5 passengers. Note the wrap-around tailgate window. It is not known for sure how this window operated.

The Oldsmobile Super 88 4-door, 9-passenger wagon. This was one of four wagon models available from Oldsmobile this year. Note the optional roof rack on this model.

A rear view of the Oldsmobile Dynamic 88 9-passenger wagon. All Oldsmobile wagons were 4-door models. All featured wrap-around quarter windows and self-contained tailgate windows. What appears to be a vent window behind the rear door is actually a fixed window.

Top of the Plymouth wagon line was the 9-passenger Sport Suburban. Plymouth wagons, as well as the whole passenger car line, featured uni-body construction. Plymouth, like the rest of the Chrysler Corporation cars, still clung to rear fender fins. This would be the last year for those fins, but they were going out in a blaze of glory.

The Plymouth Sport Suburban 6-passenger model. The self-contained tailgate window, which was pioneered by Plymouth, was standard on all Plymouth wagons. It was operated by push button on the dash or by key on the outside of the tailgate. One of the options available on the Plymouth wagon was the Aero Wheel. This was an almost rectangular shaped steering wheel. It was claimed that steering was much easier and also entrance and exit for the driver was easier.

The Plymouth Custom 4-door, 6-passenger wagon. This was the middle of the line wagon. It was also available as a 9-passenger. Optional engines included a 6-cylinder and four V-8s. Topping the V-8 list was the Sonoramic Commando V-8. This was an advanced deep-block design that used hi-frequency sound waves to provide supercharger effect. Horsepower was 330 at 4800 RPM.

The Plymouth DeLuxe 4-door, 6-passenger Suburban was only available as a 6-passenger model. This was the bottom of the line series. All engine options were available. Many of the features from the top of the line were also available.

Here is a Plymouth Custom Suburban 6-passenger wagon being used as an ambulance. Special ambulance conversion such as this were available as part of Plymouth's police package.

The lowest priced full-sized Plymouth wagon was this 2-door DeLuxe Suburban model. Overall design followed that of the sedan. Note the dash mounted rear view mirror. This was standard on all Plymouth cars. Plymouth windshields were not only of the wrap-around type, but they also had a high curved crown.

New from Plymouth this year was the compact Valiant. Two Valiant wagons were available, a 2-door and a 4-door model. Both were 6-passenger wagons. Pictured here is the 4-door version. Valiant wagons were distinctive in design.

The Pontiac Catalina Safari 9-passenger wagon. The basic body shell was shared with Oldsmobile. This was one of four wagon models available from Pontiac. The third seat was rear facing. The tailgate window was self-contained. The spare was mounted below the cargo floor. All Pontiac wagons were powered by V-8 engines. All had Hydra-matic transmissions.

The Rambler Custom Cross Country 9-passenger model. The tailgate is actually a fifth door. The fifth door design was standard with all 9-passenger Rambler wagons. It was unique for 1960. Note the third seat is rear facing. All manufacturers except Ford used the rear facing third seat this year.

The Rambler Super Cross Country was the middle of the line wagon. It was the best selling of the Rambler wagons. The roof rack was standard. The tailgate window was self-contained. One of its unique features was reclining front seats.

The Rambler Ambassador V-8 Super Cross Country wagon. Note the distinctive roof dip at the rear. The roof rack was standard. This was one of eight Rambler wagons available this year. Topping the line was the Ambassador Custom Hardtop Cross Country, which featured pillarless styling.

Lowest priced of the Rambler wagons was the American series. There were two models available in this sub-compact series. Pictured here is the Super model. It was also available in the DeLuxe, which was the cheaper model. All Rambler American wagons were 2-door, 5-passenger wagons. The roof rack on this model is standard. Wheelbase of the American wagon was 100 inches, with an overall length of 178.3 inches.

Willys continued to offer an unchanged 2-door, 6-passenger wagon. One set of quarter windows were sliders and the other fixed. The tailgate was two piece. The spare was mounted insiee against one of the rear quarter panels. The panel stampings were still the same, but the simulated wood was gone.

Studebaker also offered a compact sized wagon in this 4-door Lark version. It was a 6-passenger model. The tailgate window was self-contained. The rear doors had operational vent windows. Note that the tail lights are mounted at the beltline — the only wagon in the industry to do so.

The year 1961 marked the passing of DeSoto. Chrysler [Co]rporation halted production of the DeSoto during the [las]t week of December 1960, only a month after the [ne]w models were introduced. There was no wagon, and [onl]y 911 2-door hardtops and 2,123 4-door hardtops were [pro]duced. This culminated a production record of [2,8]56,000 cars since 1928.

[G]eneral Motors introduced compact models in the Buick, [Po]ntiac and Oldsmobile. All General Motor divisions [int]roduced new body designs for this year. Buick had [tw]o full-size wagons in the LeSabre series and three [com]pact wagons in the new Special series. Buick, Pontiac [an]d Oldsmobile compacts all shared the same body shell. [A] unique feature of the compact wagons was a hatchback [tail]gate.

[C]hevrolet introduced a wagon in its compact Corvair [ser]ies. The Corvair was first introduced in 1960 without a [wa]gon. New for this year, in addition to the Corvair wagon, [wa]s the Greenbriar Sportswagon. This was a 9-passenger [van] type wagon, powered by the rear mounted Corvair [en]gine. With the addition of the Greenbriar, Chevrolet [bo]osted its wagon offerings to five series.

[O]ldsmobile, including its newly introduced compact, the [F-8]5, offered three wagon models. Pontiac on the other [ha]nd offered four models including its new compact, [Te]mpest.

[C]hrysler Corporation had no major changes in overall [de]sign. For the most part the fins were all but gone. Dodge [an]d Plymouth both offered compact wagon models. [Ne]wly introduced this year was the Dodge compact [wa]gon, the Lancer. It was no more than a Dodge-trimmed [Pl]ymouth Valiant. The compact Plymouth Valiant was [in] its second year.

[F]ord Motor Company had twelve wagon models [ava]ilable. Four were full-sized Fords, two were compact [Fo]rd Falcons and there was a newly introduced Station [Bu]s (a van type vehicle). In the Mercury line there were [tw]o full-size wagons and two compact Mercury Comet [wa]gons.

New for this year was the Compact Buick Special wagon. It was available in three models—two standard versions, a 6-passenger and a 9-passenger, and a DeLuxe version available only as a 9-passenger model. The exteriors were all the same with differences being confined to interior trim. Pictured here is the Standard 6-passenger, Model 4035. It sold for $2,681, and 6,101 were built. The 9-passenger, Model 4045, sold for $2,762 and only 798 were produced.

The Buick Special DeLuxe 9-passenger wagon. It was new for this year, one of three Special compact models. It shared its body with Oldsmobile and Pontiac. Note the hatchback tailgate. This type of tailgate would later be revised in the 1970s. The Buick Special DeLuxe sold for $2,853, and 11,729 were produced. It proved to be the most popular of the Special wagons.

The Chevrolet Corvair 700 Series Lakewood Station Wagon was the more deluxe Corvair wagon. The inside trim made the difference between the 500 and 700 Series. Both wagons were 4-door, 6-passenger models.

Chevrolet's highest priced model for 1961 was this Impala Nomad wagon, which sold for $3,099. It was a 4-door, 9-passenger model, one of six wagon models being offered by Chevrolet. The wrap-around windshield and wrap-around quarter windows were both gone. The sedan look was somewhat gone with the elimination of the smaller quarter window which was found behind the rear door in the 1960 models.

New for this year, and appearing only this year in the 500 Series was this Corvair Lakewood station wagon. It was a 4-door, 6-passenger model. Designated as Model 535, it sold for $2,266. The spare was mounted on the inside. It was powered by a 6-cylinder rear engine.

The Chrysler Newport station wagon was available in 6 and 9-passenger form. Chrysler continued to offer pillarless styling. The 6-passenger model cost $3,541 and had a production run of 1,832. The 9-passenger version cost $3,662 and 1,571 were produced. This would be Chrysler's last year for tail fins.

The Chevrolet Greenbriar Sportswagon. This bus-type wagon used Corvair mechanical components, including the rear engine. Its carrying capacity was greater than a passenger car wagon, and it soon became a favorite with large families and outdoors lovers. A total of 18,489 were built and sold for $2,651.

Dodge entered the compact car market this year with the introduction of the Lancer. Two wagon models were offered, both 4-door, 6-passenger wagons. The higher priced model was the Lancer 770 Series, selling for $2,466. The lower priced being the 170 Series at $2,383. Lancer shared its body with Plymouth's Valiant. The body stampings were virtually identical.

The Chrysler New Yorker station wagon. In the 6-passenger version it sold for $4,764 and as a 9-passenger wagon it sold for $4,871. Only 760 of the latter were built. They remained the highest priced American made wagon. Styling of the Newport and New Yorker were the same, with the differences being in the trim.

DeSoto faced its last year of production and while there was no domestic wagon, an export model, the Diplomat, was available. The Diplomat, as in previous years, was a Dodge wagon with DeSoto trim. It was offered only as a 6-passenger model and was not available in the U.S.

Rear view of the Dodge Seneca wagon. This 4-door, 6-passenger model was the lowest priced full-sized Dodge wagon. It carried a price tag of $2,787 with the standard 6-cylinder engine and sold for $2,825 with a V-8. Note the rubber bumpers attached to the tailgate. These helped support the tailgate in the lowered position.

Polara's most expensive model was the 4-door hardtop station wagon offered in two forms. The 2-seat, 6-passenger version went for $3,294 and weighed 4,115 pounds. The 3-seat, 9-passenger version was the most expensive Dodge offered this year. It went for $3,409 and weighed 4,125 pounds. The attractive lines seen on the Polara 4-door hardtop were carried over to the station wagon model with considerable success.

Dodge offered five full-sized wagons. Pictured here is the Dart Pioneer 4-door, 6-passenger model. It was also available as a 9-passenger wagon. It sold for $2,906 as a 6-passenger and for $3,011 as a 9-passenger. All of the full-sized Dodge wagons had the same body design, with the top of the line Polara being offered as a pillarless model.

The Ford Country Sedan 6-passenger wagon. It was also available as a 9-passenger model. This wagon was one step below the Country Squire. It sold for $2,850 as compared to the Country Squire price tag of $3,100. The body design for 1961 was all new. The extreme streamlined styling of the 1960 models proved to be unpopular, so in an unprecedented move the basic body design was drastically changed after only one year.

Ford Motor Company continued to be the only manufacturer to offer simulated wood trim. Only the top of the line Country Squire was available with this trim, as was the top of the Mercury line. The Country Squire was available as a 9-passenger model, with the third seat facing forward. Only Ford and Mercury offered a forward facing third seat.

The Ford Ranch Wagon, 4-door, 6-passenger model was one of two Ranch Wagon models offered by Ford. This version sold for $2,656—$180 less than its competitive model Chevrolet.

The Ford Falcon 4-door, 6-passenger wagon was one of two compact wagons offered by Ford this year. The basic body design was unchanged from the previous year. This version sold for $2,270.

Ford's new styling proved to be a success, and all models were very attractive. The lowest priced full-sized Ford station wagon was the 2-door, 6-passenger Ranch Wagon. It sold for $2,586. Note how the tailgate window could be lowered by means of a crank on the outside.

The Ford Falcon 2-door wagon. This was the second year for the Falcon wagon. It featured a self-storing tailgate window operated by a crank on the outside. This lowest priced Falcon wagon sold for $2,225, as compared with the lowest priced Chevrolet Corvair wagon, which sold for $2,266.

Introduced this year was the Ford Econoline Station Bus. It utilized many Falcon parts and was designed to compete with the Volkswagen Bus. Seating was for 9 passengers, and with the seats removed it could carry a large amount of cargo, or camping gear, or what-have-you — a truly versatile vehicle.

The International Travelall. Designed more like a truck, it was nonetheless a passenger car vehicle — a station wagon. This was a 4-door, 8-passenger model. The tailgate was a two-piece design. The quarter windows were fixed. It was powered by a 6-cylinder engine.

Mercury's economy wagon was the Commuter, shown here parked next to its dressed-up brother, the Colony Park. The Commuter weighed 4,115 pounds, and cost $2,992 in three-seat form or $2,922 in two-seat version. The Commuters used the 6-cylinder engine as standard, but were available with any of the V-8s. All Mercury chassis this year were pre-lubricated to go 30,000 miles without additional lubrication.

A good looking station wagon was the Colony Park, shown here with optional wheel discs, skirts, and roof-top luggage rack. It was available as a three seat model for $3,189 or as a two-seater for $3,118. It weighed 4,131 pounds. The fact that Mercurys shared basic bodies with Ford this year is quickly evident when the Colony Park is compared with the Ford Country Squire.

The Comet 2-Door Station Wagon was priced at $2,310 and weighed 2,548 pounds. A three-speed manual transmission was standard, but an automatic was available.

The Comet wagons shared unit bodies and chassis with the Ford Falcon, but had different front ends and power plants. This is the 4-Door Wagon, which sold for $2,353 and weighed 2,581 pounds. The wagons were built on a 109.5-inch wheelbase and were 191.8 inches overall.

A front view of the Oldsmobile Super 88 Station Wagon. The full wheel covers were standard. Oldsmobile offered a new box strength guard-beam frame coupled with such features as: over-the-axle coil springing, live rubber body mounts, and anti-spin rear axle.

The Oldsmobile F-85 DeLuxe Station Wagon was newly introduced this year. It marked Oldsmobile's entrance into the low price field, and more correctly, into the compact car field. The F-85 wagon was a 4-door, 6-passenger model with a wheelbase of 112 inches. It was powered by a 215 cubic inch 155 HP Rockette V-8. The tailgate was a one-piece hatchback design. The tailgate window was divided into three sections. An all-vinyl interior was standard. The roof rack was an option.

The Oldsmobile Super 88 4-door, 9-passenger wagon. This was the deluxe wagon, one of three wagon models being offered by Oldsmobile this year. The tailgate had a self-storing window, which was electrically operated by a switch on the dashboard. The third seat was rear facing. The standard engine for the Super 88 Series was a new 394 cubic inch Skyrocket V-8. This was coupled with a new Hydra-matic transmission which gave smoother shifting.

The lowest priced full-sized Oldsmobile wagon was this Dynamic 88 4-door, 6-passenger model. With the rear seat folded it provided 7½ feet of cargo space. Interiors were available in a combination of vinyl and cloth or all vinyl, both color keyed to match or contrast with the outside paint. The Dynamic 88 Series was powered by a 394 cubic inch, 250 horsepower V-8, which featured an Econ-O-Way carburetor and minimum overlap camshaft to precisely monitor fuel flow.

The Plymouth wagon for 1961 was available in three series with 9 models, which included full-size and compact-size models. Pictured here is the 6-passenger wagon fitted for police use. Note the ambulance conversion. The tailgate window was self-storing.

The Plymouth Sport Suburban. This was the top of the Plymouth wagon line. It was available as a 4-door, 6-passenger or 9-passenger model. The third seat faced to the rear. The tailgate window was self-storing. Step plates were mounted on the bumpers for easier access to the third seat. The quarter windows were a wrap-around design. The four door configuration had a strong resemblance to a sedan.

The lowest priced full-size Plymouth wagon was this DeLuxe Suburban 2-door, 6-passenger model. All Plymouth wagons were of uni-body construction, providing a rattle-free car— or so the manufacturer claimed. Each body was sprayed six times and dipped seven times to repel rust and corrosion.

The Plymouth Valiant V-100 wagon was the economy compact wagon. It had a little less of the fancy trim. Quarter windows were wrap-around and the tailgate window was self-storing. Interiors of the Valiant wagons were upholstered in washable vinyl.

The Pontiac Bonneville Custom Safari was a 4-door, 6-passenger model. This was one of three full-size Pontiac wagons being offered this year, the others being a 6-passenger Catalina and a 9-passenger Catalina. With the second and/or third seats folded, a load area of over 8 feet in length and 36.2 square feet in total floor capacity was provided. The third seat faced to the rear. A wide range of V-8 power choices were available. The interiors were upholstered in vinyl, with chrome skid strips on the cargo floor.

The DeLuxe Suburban 4-door wagon was a step down from Plymouth's top of the line Sport Suburban. The body design was the same with a little less of the fancy trim. The DeLuxe was available in 6-passenger and 9-passenger versions, powered by either a Six or V-8 engine.

Plymouth offered two compact wagons for 1961. They were the Valiant V-200 and the V-100, with the V-200 being the more deluxe model. The Valiant V-200 is pictured here. Both models were 4-door, 6-passenger wagons. The design was striking and handsome.

New for this year was the Pontiac Tempest wagon. This was a 4-door, 6-passenger model. The tailgate was a one-piece hatchback design. The Tempest shared its body with Buick Special and Oldsmobile F-85. The basic features on all three wagons were the same, only the trim was different.

American Motors offered a choice of 19 Rambler wagons. Top of the line was this Ambassador Custom Cross Country. It was available as a 6-passenger or 9-passenger model. The roof rack was standard. The wheelbase was 117 inches. The Ambassador was powered by either a 250 or 270 horsepower V-8.

The Rambler Classic Custom Cross Country 9-passenger model. All 9-passenger models featured a unique fifth door instead of the traditional tailgate. Access into the third seat area was a little easier with this type of design.

The Rambler Classic 6 DeLuxe Cross Country (upper) and the Rambler Classic Super Cross Country Wagons were available as 6 or 9-passenger models. The roof racks were standard. The Super was available as either a 6 cylinder or V-8. The Classic was also available in the Custom Cross Country. With seats folded, a cargo space of 80 cubic feet was available.

The lowest priced Rambler wagon was this American 4-door DeLuxe. It was one of three American series wagons—. the other two being the Custom and the Super. The American wagon was only 173.1 inches in overall length, but had a cargo area of 64 cubic feet.

The Rambler American wagons were available in three models. Pictured here is the Custom. All were 6-passenger wagons. The roof rack was standard. The American series was powered by a 6-cylinder 90 or 125 horsepower engine.

The Studebaker Lark wagon for 1961. This is the 4-door, 6-passenger, 6-cylinder model. With the rear seat down and tailgate up, 71 inches of cargo floor length was provided. The tailgate was a two-piece design. The Studebaker was one of two American wagons that still held to this design.

Studebaker offered two wagon models this year, a 4-door and a 2-door. Both were 6-passenger models, powered by either a 6-cylinder or V-8 engine. Pictured here is the Lark Regal 4-door wagon, with optional roof rack.

The lowest priced Studebaker wagon was this Lark 2-door model. With tailgate up the length of the cargo floor was 72 inches. This was coupled with a width and height of 58 inches by 35 inches. The quarter window was split, with one of the sections being a slider.

Virtually unchanged since its introduction in 1946 was the Willys Station Wagon. It was still a 2-door, 6-passenger wagon with a two-piece tailgate. Strictly a utility vehicle, it was a little short on distinctive styling.

A 1961 Willys IVI prototype wagon. This was a mid-engine study designed by Brooks Stevens. It never went into production.

For 1962, Chevrolet and Ford both introduced mid-sized compact models — the Chevy II and Fairlane, respectively. These were a step up from the Corvair and Falcon. The Corvair and Falcon subsequently became, in effect, sub-compacts. With the addition of the Chevy II models, Chevrolet now offered a total of 11 wagons. There were five full size wagons, three Chevy II wagons, two Corvair wagons, and the Greenbriar wagon bus.

Ford extended its warrantee to 24 months. Of the 34 models available from Ford this year, 11 of these were wagons. Mercury introduced a mid-size series this year, the Meteor, but there were no wagons. Still, Mercury buyers had nine wagon models to choose from. There were four full size models and five sub-compact Comet models.

Chrysler continued unchanged in its basic design and in the number of wagon models available. There were four models from Chrysler, seven from Dodge and seven models from Plymouth. What was new from Chrysler Corporation this year was the unveiling of a new showcar — the Plymouth Cabana. This was a station wagon design study built by Ghia of Italy. Three design objectives were accomplished with this wagon. (1) It combined all the desirable station wagon features; (2) It was designed for ambulance and hearse conversion; (3) It reduced the squared, boxy rear end appearance of current station wagons. The most unique feature of this wagon was the third seat area enclosure. The tailgate was a door and there were two sliding, clear plastic roof panel sections. This aided in third seat entry and in cargo loading. This was a design similarly introduced by Brooks Stevens in 1956 in the Scimitar showcar. It was later put into production with the 1963 Studebaker wagons.

Aside from Chevrolet, the other General Motor Divisions, Buick, Pontiac and Oldsmobile remained unchanged in basic design and the number of wagon models offered.

Rambler topped all American car makers in the number of wagon models, with a total of 12 being available. There were compacts, and sub-compacts, four-door and five-door models, a choice of 6 or 9-passenger wagons, and power by either a V-8 or 6-cylinder engine.

Jeep, now part of the Kaiser Corporation, introduced a 4-door model. Now there were two wagons to choose from, a 2-door or 4-door version. Also new for this year from Jeep was the introduction of a V-8 engine, and a Turbo-Hydramatic transmission coupled to 4-wheel drive. It proved to be a powerhouse. Other companies would eventually follow with their versions of an all-terrain vehicle.

Top of the Buick wagon line was this Invicta 4-door 9-passenger model. This year Buick moved the Estate Wagons from the LeSabre series to the Invicta series. The basic design was unchanged. The third seat faced rearward. All GM cars featured a sweeping windshield post, giving the appearance of a wrap-around windshield. The roof rack was optional. The 9-passenger Invicta Estate Wagon sold for $3,917.

A rear view of the Buick Invicta wagon shows that the tailgate window was self-storing. It was power operated by a switch on the dashboard or by inserting a key into the tailgate lock. A new feature this year was the availability of bucket seats in the front.

The Buick Model 4635 was a 4-door, 6-passenger wagon. It featured two-tone vinyl upholstery, optional roof rack, and optional bucket seats. This model sold for $3,836. Even though the wagons were moved up in series there was no increase in base price.

The Buick Special 4-door, 9-passenger wagon. This compact Buick wagon continued to feature a hatchback tailgate. The third seat faced rearward. Note the placement of the spare tire. The Special wagon was also available in a 6-passenger model. In the 9-passenger form it sold for $2,736; as a 6-passenger it sold for $2,655.

The top of the Chevrolet wagon line was this 9-passenger model. The third seat faced rearward. The roof rack was optional. In this form it sold for $3,171. Chevrolet advertised the wagons as "utility wrapped up in passenger car comfort."

Checker, a taxicab manufacturer, entered the domestic passenger car market and introduced a wagon model, the Superba. This was a 4-door, 6-passenger wagon. It was non-pretentious in design and had the stark look of a practical car. It was big and roomy — no doubt the biggest, roomiest wagon on the market, with the ruggedness of a taxicab. But this was not enough, and it did not sell in volume.

The Chevrolet Bel Air wagon was available as a 4-door, 6-passenger or 9-passenger model. The tailgate window was self-storing. The third seat faced rearward. As a 6-passenger wagon, it sold for $2,926, and as a 9-passenger wagon it sold for $3,029. Chevrolet's lowest priced full size wagon, the Biscayne, sold for $2,832.

1962

Newly introduced this year was Chevrolet's Chevy II series. There were three wagon models available — the Nova 400, pictured here; the 100 and the 300. The Nova sold for $2,497. It was powered by a 6-cylinder engine.

The Chevy II 100, 4-door, 6-passenger wagon was the lowest priced wagon in this series at $2,339. Unlike comparable models from Buick, Pontiac and Oldsmobile, the Chevy II featured a tailgate with self-storing window. With the tailgate lowered, it offered 9 feet of load space. Note the mounting of the spare against the right quarter panel. The roof rack was optional.

This year Chevrolet offered the Corvair wagon in two models. This was the more expensive Monza Lakewood wagon. It was a 4-door, 6-passenger wagon with a hatchback tailgate. In this version it sold for $2,569.

The Chevrolet Corvair 700 series station wagon. This was the last year for the Corvair wagon. It proved to be unpopular. This was one of two Corvair wagons offered this year. Both were 4-door, 6-passenger models. The 700 sold for $2,407.

The Chevrolet Greenbriar station bus. This rear engined vehicle with seats removed provided 175.5 cubic feet of usable cargo space. In its basic form it sold for $2,655 — a bargain compared to the $2,569 cost of the little Corvair Monza wagon.

The Chrysler New Yorker station wagon at $4,873 was the highest priced American production wagon. It was also available in 6-passenger form for $4,766. A total of 728 of the 6-passenger models and 793 of the 9-passenger models were built.

Chrysler hit an all time high in wagon production this year turning out a record 5,634 Newport wagons. The Newport was a 4-door pillarless wagon available as a 6-passenger or 9-passenger model. It sold for $3,478 and $3,586 respectively.

Top of the Dodge station wagon line-up was this 440 4-door, 9-passenger model. It only came equipped with a V-8 engine. Wheelbase was 116 inches with an overall length of 201 inches. In this form it sold for $3,092. As a six-passenger model the cost was $2,989. The roof rack was optional.

The Chrysler Newport wagons were also available as an Enforcer Special. It was beefed up with heavier suspension, all-vinyl interior and could be ordered with a 383 cubic inch 325 horsepower V-8 engine. With this option, dual exhaust and 4-barrel carburetor were standard.

Beautiful hardtop styling graced the Custom 880 station wagon models offered in two versions. This model was the largest, most expensive and heaviest Dodge available for 1962, and had an over-all length of 251 inches. As a 3-seat, 9-passenger wagon, this car sold for $3,407, weighed 4,055 pounds and was designated a Model 659. The Custom 880, Model 658, was a 2-seat, 6-passenger wagon. It cost $3,292 and tipped the scales at 4,025 pounds.

The standard Dart station wagon was available in both the Dart and the Dart 330 Series in both the 2 and 3-seat versions and with either a Six or a V-8. Both series wagons looked alike and were offered as 4-doors only. The standard Dart Series 6-cylinder 2-seat wagon cost $2,644 and weighed 3,270 pounds. The 8-cylinder version went for $2,751 and tipped the scales at 3,435 pounds. The 330 Series 2-seat 6-cylinder wagon cost $2,739 and weighed 3,275 pounds, and the V-8 330 wagon with two seats sold for $2,848, tipping the scales at 3,500 pounds. The large 3-seat, 9-passenger 330 wagon went for $2,949 and weighed 3,435 pounds.

The Dodge Dart 330 series station wagon was one of two models in the Dart series. Both were 4-door wagons, and could be ordered as 6-passenger or 9-passenger models. There were 6-cylinder and V-8 engine options.

Appearing for the last time was the Dodge Lancer line. Pictured here is the Lancer 770 wagon. It was the most expensive Lancer model. Based on the Plymouth Valiant, and using Valiant sheet metal as well as chassis, the Lancer wagon was a 4-door, 6 or 9-passenger model. The 770 was powered by a 170 horsepower Slant Six. Its cost was $2,408.

The Dodge Lancer 170 series wagon. This was a 4-door, 6-passenger model. Note the roof overhang at the rear. The tailgate had a self-storing window. The body design of the Lancer and Plymouth Valiant was ageless and appears modern even today. The 170 wagon was the lowest priced Dodge wagon at $2,335.

Once again Ford's top of the line wagon, the Country Squire, featured simulated wood siding. Ford Motor Company continued to be the only manufacturer to feature such siding trim on its top of the line wagons. This year the Country Squire sold for $3,150. And once again Ford outsold Chevrolet in station wagons.

One step below the Country Squire was the Country Sedan. This popular Ford wagon was available as a 6 or 9-passenger model. It sold for an even $3,000. Power plant options included a choice of V-8s or economy 6-cylinder engines.

The lowest priced full size Ford wagon was this Ranch Wagon, a 4-door, 6-passenger model. The tailgate had a self-storing window. There was an optional roof rack, and a choice of V-8 or 6-cylinder power plant. It sold for $2,733.

The Ford Falcon Deluxe Wagon was a 4-door, 6-passenger vehicle. The rear doors had vent windows. The quarter windows were curved. This model sold for $2,385.

Ford upgraded its compact Falcon wagon with the addition of this Falcon Squire model. This was achieved by adding simulated wood siding. The model was very attractive and sold very well. It was available only in 4-door form and sold for $2,605. The roof rack was optional.

The Ford Falcon DeLuxe 2-door wagon sold for $2,384. It was powered by an economical 6-cylinder engine. The quarter window was divided into two sections, neither of which was movable.

A rear view of the Ford Falcon DeLuxe 2-door wagon. The tailgate had a self-storing window, which was operated by a crank on the tailgate. The Falcon wagons were a very attractive package and had no trouble outselling the competition. As a matter of fact, Chevrolet and Dodge both gave up and discontinued their compact wagons with the end of this model year.

In the Falcon series, Ford also offered this Station Bus Club Wagon. In this form it sold for $2,436. A more dressed up version was offered at $2,673.

Mercury's fancy station wagon, the Colony Park, is shown here in the design stage, minus the Custom series trim with which it was decorated. It sold for $3,289 in 9-passenger form and $3,219 in 6-passenger style. The Colony Park, which weighed 4,198 pounds, and the Commuter Wagon were the only Mercurys to weigh more than two tons this year.

Mercury's lowest price full-size wagon was the Commuter, which was listed in the Monterey series. It weighed 4,183 pounds and cost $3,110 in 9-passenger form or $3,029 in the 6-passenger version. This year, all cars in the Monterey sub-series used the 223 cubic inch Six as standard power.

The Comet Custom 4-Door Wagon sold for $2,562 and weighed 2,679 pounds. Although the 85 horsepower Six was standard, many buyers took the new, optional 170 cubic inch Six, rated at 101 horsepower at 4400 RPM.

The Oldsmobile Dynamic 88 4-door, 9-passenger wagon was one of four full size wagons available from Oldsmobile this year. The body design was virtually unchanged. The Dynamic 88 wagon was also available as a 6-passenger model.

Also in the Comet Special sub-series was the Villager Wagon, a wood-grain paneled 4-Door Station Wagon which sold for $2,710 and weighed 2,712 pounds. This model is equipped with the accessory chrome roof-top luggage rack.

A rear view of the Dynamic 88 Fiesta, 9-passenger wagon, The tailgate had a self-storing window which was activated by a switch on the dashboard or by a key in the tailgate lock. The third seat faced to the rear. The spare was stored on the right side, against the quarter panel. The interior was all-vinyl with deep-pile carpeting.

The Oldsmobile Super 88 Fiesta wagon. This is the 4-door, 6-passenger model. It was also available as a 9-passenger. With the tailgate lowered it provided 7½ feet of cargo floor. The tailgate window was self-storing. The roof rack was optional.

Oldsmobile continued to offer its compact F-85 wagon, which was available as a 6 or 9-passenger model. Pictured here is the 6-passenger version. It was powered by a Rocket V-8 155 horsepower engine. The wheelbase was 112 inches.

The Oldsmobile F-85 4-door, 9-passenger model. The F-85 shared its body with Buick and Pontiac. One of its features was the hatchback tailgate. It made entry into the third seat area easier. The roof rack was optional.

The Plymouth Cabana was a Chrysler Corporation showcar. More of a design study, it was built by Ghia of Turin, Italy, on a 1958 Plymouth chassis. The basic design was pillarless, with its four doors opening at the center. Note the sculptured fender and extreme fin – a carryover from the 1950s.

A rear view of the Plymouth Cabana showcar. The cargo area featured a unique roof. There were two sliding clear plastic panels, which improved loading and passenger access into the third seat area. It also increased the cargo carrying height. The tailgate was actually a door, and was hinged at the side.

Top of the Plymouth Station Wagon line was this Fury, 4-door model. It was available in 6 or 9-passenger form. Floor length, with tailgate closed and the seats folded flat, was 117.9 inches. The fuel tank capacity for all full size wagons was 21.5 gallons. This was the largest tank of all Plymouth models.

A rear view of the Plymouth Fury wagon. This is the 9-passenger model. The third seat faced rearward. The tailgate window was self-storing. Standard features on the Fury included an electric clock, backup lights, a highback driver's seat, and deep-pile carpeting. The Fury was also powered by a 318 cubic inch 230 horsepower V-8.

The Plymouth Belvedere 4-door, 6-passenger wagon. It was also available as a 9-passenger model. Some of the options available on Plymouth wagons included: tinted glass, air conditioning, power steering, brakes and seats, safety belts, and sure-grip differential.

Plymouth continued to offer its compact Valiant wagon. Pictured here is the 4-door, 6-passenger version. Valiants were unchanged in styling since their introduction, although the styling was quite timeless.

The lowest priced full size Plymouth wagon was this Savoy 4-door, 6-passenger model. Shown here in police dress-up, and ready for action, it was a true utility vehicle.

The Pontiac Catalina 6-passenger Safari wagon. This would be considered a stripped down model, with no roof rack, no radio, small hub caps and only optional whitewall tires. Back-up lights in the rear bumper were also optional.

A rear view of the 9-passenger Pontiac Catalina Safari. The third seat faced rearward. The tailgate window was self-storing. Pontiac cargo area was wide enough for a 4 x 8 foot piece of plywood to be carried flat. All full size wagons were powered by Pontiac's Trophy V-8, rated from 215 to 348 horsepower at 389 cubic inches.

The Rambler Ambassador 6-passenger wagon was the top of the line wagon. It featured a luxurious carpeted cargo area, and a V-8 power plant. Front seats were recliners which were available on all Rambler models. The wheelbase of the Ambassador and Classic series was 108 inches. The tailgate window was self-storing, being operated by a crank on the outside.

CATALINA 6-PASSENGER SAFARI

The Pontiac Catalina Safari 9-passenger model. This was the middle of the line full size Pontiac wagon. It was one step below the Bonneville Safari. But it was the only 9-passenger wagon available.

The Pontiac Tempest wagon shared its body with Buick and Oldsmobile compacts. The tailgate opened in hatchback fashion. This was a 4-door, 6-passenger wagon. The roof rack and whitewall tires were among the available options.

The Rambler Ambassador "400" 9-passenger wagon. The tailgate was a door, which made for easier entrance into the third seat area. The roof rack was standard. This was one of twelve wagon models offered by Rambler this year.

The Rambler Classic wagon was available as a 6 or 9-passenger model. Powered by a 127 or 138 horsepower 6-cylinder engine, its cargo capacity was 80 cubic feet, overall length was 190 inches, and the overall width, 72.4 inches.

The Rambler American wagon was available in two models, a 2-door or a 4-door. Both were 6-passenger wagons. Both had a 100-inch wheelbase, a width of 70 inches, and a cargo capacity of 64 cubic feet. The power plants available were either a 90 horsepower L-Head Six or 125 horsepower Overhead Valve Six.

The Kaiser Jeep station wagon, the Wagoneer, was designed by Brooks Stevens. This design, introduced in 1960, remains in production today under the AMC/Jeep banner. The Jeep wagon has had only two designs since its inception in 1946. Both were products of Brooks Stevens. Mr. Stevens claims that this wagon remains the only true wagon in the industry today, in that it is not a derivative of a manufacturer's standard sedan, but was designed and engineered strictly and exclusively for station wagon purposes.

The Jeep Wagoneer 4-door Custom Wagon was available with 2 or 4-wheel drive. And, for the first time, it offered a 250 horsepower V-8 coupled with Turbo Hydra-matic. The Wagoneer was one of the most versatile wagons available.

Studebaker became the U. S. distributor for Mercedes-Benz, and the influence of this move could be plainly seen in the grille treatment of the 1962 models. Pictured here is the Studebaker Lark wagon for 1962. This was a 4-door, 6-passenger model, powered by either a 6-cylinder engine or a choice of two V-8s. Cargo capacity was 72 cubic feet. The roof rack was optional.

The Jeep Wagoneer 2-door wagon was a 6-passenger vehicle available with 2 or 4-wheel drive. The Jeep wagon was aimed at a market that truly used the wagons for work and play, no matter what the work or the play. It was advertised as a go-anywhere wagon. The interiors were all-vinyl.

The introduction of the extended manufacturer's warranty occurred in 1963. Chrysler Corp. announced "America's first five-year or 50,000 mile automobile warranty." This warranty applied to all Chrysler, Dodge and Plymouth passenger cars. It covered the engine and drive train.

This year Chrysler offered two wagon models. Dodge had seven full size and two compact wagons. Plymouth offered three full size and two compact wagons.

Rambler won Motor Trend Magazine's "Car of the Year" award. The award was given for "outstanding design achievement and engineering leadership." Ten wagon models were available from Rambler. These included 6 and 9-passenger versions with two, four, or five doors.

The newest station wagon innovation came from Studebaker. Newly introduced for 1963 was the "Sliding Roof" Lark Wagonaire. The sliding roof was a Brooks Stevens design first introduced on a show car in 1956. The concept of a sliding roof panel over the cargo area was brilliant – and a very practical, very good idea. It is surprising that other manufacturers did not adopt this

idea. Studebaker offered two wagon models this ye one each in the Regal and Daytona series.

Ford continued to be the only manufacturer to feat simulated wood siding on its top of the line wago Ford and Mercury offered a combined total of no l than 25 wagon models. This covered a complete ral from full size wagons, through mid size, into the sm compacts, with a couple of van-type wagons available make sure all bases of the market were covered.

General Motors wagons remained unchanged. divisions continued to offer the same models and num of wagons. An interesting note about 1963. It never cea to be amazing that with the obviously infinite number choices of names for a model car, auto manufactur have continued to come up with names used in the pa competitors' discarded names, or names similar to wl somebody else was currently using: A case in poi Studebakre offered the Lark Wagonaire, while Jeep v offering the Wagoneer. Which one had the grea imagination?

The Buick Invicta Estate Wagon was available only as a 6-passenger model. This was Buick's top of the line wagon. The noticeable differences between this model and the lesser LeSabre wagon were the large front turning lights and the full length body side moulding. The Invicta was powered by a 325 horsepower, 401 cubic inch V-8 engine. Its cost was $3,969.

The Buick LeSabre Estate Wagon. Two models were available in this series—a 6-passenger and a 9-passenger. Shown here is a rear inside view of the nine-passenger version. The third seat faced to the rear while the luggage rack was optional. Cost of the LeSabre 9-passenger wagon was $3,526.

There were three wagon models offered in the Buick Special series. There were two standard models and one deluxe. A 6 and 9-passenger version was offered in the standard models, while only a 6-passenger was available in the deluxe. The tailgate continued to be a one-piece hatchback gate. The roof rack was optional. The deluxe model cost $2,818, and its standard counterpart cost $2,659. Both models were available with V-6 or V-8 engines.

A rear view of the Chevrolet Bel Air wagon. This model was in the middle range of full size Chevrolet wagons. The cost in 9-passenger form was $3,028. As a 6-passenger wagon the cost was $2,926. Both 6-cylinder and V-8 engines were available. The roof rack was optional.

The top of the line Chevrolet Impala wagon was available as a 6 or 9-passenger model. Cost of the 6-passenger model was $3,067 and the 9-passenger $3,170. The third seat of the 9-passenger version faced to the rear. A luggage rack was optional.

The Chevrolet Chevy II 300 wagon. This was the middle range compact wagon. In 9-passenger version it carried a price tag of $2,575, only $255 less than a full size Chevrolet Biscayne wagon. The tailgate had a crank down rear window. A roof rack was optional.

One of three Chevy II wagons, this Nova 400 was the top of the line. It was available in 6 or 9-passenger form. Either a 4-cylinder or 6-cylinder engine could be ordered. A total of 67,347 Chevy II 6-passenger wagons were produced, while only 7,927 of the 9-passenger models were made. This was a combined total of all Chevy II wagons.

For off the road traveling in station wagon style, Chevrolet offered the Carryall Suburban model. Equipped with four-wheel-drive this big 9-passenger wagon could go anywhere.

The Chevrolet Greenbrier Sport Wagon had a 179.7-inch wheelbase and was powered by the air cooled Corvair rear engine. It sold for $2,655. A total of 13,761 were produced. The van-type wagon was ideal for sportsmen and large families alike.

The Chrysler New Yorker station wagon continued to offer pillarless styling. The New Yorker wagon was available as a 6 or 9-passenger model. In 9-passenger form it sold for $4,815, making it the highest priced American wagon.

Chrysler set a production record in station wagons this year by producing 6,566 of these Newport models. The Newport wagon was available as a 6 or 9-passenger model. In the latter version it cost $3,586, and as a 6-passenger the cost was $3,478. Wheelbase of the Newport wagon was 219.4 inches, and like its big brother, the New Yorker, it featured pillarless styling.

The top of the Dodge station wagon line was this Custom 880 9-passenger model. It was also available as a 6-passenger wagon. The Dodge 880 wagons boasted a cargo deck length of more than 10 feet from back of front seat to open end of tailgate. The cargo opening was 49.2 inches and total load capacity was 91.5 cubic feet. Among options available on the Dodge this year was the "Auto-Pilot," a cruise control for turnpike traveling.

The Series 440, when offered as a 9-passenger, three seat wagon was designated a Model 667. This car sold for $2,956 while tipping the scales at 3,552 pounds. The 330 Series 9-passenger 6-cylinder wagon weighed 3,358 pounds, cost $2,749 and was called a Model 457. Model 657 was the 330 Series 9-passenger, three seat V-8 wagon. In this form the car cost $2,857 while tipping the scales at 3,543 pounds. In the foreground is the 440 wagon while the 330 version lurks in the background.

The Dodge 880 6-passenger Sedan Wagon, unlike the Custom 880 models did not feature the pillarless hardtop styling. The standard power plant was a 361 cubic inch V-8. It could be coupled with a 3-speed manual or automatic Torqueflite transmission. If this wasn't enough, there was an optional 383 cubic inch rated at 305 horsepower.

Standard size station wagons were offered by Dodge in both the 330 and the 440 Series. The Series 330 wagons were available with either the V-8 or a Six, while Series 440 models were offered as V-8 wagons only. The 330 6-cylinder 6-passenger wagon cost $2,748, weighed 3,293 pounds and was designated a Model 456. The V-8, 6-passenger 330 wagon went for $2,756 while weighing 3,478 pounds. The more luxurious 440 wagon went for $2,854 as a two seat wagon while weighing 3,487 pounds. This car was the Model 666, while the two seat V-8 330 wagon was called the Model 656.

The Dodge Dart 270 Wagon was one of two compact wagons offered by Dodge. The lesser model was the Dart 170. Both offered 68.9 cubic feet of cargo space. An optional power tailgate window was offered, along with an optional luggage rack. The interiors of both models were upholstered in vinyl.

Although the Dart station wagons rode on the same 111-inch wheelbase as the sedans, they had an over-all length of 190.2 inches. The largest, heaviest, and most costly of the 270 Series models was the station wagon Model 776. This car, seen with optional roof rack and radio as well as custom wheel covers, is a striking example of the attractive lines which adorned the Dart wagon. The standard 270 station wagon cost $2,433 and weighed 2,745 pounds.

The Dodge D-100 Town Wagon was a utility wagon mounted on a ¾-ton truck chassis. The Town Wagon was direct competition for the Chevrolet Carryall and the International Traveler.

The Ford Country Squire remained as Ford's top of the line wagon. And, like all other Ford deluxe wagons, it featured simulated wood siding. As a 9-passenger wagon it carried a price tag of $3,150. A roof rack was optional.

The Deluxe version of Ford's mid sized wagon models was this Fairlane 500 Squire Wagon. The mid sized series was newly introduced this year. The 500 wagons were available only with a V-8. This model sold for $2,890.

Runner up to the Country Squire was this Ford Galaxie Country Sedan. It was available as a 6 or 9-passenger model. A power tailgate window was optional. Ford wagons this year had high styling. The Country Sedan sold for $3,000. This was $28 less than its Chevrolet counterpart.

Rear view of the Fairlane Ranch Wagon, which was the low priced mid sized wagon, selling at $2,630. The Ranch Wagon was officially placed in the Fairlane series this year. Cargo carrying capacity was 86.2 cubic feet, with a storage compartment of 6.7 cubic feet located below the cargo floor.

The Ford Fairlane 500 Wagon was a step down from the Squire model. Rear doors featured vent windows. The tailgate had a self-storing window with optional power assist. A roof rack was also optional, as were the fancy wheel covers shown here.

The Ford Falcon Squire Wagon was the top of the line Falcon wagon. The compact series offered four wagon models. The Squire sold for $2,670. This was $176 more than the Chevy II Nova wagon. The simulated wood siding was a combination of decal paneling and fiberglass framing—a far cry from real maple and mahogany.

Lowest priced of the Falcon wagons was this 2-door model. It carried a price tag of $2,300. The window to the immediate rear of the door was movable. The fancy wheel covers on this example were an added cost option.

The Falcon DeLuxe 4-door wagon had a tailgate window that was self-storing and operated by a crank located on the outside of the tailgate. Rear doors featured vent windows, and the quarter window was curved. This model sold for $2,430.

The Falcon Club Wagon. In addition to the front doors, there were a pair of side doors on the right, or the passenger side. It also had a pair of rear doors. The "mini" bus could carry up to 10 passengers, with an abundance of luggage space. It sold for $2,440.

Ford of England introduced two wagon models. Pictured here is the Consul Estate Wagon. Ford was gambling that the wagon would become as popular in Europe as it did in the United States. Note how the Falcon hood styling was carried over on this model.

A step up from the Consul Estate Wagon was this Ford of England Consul Cortina Estate Wagon. Simulated wood trim was a new innovation for Europe, but never really caught on in England.

The International Harvester Travelall was a utility station wagon based on a ¾-ton truck chassis. It boasted that in addition to the cargo capacity, it could haul a boat trailer without fish-tailing.

The two-tone paint job marked this model as the DeLuxe International Harvester Travelall. The cargo space behind the front seat was a whopping 124 cubic feet. Note that the gas tank was located up front, with the filler cap on the front fender. The Travelall was built on International's Model 1000 light truck chassis, and proved to be a very dependable and hard working vehicle for users who required a rugged high capacity wagon. In addition to its large cargo capacity, the International Travelall could carry six passengers in great comfort. The Travelall featured four doors and a one-piece tailgate with self-storing window.

Meteor's brand new fancy-pants wagon was the Country Cruiser, a wood-grain paneled version of the Custom 4-Door Wagon. Weighing 3,453, it not only was Meteor's heaviest vehicle, it was also the only Meteor wagon available in either 6 or 9-passenger style. The 6-passenger model cost $2,990, while the 9-passenger version cost $3,034. The 9-passenger style was also the only Meteor with a price base above $3,000. The chrome luggage rack was an accessory.

The newly designed Meteor Custom Wagon was available in 4-door style only, the 2-door version being found only in the plain Meteor sub-series. It featured chrome window edges, rockers and wheel cut-out rims. It cost $2,823 and weighed 3,382 pounds. All Meteor wagons used a 115.5-inch wheelbase and were 202.3 inches overall.

The most expensive Comet was the Custom Villager Wagon, priced at $2,754. The 2,750-pound vehicle featured wood-grain paneling and interior trim slightly more luxurious than that found on the Custom 4-Door Wagon. It was available only in 4-door style.

The Comet Custom 2-Door Station Wagon was a dolled-up version of the economy Comet 2-Door Wagon. It sold for $2,527 and weighed 2,680 pounds. The spare tire was carried upright at the right rear of the cargo area. The Comet wagons were available in 6-passenger style only.

The Comet series retained its two wagon models. They were the 4-Door Wagon, shown here, which cost $2,483 and weighed 2,700 pounds, and the 2-Door Wagon, which cost $2,440 and weighed 2,665 pounds. The wagons used a 109.5-inch wheelbase and had an overall length of 191.8 inches.

The Oldsmobile Super 88 Station Wagon was a prestige model. It is shown here with optional roof rack. Interiors were available in either cloth and Morocceen or all-Morocceen. Morocceen was a deluxe grade of vinyl. Standard power plant for the Super 88 was a 330 horsepower Skyrocket V-8. The cargo area had a big 122.7 inches of loading room. And an optional split second seat could be ordered. It split 1/3-2/3 for added versatility, like carrying skis inside, flat, and not giving up the rear seat.

The Oldsmobile Dynamic 88 Fiesta Wagon was available as a 6 or 9-passenger model. Standard engine for the Dynamic 88 was a 280 horsepower rocket V-8. The wheelbase was 123 inches. In addition to a large cargo floor there was an 8 cubic foot locker located below the cargo floor in all 6-passenger models. The tailgate window was power operated. A luggage rack was optional and other options included: cruise control, power antenna, tilt steering wheel, power seats and windows, guide-matic headlight control, air conditioning, self-adjusting brakes, and AM/FM radio.

The Oldsmobile F-85 DeLuxe Station Wagon was the compact series. There were two models, a Standard and a DeLuxe. The spare tire was carried in a compartment at the rear of the right rear fender. Note the tire profile protruding below the fender line. The F-85 DeLuxe wagon came only as a 4-door model. The wheelbase was 112 inches. The roof was optional. The standard engine was a 155 horsepower V-8, with 215 cubic inch displacement. A manual or Hydra-matic transmission was available.

A rear view of the Oldsmobile F-85 wagon. The tailgate was a one-piece hatchback design. Note the spoiler located on the roof, above the tailgate. This helped keep the rear window clean. The roof rack was optional.

The Pontiac Tempest Wagon was Pontiac's compact offering. Design features were similar to the Buick Special and the Oldsmobile. F-85. It was only available as a 4-door. The tailgate was of the one-piece hatchback design. A roof rack was optional.

The Pontiac Catalina Safari Wagon was a step down from the Bonneville Safari. Both 6 and 9-passenger versions of the Catalina Safari were available. Pictured here is the 9-passenger model. The tailgate window was self-storing with option power assist. A roof rack was optional.

The Plymouth Valiant V-200 Station Wagon was one of two Valiant wagons. Both were 4-door models. The V-200 was the more DeLuxe. Both had rear door vent windows and a self-storing tailgate window. The Valiant was Plymouth's compact car series. There were three full size Plymouth wagons – the Fury, the top of the line; the Belvedere; and the Savoy. All were 4-door models in 6 and 9-passenger versions. Plymouth and its corporate brothers offered a 5-year, 50,000 mile warranty, thereby leading the way to industry-wide extended warranties.

The Rambler Ambassador 990. Standard on all Ambassador models was a V-8 power plant. Rambler won Motor Trend Magazine's "Car of the Year" award. The roof rack was standard. Bucket seats and a console were available as options.

The lowest priced Rambler wagon was the American series. There were two wagon models in this series – a Standard 2-door model and a DeLuxe 4-door model. Both were powered by an economical 6-cylinder engine.

1963

The Rambler Classic 660 wagon was available as a 6 or 9-passenger model. The 6-passenger version featured a fifth door instead of a tailgate. The Classic was available with either a 6-cylinder or V-8 engine. The roof rack was standard. Reclining front seats were optional.

The only wagon innovation this year came from Studebaker. Studebaker pioneered the sliding roof panel. This was an excellent idea. Unfortunately, the rest of the industry did not follow suit.

The Studebaker Daytona Lark Wagonaire. The sliding roof panel was a Brooks Stevens design that first appeared on a show car in 1956. Note the assist step hanging from the tailgate. This step was built into the tailgate and folded out of the way when not in use. Studebaker wagons were available only as 6-passenger models.

The Studebaker Regal Lark Wagonaire was one of two wagon models offered by Studebaker. Both had basically the same features; however, one was trimmed differently than the other. This picture shows the practicality of the sliding roof panel.

Newest addition to the Willys Jeep line was this Wagoneer. It was available as a 2-door or a 4-door model. With four-wheel-drive the Wagoneer became an all-terrain vehicle. Rear vent windows were featured in both the 2 and 4-door models. The tailgate window was self-storing. The Wagoneer represented the first real change in Jeep station wagon design since 1946.

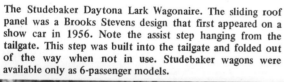

Automotive history was made this year with the introduction of the Ford Mustang. Introduced in April of 1964, was designated a 1965 model. The Mustang was destined become the most successful auto ever built. No other has surpassed its first year sales and production record. fortunately, there was no station wagon model. With exception of the Mustang, 1964 was pretty much acelift year for the entire auto industry.

ord offered a total of nine passenger car wagons plus a n-type wagon. The wagons came in three sizes—the full e Country Squire and Country Sedan, the mid-size rlane wagons, and the compact Falcon wagons. All gon models were 4-door versions, with the exception of lowest priced Falcon, which was the only 2-door ssenger car wagon offered by Ford. Every top-of-the-line del had simulated wood side panels. Mercury had a line-of four wagon models—two full size and two compacts. e full size Colony Park continued to be Mercury's -of-the-line wagon. The Comet Villager was the prestige rcury compact. Both models sported simulated wood e panels.

ll General Motors Divisions had unchanged wagon dels, with the exception of Oldsmobile and Buick. is year, Oldsmobile introduced the Vista-Cruiser. The sta-Cruiser was an F-85 model with tinted transparent ne windows along the perimeter of the roof panel, but ly over the second and third seat areas. The third seat o faced forward, permitting entry into this area by way the rear doors, rather than the tailgate. The Vista-uiser was one of two F-85 models available this year. w for this year from Buick was the Skylark Sportwagon, ich shared the Oldsmobile F-85 Vista-Cruiser body.

hrysler Corporation offered an array of wagons. There re two Chrysler models, the Newport and New Yorker. dge offered wagon models in four different series, luding the compact Dart series, which had two wagon dels. Plymouth had wagon models available in the Fury, lvedere and Savoy series, as well as two models in the mpact Valiant series. Chrysler Corporation continued to er the extended 5-year/50,000 mile warranty.

Rambler's wagon line-up included a total of six wagon dels in three different series. One of the unique tions available from Rambler was the "Twin Stick or Shift" — a combination of a 3-speed transmission d overdrive which gave five forward speeds. The Twin cks were housed in a floor console. One stick controlled gear selection, the other controlled the overdrive. This tion should be a rare find today for the car collector. debaker continued to offer the Wagonaire, with sliding f panel, and also had a wagon without the sliding roof. p continued with the Wagoneer model, and Inter-tional offered the Travelall. All of these models were changed from the previous year.

The Buick Special 4-door, 6-passenger wagon was Buick's lowest priced station wagon. Although the appearance was austere by comparison, it was as functional as its higher priced sisters. Designated the standard model, it sold for $2,760.

A step up from the standard model was this Buick Special DeLuxe wagon. It too was a 4-door, 6-passenger wagon. Only two models were offered in the Special series this year. The roof rack was optional. The Special DeLuxe sold for $2,858.

Newest of the Buick wagons was the Skylark Sportwagon. It featured a domed roof panel with sky lights. The Skylark shared its body with the Oldsmobile Vista-Cruiser. There were four versions of the Sportwagon—two Standard models and two Custom models. Each offered both a 6 and 9-passenger body. The Custom 9-passenger wagon sold for $3,286. Pictured here are details of the domed roof and the split second seat. The third seat faced forward and the split second seat provided easy entry to that area.

The top of the Chevrolet wagon line was this Impala model. It was available as a 6 or 9-passenger wagon. The 6-passenger version sold for $2,970 and the 9-passenger model sold for $3,181.

Runner-up to the Impala was this Chevrolet Bel Air model, available in either 6 or 9-passenger version and powered by either an economy Six or a V-8. The roof rack was optional. The 6-passenger model sold for $2,828, while its 9-passenger counterpart was priced at $3,039. The tailgate had a self-storing window. The third seat faced rearward, unchanged from previous years. The spare tire was housed in a compartment over the right rear wheel.

At the bottom of the Chevrolet full size line of station wagons was the Biscayne. Except for some minor trim differences, it was hard to distinguish the Biscayne from the Bel Air model. The Biscayne was available only in 6-passenger form. It weighed 3,700 pounds and sold for $2,871.

One of four wagon models in Chevrolet's mid size Chevelle line was this Model 300, a 4-door, 6-passenger vehicle. It had a self-storing tailgate window and a price tag of $2,674.

The Chevelle Series 300 2-door wagon was the lowest priced mid size Chevrolet wagon. It sold for $2,636. This was the only 2-door Chevrolet wagon available. It marked a return to this style.

Chevrolet's lowest priced wagon was this 4-door 6-passenger Chevy II 100 model. It was only available in this form and was one of two compact wagons being offered by Chevrolet. The power plant was an economy 6-cylinder engine. Cost of this wagon was $2,406. Production of the Chevrolet compact

wagon was almost cut in half this year, as a total of only 35,700 were built. The little Chevy was running into strong competition. Some of the Chevy II wagon features included a self-storing tailgate window and an optional roof rack.

For those who wanted a little more out of a station wagon, Chevrolet continued to offer the Suburban Carryall. Based on the ¾-ton truck chassis, it combined roominess with ruggedness. Buyers had a choice of a tailgate or panel delivery type rear doors. The quarter windows were of the sliding type.

Appearing so late in the year that it is sometimes classed as a 1965 vehicle was the Chevyvan Carryall, a forward engine version of the Greenbrier wagon. The six-door wagon offered vast load capacity plus station wagon seating via the use of removable seats.

Chrysler continued to feature pillarless hardtop styling in their wagons. Pictured here is the New Yorker Town and Country wagon. This was the top of the line and 2,853 were built. They sold for $4,828 in the 9-passenger version, once again making Chrysler the highest priced American production wagon. The 6-passenger model sold for $4,721. The third seat faced to the rear, and assist handles were attached to the rear window pillars. These helped entry into the third seat area. All New Yorker models were powered by a 413 cubic inch V-8, rated at 340 horsepower. The roof rack was standard.

The Checker Superba wagon was a 4-door, 6-passenger model. It was the largest passenger car wagon available. Cargo capacity was greater than any other domestic wagon. Note the positioning of the luggage rack — to the extreme forward, rather than to the rear. Because of its height, loading of the roof rack was easier when standing on the door sill.

The Chrysler Newport Town and Country wagon hit another production record when a total of 6,761 were built. Of the total production, 3,041 were 9-passenger models which carried a price tag of $3,521, while 3,720 of the 6-passenger version were built. These sold for $3,414.

Automotive Conversions of Troy, Mich. was the builder of this Chrysler Amblewagon, ambulance conversion. They began with a Newport station wagon. The Amblewagon conversions were available through Chrysler dealers on a special-order-only basis.

The Dodge 880 Custom Hardtop wagon was offered in two versions. These wagons used the 122-inch wheelbase chassis but had an over-all length of 216.3 inches and a width of 80 inches. The Model 559 was a three seat, 9-passenger hardtop that sold for $3,420 and weighed 4,230 pounds. The 6-passenger, two seat version was designated a Model 558. It cost $3,305 and weighed 4,135 pounds. As with previous Dodge 880 models, the 1964 version shared a body shell with the large Chryslers.

The Dodge 880 Series also offered a station wagon. Model 557, a three seat, 9-passenger sedan type wagon sold for $3,270 and weighed 4,185 pounds. The two seat, 6-passenger version, Model 556, cost $3,155 and weighed 4,135 pounds.

The Dodge 330 was available as Dodge's lowest priced station wagon, in two versions. The 6-cylinder 330 Dodge Model 456 was a two seat, 6-passenger wagon weighing 3,375 pounds and costing $2,654. The 9-passenger 6-cylinder 330 wagon went for $2,755, weighed 3,445 pounds and was a Model 457. With the Series 330 standard V-8, this wagon was classified as a Model 657 when a 9-passenger version. It cost $2,863 and weighed 3,560 pounds. As a two-seat, 6-passenger wagon, the 330 V-8 was designated a Model 656 and sold for $2,762 while weighing 3,555 pounds. In any of these versions, the 330 station wagon was the least costly of any Dodge wagon offered in 1964. The lack of chrome trim immediately distinguishes this car as a Series 330.

The Dodge 440 station wagon was not available with a Slant Six engine, and all versions were fitted with the standard V-8. This was a 318 cubic inch, 230 horsepower engine equipped with a two barrel carburetor and a single exhaust system. The 440 wagon was offered in two versions. The 9-passenger version featured a rear facing third seat and carried a price tag of $2,962. Weighing 3,620 pounds, this wagon was designated a Model 667. The 440 Model 666 was a two seat, 6-passenger wagon which cost $2,861 and weighed 3,615 pounds.

Only new taillights gave away the Dart 270 station wagon as a 1964 model when viewed from the rear. The tailgate window was key operated and would electrically lower into the lower half of the tailgate. This 4-door wagon was designated a Model 776 within the 270 Series. Weighing 2,740 pounds and going for $2,414, this wagon was among the more expensive of the Darts for 1964. Dart wagons used a wheelbase of 106 inches as opposed to the 111 inches under sedans.

One of the most attractive of the Series 170 Darts was the Model 756 station wagon. Selling for $2,315 and weighing 2,730 pounds, this little wagon was the lowest cost and lightest of all 1964 Dodge wagons. The new grille and other minor trim alterations are highly visible in this view.

The Ford Country Squire wagon was available as a 6 or 9-passenger model. Wood side paneling once again marked this model as the top of the line. This 4-door, 9-passenger model was powered by a high performance "Thunderbird" V-8 engine. Note how the simulated wood framing is used to accent the front fender crease. On the Galaxie models a chrome strip was used to do the same thing.

1964

The Ford Country sedan was a 4-door, 6-passenger model, available with 6-cylinder or V-8 engine. The body was identical to the Country Squire, less the simulated wood. This was one step down from the Country Squire. The Country Sedan sold for $3,000, while the Squire model sold for $3,150.

This model was the top of the line for Ford's mid size wagons—the Fairlane Squire. Its distinctive simulated wood side trim immediately set it apart from other models. The rear door vent type windows were non-functional. This model sold for $2,875.

The lowest priced Ford Fairlane wagon was this Ranch Wagon model. It was a 4-door, 6-passenger wagon. The tailgate window was self-storing. There was more than ample storage capacity. This version sold for $2,620, which was $255 less than the Squire model.

The Ford Fairlane 500 Custom Ranch Wagon was a step down from the Squire model and was one of three Fairlane wagons. It was attractively trimmed, and was available with either a 289 V-8 or an economical 6-cylinder engine. Price tag for the Custom Ranch Wagon was $2,700.

The Ford Falcon DeLuxe 4-door wagon was one of four Falcon wagons available this year. The Falcon model was Ford's compact car. The tailgate window was self-storing, and lowered by means of a crank on the outside of the tailgate. The rear door vent type windows were non-functional. The DeLuxe sold for $2,435.

The lowest priced Ford station wagon was this Falcon 2-door Standard model. It sold for $2,315, as compared to a price tag of $3,150 for the full size Country Squire. The 2-door Falcon was a 6-passenger model. The two quarter windows were fixed.

The Ford DeLuxe Club Wagon features included one door on the left and three doors on the right. The two center windows were functional. It was priced at $2,675. The driver sat directly over the front wheels.

The Ford Cortina 4-door, 5-passenger wagon was manufactured by Ford of England. It was not imported into this country. It had only limited appeal in England.

An ad for the International Travelall read "Will you buy it for love. If you love hunting, fishing, boating, skiing, camping, exploring — you couldn't do it better than in a TRAVELALL." The rugged 4-door, 9-passenger wagon, equipped with four-wheel-drive, could go anywhere.

The International Travelall was a 4-door, 9-passenger wagon. It was available with either an economy 6-cylinder or V-8 engine, and with 4-wheel-drive and trailer pulling package. It was made to compete with the Chevy Carryall and the GMC Suburban. Note the gas filler cap was located in the front fender. Dual gas tanks were also available, located in the front fender panels.

Mercury's heaviest vehicle was the Colony Park Wagon, which weighed 4,285 pounds. It was available as a 6-passenger model for $3,423, or as a 9-passenger car at $3,493. The chrome roof rack was an accessory.

Comet's functional wagon was the same vehicle as the Villager but without the wood-type trim and lacking a few interior refinements. It cost $2,539 and weighed 2,741 pounds. Comet dropped its 2-door wagon models this year and offered only these two 4-door styles, both available in 6-passenger style only. They used a wheelbase of 109.5 inches and were 191.8 inches overall.

Comet's fancy wagon was the wood-trimmed Villager, shown here with the accessory chrome roof rack. Priced at $2,723 and weighing 2,745 pounds, it was the most expensive Comet produced. Optional trim, not shown here, included three chrome portholes, similar to those used on the 202 sub-series, mounted on the front fender wood applique.

Mercury's plain wagon was the Commuter, which weighed 4,269 pounds. In 6-passenger form it sold for $3,225, while in 9-passenger style it cost $3,295. This model sports accessory cargo ribs on its roof. The Mercury station wagons used the same 120-inch wheelbase as did the cars, but were only 210.3 inches overall.

The Oldsmobile Dynamic 88 Fiesta Wagon was a 9-passenger model. It featured a concealed luggage compartment that locked, a divided second seat, and a roof rack. All were available at extra cost. The combination of fabric and vinyl upholstery was also optional. A power operated self-storing tailgate window was standard on 9-passenger models. It was an extra cost option on the 6-passenger wagon. The standard engine for the Dynamic 88 line was the 280 HP Rocket V-8. A full coil suspension was also standard.

The Oldsmobile F-85 DeLuxe Station Wagon. The roof rack was optional. Cargo capacity was increased by 20% and 87.8 cubic feet of cargo space was now available. The hatchback tailgate was gone. In its place was a swing-down tailgate with self-storing window. This was the conventional way of handling the tailgate.

Announced as a mid-year introduction was the all-new "Vista-Cruiser." It was based on the Oldsmobile F-85 wagon. A domed vista roof was added. With the addition of the domed roof, cargo capacity was increased to 100 cubic feet. The Vista-Cruiser was available in either a 6-passenger or 9-passenger model. The Standard engine was a Jetfire Rocket rated at 290 horsepower. The third seat faced forward and the second seat was split to provide easy access.

The Pontiac Bonneville Safari Wagon was the top of the line wagon. It was available only as a 4-door, 6-passenger model, and was powered by a Trophy V-8, a standard 235 HP engine or an optional 421 cubic inch, 370 HP hustler. The tailgate had a self-storing window that was power operated.

The Pontiac Tempest 4-door, 6-passenger wagon. The only real change in this model was in the tailgate design. The hatchback type of tailgate was dropped in favor of the more conventional swing down gate with self-storing window. There was an optional roof rack available.

The Plymouth Belvedere 4-door wagon was available in either 6 or 9-passenger version, powered by either a 6-cylinder or V-8 engine. One of its features was uni-body construction. Plymouths were also equipped with torsion-bar front suspension.

Plymouth's lowest priced full size wagon was the Savoy 2-door, 6-passenger model, shown equipped with optional roof rack and trailer towing package. Plymouth continued to offer its 5-year, 50,000 mile factory warranty.

One of two Catalina Safari wagons offered by Pontiac this year was this 4-door, 6-passenger wagon. A 9-passenger version was also available. The third seat still faced to the rear. A roof rack was optional. Cargo capacity was a huge 96.3 cubic feet. Among the options available were AM/FM radio with rear speakers, power steering and brakes, power windows, and a power vent window, tilt steering wheel, a trailer hauling package and heavy duty suspension.

Top of the Plymouth lineup of wagons was this Fury model, available as a 6 or 9-passenger wagon. The roof rack was optional as were the rear window wind deflectors. Note their position on the tailgate window posts. These deflectors helped keep the rear window clean. The third seat still faced to the rear. The overall length was 211.5 inches on a 116-inch wheelbase.

Plymouth wagons were also popular with police departments. Pictured here is the Savoy 4-door, 6-passenger model, equipped with a 318 cubic inch 230 horsepower V-8. Features included aluminized muffler and tailpipe; 32,000 mile lubrication cycles and 4,000 mile oil changes, plus an alternator instead of a generator.

One of two compact wagons offered by Plymouth was the Valiant V-200. This was the DeLuxe model. It was a 4-door, 6-passenger wagon. The roof rack was optional.

1964

The Plymouth Valiant V-100 wagon was this 4-door, 6-passenger model. It was the lowest priced Plymouth wagon. It was equipped with a 170 cubic inch economy 6-cylinder engine, rated at 101 horsepower.

The Rambler Classic 770 Cross Country wagon was one of three Classic wagons. Also available were the 660 and 550 wagons, in 6 or 9-passenger models. A 127 horsepower Six or 198 horsepower V-8 were the engine choices.

The Rambler Classic 550 Cross Country was the lowest priced Classic series wagon. Pictured here is the 6-passenger model. The roof rack was standard. Featured options included a floor console with twin-stick shift and bucket seats. The twin-stick option made available five forward speeds. Cargo space was generous at 80 cubic feet.

One of two Rambler American series wagons was the DeLuxe 330 wagon. The Rambler American was completely redesigned this year. Cargo capacity was 75 cubic feet. The tailgate was the conventional swing-down type with self-storing window. This year the American was enlarged to carry six passengers. The roof rack was standard on the 330 model. Construction continued to be uni-body with deep dip rust-proofing.

Lowest priced Rambler wagon was this American 220 model, a 4-door, 6-passenger version. The roof rack was optional. Choice of economy engines were a 90 horsepower, 125 horsepower or 138 horsepower 6-cylinder. Wheelbase of the American wagon was 106 inches with an overall length of 177.25 inches. Height was 54.5 inches.

Studebaker continued to offer the Brooks Stevens designed wagon in two series, the Challenger and Daytona. Engine options included the economy Six or the 259 horsepower V-8. All wagon models were 4-door, 6-passenger models. The forward mounted roof rack was optional. The Brooks Stevens designed sliding rear roof section was one of the most unique wagon features since the introduction of the self-storing tailgate window back in 1950. Note that with the sliding roof in the open position and the tailgate down, a handy swing down step was built into the gate and swung down for easy access into the cargo area. It is surprising that other manufacturers did not adopt the sliding roof idea. These wagons will surely become real collectors items.

The Buick Special wagon was offered as a standard and DeLuxe model. Pictured here is the DeLuxe version priced at $2,796. The Standard Model sold for $2,699. Both wagons were 4-door, 6-passenger models. The roof rack was optional.

Buick wagons were available only in the Special series. Buick continued to feature their domed roof wagon, the Skyroof. It was available as a 6 or 9-passenger model. Pictured here is the 9-passenger version which sold for $3,214.

The Buick Skyroof Sportwagon. This is the 6-passenger model. It was priced at $3,092. There were two other Skyroof models in addition to the Custom models. There were two standard versions, each available as a 6 or 9-passenger wagon. These sold for $2,925 and $3,056 respectively. The Skyroof wagon shared its body with the Oldsmobile Vista-Cruiser wagon.

Few changes took place in 1965. Ford introduced a new body design but continued to offer the same lineup of wagon models. The 10-passenger Country Squire and Country Sedan models had two facing third seats, which was unique. These were likened to the early jitney wagons of the teens and twenties. All top of the line Ford and Mercury wagons were distinguished by simulated wood siding.

Buick and Oldsmobile continued to offer their domed vista roof models. The Buick model was called the Skyroof and the Oldsmobile was called the Vista Cruiser. Both Buick and Oldsmobile limited their wagon models to the compact series. Chevrolet and Pontiac on the other hand offered wagons in all of their series. There was a full size and a compact Pontiac wagon, while Chevrolet had a wide range of wagons, from the full size Impala to the compact Chevy II, not to mention the Chevy Van and Suburban Carryall.

Chrysler, like most of the industry, introduced a new body design this year, which produced a cleaner looking wagon. Dodge and Plymouth offered a full range of wagon models, from full size to mid-size, to compact. Dodge also offered two Sportsman van-type wagons, plus the Town Wagon series, which competed with the Chevy Carryall and International Travelall.

As for the independents, Rambler remained pretty much unchanged, marketing the same lineup of wagons as in the previous year. There were three Rambler series, the Ambassador, the Classic, and the American. All Rambler wagons were 4-door models. Checker had two wagons, the Superba and the Marathon. The Checker wagon was the largest passenger car wagon in the industry. Because of its height, the roof rack on the Checker was placed over the forward roof section. One could then reach the roof rack by opening a door and standing on the sill plate. Studebaker discontinued production of their wagons, although they did build two prototypes. Willys continued to offer the Wagoneer, and International continued with the Travelall.

Chevrolet offered five full-size wagon models this year. The Bel Air, pictured here, was the mid-priced model. Available as either a 6 or 9-passenger wagon, the 6-passenger sold for $2,770, while the 9-passenger sold for $2,976. Both models were available with 6-cylinder or V-8 engines. All full-size wagons had the same body dimensions, with the same cargo capacities. They varied only in trim treatment.

The 1965 Chevrolet Impala Station Wagon was Chevrolet's top of the line wagon. The basic body design was new for this year. The three tail light design included a back-up light as the middle lense. The Impala was available in both 6 and 9 passenger form.

A rear view of the full-size Chevrolet wagon. With the tailgate lowered, a full 4 x 8 foot sheet of plywood could be carried flat. The 6-passenger model offered an optional lockable compartment. The spare tire was mounted in the right rear wheel well. Chevrolet had three distinctive round tail lights; two of these were located on the tailgate. One of the three lights served as a back-up light.

The Chevelle 300 DeLuxe 4-door, 6-passenger wagon was part of Chevrolet's mid-size series. It was also available as a 2-door wagon. The 4-door wagon was considered the DeLuxe version while the 2-door was the Standard model. The DeLuxe 4-door model sold for $2,511, equipped with a 6-cylinder engine. With a V-8 it was priced at $2,626.

The lowest priced full-size Chevrolet wagon was this Biscayne model. Available only as a 6-passenger wagon, it sold for $2,707, equipped with a 6-cylinder engine. Trim on the Biscayne was sparce. There was an optional roof rack available.

The Chevrolet Chevelle Malibu was the top of the line for the mid-size wagon series. The Malibu was a 4-door, 6-passenger wagon that sold for $2,695. The tailgate window was self-storing. An optional roof rack was available.

The Chevrolet Chevy II Nova wagon was one of two wagons available in the compact series. The other was designated the Chevy II 100 wagon. It was the lowest priced Chevrolet wagon, priced at $2,363. The more DeLuxe Nova was priced at $2,456 with a 6-cylinder engine, and $2,562 with a V-8.

Chevrolet also offered a van-type wagon. This was actually more of a mini-bus. There were three doors on the passenger side, one on the driver's side and a pair in the rear. Seats could also be removed for greater cargo area.

Still one of the more popular Chevrolet Commercial bodies was this Carryall wagon. It was available with either panel rear doors or a tailgate. The quarter windows were either fixed or the slider type.

The New Yorker Town and Country was Chrysler's prestige wagon. It was the most expensive American production wagon, selling for $4,856 in the 9-passenger version. A total of 1,697 9-passenger wagons were built out of a total production run of 3,056 units. Note that with the new body design, the hardtop styling was dropped.

The Checker Marathon 4-door, 6-passenger Station Wagon. The Checker wagons were the largest in the industry when it came to passenger car type wagons, as opposed to the Carryall type wagon.

The Checker Superba wagon. This 4-door, 6-passenger wagon was the top of the line wagon for Checker. It differed from the Marathon only in the addition of trim. The roof rack was placed on the forward section of the roof, because of the wagon's height.

The Chrysler Newport Town and Country wagon. Chrysler introduced a new body design this year which made for a more pleasing-looking wagon. This was reflected in the sales, as a new record was set. A total of 8,421 units were built this year. The Newport wagon was available as either a 6 or 9-passenger model. It sold for $3,470 and $3,576 respectively.

The Dodge Custom 880 was the largest and most expensive Dodge wagon available this year. This year marked the introduction of simulated wood grain siding for Dodge. The roof rack was optional.

Dodge also offered a station wagon in the Polara Series, and this car was available in two 4-door versions. The large 3-seat, 9-passenger version cost $3,259, weighed 4,335 pounds and was dubbed the Model D57. The same car was called a Model D56 when fitted with only two seats to accommodate six passengers. This form went for $3,153 and tipped the scales at 4,270 pounds. Like all of the other Polara models, the wagon rode on a wheelbase of 121 inches but had an over-all length of 217.1 inches. The rear compartment on these wagons offered a full 96.9 cubic feet for cargo when all seats were folded down.

Dodge's new intermediate size Coronet 4-door, 2-seat, 6-passenger station wagon was designated Model W56, when fitted with the standard 6-cylinder engine. It went for $2,592 and weighed 3,446 pounds. The V-8 version of this car went for $2,688 and tipped the scales at 3,546 pounds. The standard Six for the Coronet was the 225 cubic inch Slant Six that developed 145 horsepower. The standard V-8 offering was the 273 cubic inch 180 horsepower engine, while other V-8's were offered ranging in horsepower up to 425.

Handsome is as handsome does, and the Dart 270 station wagon, Model L76, was a handsome little wagon indeed. Like all Dart wagons, this version was a 4-door, 2-seat, 6-passenger car with a wheelbase of 106 inches. As a 6-cylinder car the 270 wagon cost $2,506. The V-8 version went for $2,637 and tipped the scales at 2,935 pounds. The roof mounted rack was an optional extra. Notice the little V-8 insignia mounted on the front fender just forward of the door. These plaques were placed on all Darts adorned with a V-8.

The Dodge Coronet 440 Wagon was available either in 6 or 9-passenger form. As a 6-passenger wagon with six-cylinder engine, it sold for $2,674. As a 9-passenger model, it sold for $2,868.

The Dart Series also held Dodge's lowest cost station wagon, which sold for $2,407 in 6-cylinder form. This car, when fitted with the 273 cubic inch, 180 horsepower V-8, cost $2,538 and weighed 2,930 pounds. The Dart Series station wagon was dubbed a Model L56. This version is seen complete with the optional roof rack, wheel covers, and whitewall tires.

The Dodge A-100 Sportsman Wagon, when equipped with trailer towing package, made a super station wagon.

The Dodge Sportsman and Custom Sportsman. These van-type wagons featured vinyl bucket seats, seating for up to eight, right side door step, self-adjusting brakes and oriflow shock absorbers. The Sportsman wagons were in addition to two full-size, two mid-size and two compact passenger car type wagons, offered by Dodge this year. Dodge also returned to featuring simulated wood siding on the Custom 880 wagon.

The Ford Ranch Wagon was the lowest priced full-size wagon available from Ford this year. It was available only in 6-passenger version. Some of the features of the full-size Ford wagon included built-in air deflectors, dual-facing rear seats in 10-passenger models. The top of the line Country Squire sold for $3,200, the Country Sedan for $3,000, and the Ranch Wagon for $2,850.

A rear view of the Ford Country Squire. The roof rack was optional. Note that the third seat was actually two facing seats. Ford considered a Country Squire with this seat a 10-passenger model. This arrangement was unconventional, as all other manufacturers had their third seat facing to the rear.

The Ford Fairlane 500 wagon was available as a 6 or 9-passenger model. This was Ford's mid-size series. The third seat faced to the rear. Price tag for this wagon was $2,700.

A rear view of the Ford Fairlane 500 Ranch Wagon. The tailgate had a self-storing window. Six-cylinder or V-8 engines were available. A roof rack was optional. Interiors were upholstered in rich vinyls.

1965

The Ford Fairlane Ranch Wagon is shown here in clay car prototype form. This was the lowest priced mid-size wagon. It sold for $2,620 and was available only as a 6-passenger, 4-door model.

The Ford Falcon Squire wagon. This 4-door, 6-passenger wagon was the top of the line in Ford's compact series. The roof rack was optional. The simulated wood siding was standard. It was a most distinctive compact wagon. Ford had a knack for applying simulated wood siding in just the right places.

One step up from the bottom of the Falcon wagon line was this Falcon DeLuxe 4-door mode. It sold for $2,455. The rear door vent style windows were fixed. This is a prototype model, photographed in the styling studio.

The Ford Falcon Futura Wagon was one of four Falcon wagons available this year. The Futura had distinctive side molding trim, rich vinyl upholstery and full carpeting. Tailgate window was self-storing. An optional roof rack was available.

It had to come to this. The success of the Ford Mustang inspired all kinds of custom versions. The Mustang Station Wagon was designed by Robert Cumberford and built from a stock 1965 notch-back by Carrozzeria Intermeccancia in Italy. If Ford had considered expanding the Mustang line this conversion would have been better than most. However, the car could hardly qualify as a functional working wagon.

A rear view of the custom built Mustang Station Wagon designed by Robert Cumberford. The wagon configuration lends itself well to the Mustang design. Photo courtesy Road and Track magazine. It appeared for the first time in the May, 1969 issue.

The Mercury Colony Park Station Wagon was available as either a 6 or 9-passenger wagon. Price tag for the 6-passenger version was $3,364. The 9-passenger version was $3,439. The wood grain siding design left something to be desired.

The plain full size Mercury wagon was known as the Commuter. It, too, was available as either a 6 or 9-passenger wagon, selling for $3,169 and $3,245, respectively. Special wind deflectors were designed into the quarter post. This helped keep the rear window clean.

The highest priced model in the Mercury Comet series was this Comet Villager Wagon. Available only as a 6-passenger model, it cost $2,808. The wood grain siding was standard. The wheelbase was 109.5 inches, with an overall length of 191.8 inches.

The Oldsmobile F-85 DeLuxe Station Wagon. Oldsmobile confined its wagon models to the F-85 series. There were a total of six Oldsmobile wagon models available this year. One step down from the F-85 DeLuxe was the F-85 Standard. Both were 4-door, 6-passenger models, which differed only in trim.

The Oldsmobile Vista-Cruiser Custom 6-passenger model. This was one of four Vista-Cruiser models available this year.

Top of the Oldsmobile wagon line was this Vista-Cruiser Custom 9-passenger model. The cargo area was nearly five feet wide and over eight feet long. The raised Vista-Roof accommodated tall items. The second seat folded easily, and the cargo area was carpeted. Vista-Cruiser interiors were also very distinctive.

The Plymouth Fury III 4-door, 9-passenger Station Wagon was the top of the line and one of five Fury wagon models. It was seven inches longer overall than other models in the line. It sat on a two-inch longer wheelbase. The roof rack was optional. The cargo floor was covered with distinctive vinyl floor covering.

The Plymouth Fury I wagon was adaptable to Police work. This wagon along with the Fury I sedan were specially outfitted for Police units and were included in the Plymouth Police catalog.

The Plymouth Belvedere II 9-passenger wagon. This was one of four Belvedere wagon models. They were available with either the 273 cubic inch V-8 or 225 cubic inch economy 6-cylinder engines. Standard equipment included a manual 3-speed transmission.

The Plymouth Belvedere I wagon was also found in the Plymouth Police catalog. Along with the Belvedere I 4-door sedan, it was specially outfitted for police work with heavy duty suspension, police special engine, heavy duty interior fabrics, and other optional equipment not generally available to the public.

The Plymouth Fury II 6-passenger wagon. The roof rack was optional. Note the rear bumper rubber step plates. Plymouth was the only wagon to offer these passenger assists. The Plymouth wagon was advertised as having "passenger car style inside and out."

The Plymouth Fury I 6-passenger wagon was the lowest priced full-size model. It was the same size as the Fury III but lacked the plush appointments.

The 6-passenger Plymouth Belvedere wagon. Popular optional equipment for the Belvedere wagon included: A choice of V-8 or 6-cylinder engine, AM/FM radio, tinted glass, air conditioning, roof rack, 3-speed column mounted automatic transmission or 4-speed manual with Hurst floor shifter. Floor length with tailgate open and all seats folded was 117.9 inches. The wheelbase of the Belvedere wagon was 116 inches.

1965

There were two Plymouth Valiant wagons available this year. This is the Valiant 200 wagon. It was the top of the line. Note the curved quarter windows and wind deflectors mounted on the tailgate window posts. Valiant wagons were available only in the 6-passenger form.

Lowest priced Plymouth wagon was this compact Valiant 100 wagon model. It was a 4-door, 6-passenger wagon. The vent-type window in the rear door was fixed; the quarter window was curved. Valiant wagons followed the sedan design very closely. An optional roof rack was also available. The car had an overall length of 208.5 inches and an overall height of 55 inches. The floor width between the rear wheel housings was 45 inches.

The Pontiac Catalina Safari wagon is shown here with optional roof rack. A Cordova vinyl roof covering was also available in black or beige, with or without the roof rack. The Catalina wagon was available as a 6 or 9-passenger model, whereas the Bonneville was only available as a 6 passenger.

The Pontiac Bonneville Safari was the Pontiac top of the line wagon. The wheelbase was 121 inches and it boasted more than 90 cubic feet of cargo space. The Bonneville Safari was equipped with a 333 horsepower V-8 engine, coupled with a hydra-matic transmission. A roof rack was also available along with a whole list of options that included 4-speed transmissions, power brakes, steering, windows, and air conditioning, to name but a few.

The Pontiac Tempest Safari wagon. There were two Tempest wagons – the Safari and the Custom Safari. Pictured here is the latter. It was available with a 140 horsepower Six or choice of either a 250 horsepower V-8 or 285 horsepower V-8. Deep pile carpeting, padded vinyl cargo mat, bright metal skid strips, and Morrokide upholstered interiors were standard.

The Rambler Ambassador 880 Cross Country is shown with optional third seat and fifth door. This model was a step down from the more luxurious 990 Cross Country, differing only in trim.

The Rambler Ambassador 990 Cross Country was Rambler's top of the line wagon. It was available as either a 6 or 9-passenger wagon. The roof rack was standard.

A rear view of the Rambler Classic 550 Cross Country wagon. The tailgate window was self-storing, with an optional power assist. A manual exterior mounted window crank was standard. All Rambler wagons featured uni-body construction.

The Rambler Classic 770 wagon. One of its features was a lockable compartment found under the cargo floor in 6-passenger models. The luggage rack was standard. The Rambler Classic series was the mid-price range for Rambler wagons. The 6-cylinder engine was the basic powerplant.

The Rambler American 330 wagon was one of two American series wagons. It was the more deluxe of the two. Features included a standard roof rack, body side moulding and bright metal window trim.

The lowest priced Rambler wagon was this American 220 model. It was merely a stripped down version of the deluxe 330 model, with the difference being the absence of bright metal trim and the standard roof rack.

Studebaker did not have a production wagon for 1965, but they did manage to build two prototype Lark wagons. Pictured here is one of these. The simulated wood trim was low on this model lending to an overall low profile appearance.

Jeep continued to offer its Wagoneer. The Jeep wagon was portrayed as a rugged off-the-road vehicle as well as a tame city car, at home as a family car or a cross-country hauler. It was available with four-wheel-drive. The rear door vent-type windows were operational. The Jeep wagon was a basic 4-door, 6-passenger model.

One of two Studebaker prototype wagons for 1965. Neither model reached production. The simulated wood trim on this model looked very attractive. The overall design had a good appearance, and there is little doubt that the wagon would have met with favorable public reaction. Studebaker closed down its South Bend facilities at the end of 1964, and production of Studebaker cars was confined to Canada for a brief period thereafter.

The Buick Special DeLuxe wagon was a 4-door, 6-passenger model. The tailgate window was self-storing. Official designation was Model 43635. The cost of this unit was $2,853.

The Buick Special wagon was the standard version of the two wagons available in the Special series. The two wagons, the DeLuxe and the Standard, differed only in the placement of the Special nameplate (the Standard had the nameplate on the rear fender) and a body side moulding. The Standard sold for $2,764. The spare was housed over the right rear wheel housing, which was conventional for wagons of this decade.

The Buick Sportwagon was Buick's top of the line wagon. It shared its body with Oldsmobile, and sported a domed vista roof. This year Buick offered a simulated wood grain option. This model sold for $3,295 in 9-passenger form.

1966 will be marked as a milestone in station wago development. It was this year that Ford introduced th "Doorgate." Asserting themselves again as the wago master, Ford revolutionized the tailgate with a ve practical innovation they called the "Magic Doorgate Up till this time there was the tailgate, the tailgate/liftgat the tailgate with self-storing window, the fifth door, an now the doorgate. The doorgate was simply this: th tailgate with self-storing window could now be used as tailgate when load capacity needed to be increased, or fo extra long loads, etc. Or, it could be opened like a doc for easier entry into the third seat area, or for easi unloading of smaller cargo. Other manufacturers wou soon follow this lead and develop their own doorgate

All General Motors divisions continued unchange Pontiac offered a new option for its Bonneville wagon — vinyl covered roof with or without a roof rack. Oth makes would follow with the same option. Fortunatel this was not a very popular option. Buick and Oldsmobi once again confined the wagon models to their compa series, the Special and F-85 respectively.

Chrysler wagons remained unchanged, having received new body design the year before. Dodge marched in 1966 with the Dodge Rebellion, and urged everyone join. The Dodge Monaco model featured simulated woo siding. This was the top of the line Dodge wagon. Fo was no longer unique with simulated wood siding. personally believe other manufacturers considered th retention of the woodie look by Ford as part of the success in marketing station wagons. Others would soc join Dodge in following the Ford lead. Plymouth, like i coprorate brother Dodge, offered a full line of wago suited to everyone's taste and pocketbook, ranging fro the full size Fury to the compact Valiant.

The independents continued almost unchanged for 196 Rambler offered the same lineup of wagons as did Checke International and Willys. Willys Jeep was now Kais Jeep. And Jeep lauded their four-wheel drive feature "You get twice the 'grip' on slippery streets with 4-wheel drive Jeep Wagoneer."

The Standard version of the Buick Sportwagon was a 6-passenger model which sold for $3,173. All Sportwagons had a wheelbase of 120 inches and featured a newly designed interior, new instrument panels and new seat belts. It also had a lockable luggage compartment under the cargo floor. The roof rack was optional. Note the 60/40 split second seat.

Buick dealers were also importing the Opel, a GM product produced in Germany. This Opel Kadett wagon was the highest priced model in the line, selling for $1,898. It had a standard 4-cylinder, 54 horsepower engine. The roof rack was an option. It had a payload of 794 pounds.

Simulated woodgrain trim returned to Chevrolet's top of the line wagon this year. This was the Caprice 9-passenger model. In this form the wagon sold for $3,347. In a 6-passenger version the price tag was $3,234.

With the introduction of the Caprice, the Chevrolet Impala wagon was no longer the top of the line. The Impala was available in either 6 or 9-passenger form. It sold for $3,189 as a 9-passenger, and $3,076 as a 6-passenger wagon.

The Chevrolet Impala 9-passenger wagon. DeLuxe wheel covers and wrap around tail lights were some of its features. An optional roof rack was also available.

Similar to the Impala but yet another step down was this Chevrolet Bel Air wagon. It was available as a 9-passenger model for $3,053, or as a 6-passenger model for $2,940. This was Chevrolet's most popular full size wagon.

The Chevrolet Malibu Station wagon. This was the top of the line for the mid-size Chevelle series. This was a 6-passenger model which sold for $2,756.

The lowest priced wagon in the Chevrolet Chevelle series was this 300 DeLuxe mode. It was a 4-door, 6-passenger wagon which sold for $2,681. The tailgate window was self-storing. The roof rack was optional. The 2-door wagon had been dropped from the line because of poor sales.

Chevrolet offered two wagon models in the compact Chevy II series, the 100 and the Nova, which is pictured here. The Nova sold for $2,623, while the 100 sold for $2,536. The tailgate window was self-storing. Both models were 6-passenger wagons.

The Chevrolet Carryall continued to remain popular. It was available as either a station wagon or panel delivery. It was also available with the Series K10 4-wheel-drive chassis.

The Checker Marathon wagon was a 4-door, 6-passenger model. The Checker wagon was still the largest passenger car type wagon available. It had the largest headroom and biggest cargo area of any American-made production wagon.

Although not classified as a station wagon, Chevrolet also offered this camping vehicle which was based on the Chevyvan. It was self-contained and could sleep four. In standard form, in the conventional roof and seats, it served as Chevrolet's version of the van/bus type of vehicle.

An interesting version of the Chevrolet Carryall was this ambulance conversion. Note the addition of an extra set of doors. These are actually cab doors. The interior was solid formica and offered 60 inches of headroom. It was built by the Centurion Co. of Memphis.

Chrysler wagons were unchanged for 1965. This is the Newport model, available as a 6 or 9-passenger wagon. Chrysler wagons used a 121-inch wheelbase and were 219.6 inches overall. The Chrysler wagon continued to remain the most expensive production wagon in America. The 9-passenger version sold for $4,192.

The most luxurious and most expensive Dodge wagon was this Monaco model. In 9-passenger form it sold for $3,286. The simulated wood trim was standard. The roof rack was optional. The Dodge Monaco wagon was the same size as the Chrysler Newport, shared many of its component parts, but cost almost $1,000 less.

The Dodge Polara 4-door, 6-passenger wagon was also available as a 9-passenger model. This was a step down from the top of the line. In 9-passenger form it sold for $3,160. It was powered by a 383 cubic inch V-8. An optional roof rack was also available. It used a 121-inch wheelbase.

The Dodge Coronet 440 wagon. Either 6 or 9-passenger models were available. The V-8 engine was available with either model. But the 6-cylinder engine could only be had with the 6-passenger model.

The Dodge Coronet DeLuxe station wagon. It was available only as a 6-passenger model, powered by either a V-8 or 6-cylinder engine. It sold for $2,725.

The Dodge Town Wagon was based on the D-100 truck chassis. The Town Wagon was competition for the Chevrolet Carryall. The D-100 was also available as a panel delivery truck, shown in the background.

Dart 270 wagon. 6 or 273 V8 power. 2-seat model only.

The Dodge Dart series wagons came in two models – the Standard and the 270. Both were 4-door, 6-passenger wagons. The Dart wagons shared their bodies with the Plymouth Valiant wagons. Tailgate windows were self-storing and the quarter windows were wrap around. The 270 sold for $2,661, and the Standard sold for $2,564.

Ford offered 13 wagons this year. Topping the line was this Country Squire 10-passenger model. The simulated wood grain siding was traditionally standard, the roof rack was optional. Dual facing third seats were standard.

New from Ford this year was the Magic Doorgate. It was the newest thing in tailgate design since the self-storing window in 1950. It was a dual action device that could be operated as a door or a tailgate. It is shown here as a door. The window was self-storing. Entry into the third seat area was much easier.

The top of Ford's mid-size Fairlane series was this Fairlane 500 Squire Wagon. The simulated wood trim was standard and became synonymous with the use of the Squire designation. It was pleasing and well-placed. The "Magic Doorgate" was also standard on Fairlane wagons. This model sold for $2,900.

1966

The Ford Country Sedan. This model wagon was a step down from the Country Squire. The dual action "Magic Doorgate" is in the tailgate position. Note the dual facing third seats. This was classed as a 10-passenger wagon. The roof rack was optional. The Country Sedan sold for $3,100, while the top of the line Country Squire sold for $3,350. This compares to $3,347 for the Chevrolet Caprice and $3,189 for the Impala.

Ford's top compact wagon was this Falcon Futura. The Falcon Squire model was discontinued. The "Magic Doorgate" was not available on Falcon wagons. The roof rack was optional. This model sold for $2,555.

The Ford Falcon Club Wagon. This van-type wagon had room for at least 11 passengers. There were three doors on the right side and one on the left plus two doors at the rear.

The Ford Falcon wagon. This 4-door, 6-passenger wagon was Ford's lowest priced passenger car type wagon, selling for $2,445. The roof rack was optional.

Top of the Mercury wagon line was the Colony Park. It was virtually unchanged from the previous year. In 6-passenger version it cost $3,500, while in 9-passenger version it cost $3,600. The wheelbase was 119 inches with an overall length of 216.5 inches.

Topping the Oldsmobile lineup of wagons was this Vista-Cruiser model. It was available as a 6 or 9-passenger wagon and was one of four Vista-Cruiser models. The domed roof body was shared with the Buick Sportwagon. There was over 100 cubic feet of cargo space. Standard engine was a 320 horsepower Rocket V-8.

The Pontiac Bonneville Safari Wagon with optional roof rack and vinyl covered roof. This was the top of the line wagon. It was available only as a 6-passenger model. In addition to the Bonneville, Pontiac also offered two Catalina wagons and two compact Tempest wagons.

The Mercury Villager 4-door, 6-passenger wagon was the most expensive wagon in the Comet series. It sold for $2,895, and had a standard 200 cubic inch, 120 horsepower, 6-cylinder engine. The roof rack was optional. The simulated wood trim was standard.

The Oldsmobile F-85 DeLuxe Station Wagon was one of two F-85 wagons available this year. Both were 6-passenger models. They differed mainly in trim. The F-85 was available with either a Six or V-8 engine.

The Pontiac Catalina Saafri wagon, in 6-passenger form, was one of two Catalina wagons available. In addition to the Catalina, Pontiac also offered the luxury Bonneville Safari. All Pontiac wagons were unchanged in design this year.

The Pontiac Tempest wagon was available in two versions — a deluxe and a standard. The difference was in the trim. Both were 6-passenger models, and unchanged from the previous year.

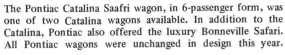

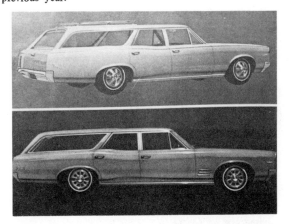

The Plymouth Belvedere I Station Wagon was a 4-door, 6-passenger model. The tailgate window is self-storing. An optional roof rack was available. There was a choice of 6-cylinder or V-8 engines.

At the top of the Plymouth mid-size line was this Belvedere II wagon. It was available as either a 6 or 9-passenger model. The Belvedere wagon had a wheelbase of 117 inches, the same as the Dodge Coronet series.

The Plymouth Fury I station wagon was the lowest priced full-size Plymouth wagon. It was available only in 6-passenger form. Top of the full size line was the Fury III wagon, available as a 6 or 9-passenger model. Six-cylinder or V-8 engines were available.

The Plymouth Valiant 100 4-door, 6-passenger wagon. This was one of two Valiant wagons available. The Valiant shared its body with the Dodge Dart. An optional roof rack could be purchased. Standard engine was a 170 cubic inch 6-cylinder.

The Rambler Classic 660 4-door 6-passenger wagon was one of the most popular Rambler wagon models. The roof rack was standard. The vent type window in the rear door was not functional.

This stripped down version of the Jeep Wagoneer was the company's utility model. Four-wheel-drive and a roof rack were two of the most favored options, though the vehicle came with conventional rear-wheel drive as standard equipment.

The Rambler Ambassador 990 4-door, 9-passenger wagon. This was the top of the line Rambler wagon. The roof rack was standard as was the fifth door. Tinted glass and air conditioning were some of the many options.

The Jeep Super Wagoneer. This jazzed up version of the Jeep wagon featured a vinyl covered roof, a roof rack, mag wheels, four-wheel-drive, a V-8 engine and wood grain accent strip. The rear door vent window was functional.

y 1967 most manufacturers were offering wood grain
lique on their top of the line wagons. This feature
uld continue to grow in popularity in the years to
ne. Options were big in 1967, and the auto makers
tainly provided a wide choice to the prospective buyer.
ontiac options included such things as: power tailgate
ndow, roof rack (a permanent one or a removable one),
gage carrier cover, removable ski rack carrier, tailgate
ndow wind deflector, luggage compartment lock (avail-
e only on 6 passenger models), and vinyl roof covering.
w these were just the run of the mill options that most
her makers offered. However, there were some goodie
tions too, such as a stereo tape player, and a utility pad
this was a thick pad to be placed on the cargo floor so as
t to mar it. For picincs, an owner could also remove this
d and use it as a ground cover. Then there was the rear
eaker, with fader switch to vary the volume. Or, how
out window screens? There were rool-up screens avail-
le for the rear doors an; the tailgate. The rear door
eens attached permanently to the window frames, while
e tailgate screen was held in place by raising the window
rtly. The screens were great for campers. Also great for
mpers was the utility lamp. It stored under the hood,
d 17 feet of cord, and served as a emergency trouble
ht or a campers light.

Rambler also had an array of options to make a wagon
re than just a utility vehicle. Rambler offered such
tions as a sport console, sports steering wheel, a
chometer, folding front seat center arm rest, cruise con-
l, tilt steering, head rests, reclining bucket seats,
oulder safety belts, AM/FM all transistor radio, posi-
action rear end, trailer hitches, window screens, plus the
ual air conditioning, power steering, brakes, windows,
avy duty suspensions, and more. Rambler also went one
p further, when in February it introduced three distinct
agon models. Each one was marked with distinctive
nulated wood siding, each different from the other.
ere was the Briarcliff, which was sold in the east, the
ariner which was sold in the coastal areas, and the
esterner, sold in the mid-west and southwest. No more
an 600 of each model were built.

This was 1967, and yet things haven't changed all that
uch today. There are no really new options. No new
odies or gadgets. From the car collectors standpoint, a
967 wagon equipped with many or all of these options
ould indeed be very collectable today.

The Buick Sportwagon. Simulated wood siding was added
this year. The Sportwagon was still considered the top of the
line. However, there was no separate distinction as to model.
All wagons were considered standard with special trim
packages. Note the optional roof rack and wire wheel covers.
The Sportwagon was available as a 6-passenger and 9-
passenger model. As the former, it cost $3,202; as the latter,
it carried a price tag of $3,340.

The Buick Special DeLuxe station wagon was available in
either Standard or DeLuxe form. The big difference between
the Special DeLuxe and the Sportwagon was in the roof
design, the Sportwagon having the vista-dome. Both models
were 4-door wagons. In the Standard form the Special
DeLuxe cost $2,812; in DeLuxe form it ran $2,901.

This is a custom built Cadillac wagon, using the Eldorado
chassis. The Nomad type wagon was built by Kustomcraft
of Littleton, Colo. It is owned by Miller Motors of Exeter,
N.H. The wagon is painted in white pearlessent, which
makes it very striking.

Buick continued to offer the Opel Kadett wagon. This little
German import was manufactured by GM in West Germany
for U.S. distribution through Buick dealers. The wagon
was a 2-door, 6-passenger model. The roof rack was optional.
Base price of the Opel Kadett was $1,980.

A rear view of the Cadillac Eldorado Wagon. Note the familiar Nomad look, and the absence of a rear bumper. The roof is extended over the windshield in visor-like fashion. This one-off wagon is owned by Miller Motors of Exeter, N. H.

For the second year in a row, Chevrolet's top of the line wagon, the Caprice, featured simulated wood siding. This most expensive of Chevrolet wagons was listed at $3,413 in basic form. A roof rack was optional. It was available as either a 6-passenger or 9-passenger wagon.

One step below the Caprice was the Chevrolet Impala wagon. Available as a 9-passenger model, its cost was $3,413. As a 6-passenger, it had a price tag of $3,301. Both versions weighed 3,950 pounds.

The Chevrolet Bel Air 9-passenger 4-door station wagon. The roof rack was optional. Sandwiched in between the Impala and the low price Biscayne, the Bel Air commanded a base price of $2,986 in 6-passenger form, while the 9-passenger version sold for $3,074.

The lowest priced full size Chevrolet wagon was this Biscayne model, a 4-door 6-passenger wagon. Features included an all-vinyl interior and a choice of four different body colors. It sold for $2,923.

In the Chevrolet mid-size Chevelle series, the top of the line was this Concors model. It was a dressed up version of the Malibu wagon. Features included a simulated wood side trim, and chrome rocker moulding. Price tag for this version was $2,933.

With the introduction of the new Chevelle Concours model, this Malibu was now the mid-priced Chevelle wagon. It was available in 4-door form only and had a one-piece tailgate with self-storing window. It sold for $2,801.

This is the Chevrolet compact Chevy II wagon. There were two Chevy II wagons available. The one pictured here is the Nova, which was the top of the line, at $2,671. The rear door vent window was not functional. A roof rack was available at extra cost. Full wheel covers were standard.

Pictured here are two versions of the Chevrolet Carryall Suburban. The series CS/CE 20906 with panel-type rear doors and the series CS/CE 10906 with a station wagon-type tailgate. The roof rack on this latter model is optional. Seating capacity was for 9 passengers. The Carryall continued to have two doors on the right side, but only one on the left.

For the first time in several years the Chrysler Newport wagon did not set production records. Only 14,703 were produced. Two versions were available — a 6-passenger and a 9-passenger. Both were in the 4-door form. The roof rack was optional, but power brakes were standard. The 6-passenger model sold for $4,264, while the 9-passenger model sold for $4,369. Both models used a 122-inch wheelbase.

The Dodge Monaco station wagon was the top of the line. Features included wood grain siding, simulated of course, power operated tailgate window and front disc brakes. The rack was optional, as were front bucket seats and air conditioning. The Monaco was available in either 6-passenger or 9-passenger version.

The most expensive of the Coronet station wagons was the Series 440 3-seat, 9-passenger Model 46. Selling for $2,975 and weighing 3,705 pounds, this version of the 440 wagon was powered by a V-8 engine. This 9-passenger was not offered as a 6-cylinder car but the 6-seater was. The 6-seat Coronet 440 wagon was dubbed a Model 45 and, with a Slant Six, sold for $2,771. It weighed 3,495 pounds, while the 8-cylinder version of this car went for $2,865 and tipped the scales at 3,605 pounds.

The Dodge Polara wagon was identical to the Monaco, less the simulated wood grain siding. Optional items included speed control, 3-speed electric wipers, electric door locks, 6-way power seats, front bucket seats and a roof rack. The 318 cubic inch V-8 engine was standard with 2-barrel carb. A 383 cubic inch V-8 was optional. Both the Monaco and Polara wagons used a 122-inch chassis, which was also shared with the Chrysler Newport Wagon.

There were two versions of the Dodge Sportsman wagon, the Sportsman and the Custom Sportsman, which is pictured here. Standard equipment included a 101 horsepower, 170-cubic inch six-cylinder engine with manual 3-speed transmission.

Universal Coach Corp. of Detroit converted many Polara station wagons into attractive and relatively inexpensive ambulances and hearses this year. This is a combination vehicle, shown here in hearse trim, but also convertible to ambulance service. Standard equipment included vinyl rear roof, draperies, tailgate protection bar, cot holders, split rear seat, and floor plates. Stretchers, lights, and siren were optional.

The standard hearse in the offerings of Universal Coach Corp. of Detroit was this landau model, built on a converted Polara station wagon. The rear roof portion was vinyl covered. Dummy chrome landau irons occupied the space formerly taken by the large rear quarter windows. These relatively inexpensive hearses appealed to funeral homes in small towns or where finances were limited. Universal also converted Coronet station wagons in the same manner.

This is the Ford Country Squire 10-passenger station wagon. By stubbornly hanging onto the simulated wood trim, Ford managed to prove over the years that a woodie trim, real or not, was indeed the best packaging for a wagon. This year many other manufacturers returned to the use of simulated wood trim. From now on it would become a designation of a top of the line model.

The Ford Country Sedan was available in 6-passenger or 9-passenger form. The roof rack was optional as were the deluxe wheel dovers. The Country Sedan was priced at $3,150 as compared with the Country Squire at $3,450.

Topping the Ford mid-size series was the Fairlane 500 Squire Wagon, featuring simulated wood siding. The full wheel covers and roof rack were optional. The vent-like windows in the rear doors were not functional.

The lowest priced Ford wagon was this compact Falcon Futura. It sold for $2,600 and was $71 cheaper than the Chevy II Nova wagon. This year the Falcon received the door/gate as standard equipment. The roof rack was optional. The vent-like window in the rear door was not functional.

The Ford Fairlane 500 DeLuxe Wagon was a 4-door, 6-passenger model. Features included a body side moulding strip which appeared on the other Fairlane 500 models. A six-cylinder or V-8 engine was available. Price tag for the Fairlane 500 DeLuxe wagon was $2,825, or $185 less than the Squire model.

Mercury's heaviest vehicle, weighing 4,297 pounds, was the Commuter wagon, shown here equipped with an optional vinyl top and chrome roof rack. In standard form, it cost $3,385 in 3-seat style, or $3,289 as a 2-seater. Both the Commuter and the Park Lane used the 390 cubic inch V-8 as standard power.

The Colony Park used very wide wood grain wood applique, bordered by chrome ribs all around. Weighing 4,294, it was available as a 3-seat vehicle for $3,752 or in 2-seat form for $3,650. This model features an accessory vinyl top and roof-top cargo rack. Both the Colony Park and the Commuter used a 119-inch wheelbase and were 213.5 inches overall.

Comet's prestige wagon was the Villager, shown here with optional wheel discs and cargo rack. Both the Villager and the Voyager used a 113-inch wheelbase and were 199.9 inches overall. The Villager cost $2,947 and weighed 3,413 pounds.

The Comet Voyager wagon used front fender trim similar but not identical to that used on the Caliente sub-series. With tailgate lowered, it offered 109.5 inches of flat floor space. As shown, but without the cargo rack, it cost $2,710 and weighed 3,391 pounds.

The Oldsmobile Cutlass 4-door, 6-passenger wagon features included a rocker moulding, fender lip mouldings, and full wheel covers. The tailgate had a self-storing window. The spare was housed on the inside above the right rear wheel. A roof rack was optional.

Identical to the Chevrolet Suburban Carryall, and differing in grille and trim only, was the GMC wagon. It could carry up to eight passengers and could be fitted for off the road operation. The roof rack was optional. The tailgate was a two-piece type.

The top of the Oldsmobile line of wagons was this Vista-Cruiser, featuring a vista dome roof. Simulated wood trim was introduced this year. The roof rack was optional. The Vista-Cruiser was available either as a 6-passenger or a 9-passenger model.

New from Pontiac this year was this Executive Safari wagon. This 4-door model was available as a 6-passenger or 9-passenger wagon. It boasted 100 cubic feet of cargo space. It featured simulated walnut wood grain siding and an energy absorbing steering column which was newly introduced on all GM cars this year. Among the options available were a matching vinyl roof and roof rack.

The Tempest Safari was Pontiac's compact wagon. It was one of four distinct wagon models offered by Pontiac this year, which included the Bonneville, the Executive, the Catalina and the Tempest. The simulated wood grain siding distinguished this model as being the posh Tempest Wagon.

The Plymouth Fury II 9-passenger and Fury I 6-passenger wagons. The Fury I was the lowest priced full size Plymouth wagon. A 225 cubic inch six-cylinder engine was standard.

The Plymouth Fury III Station Wagon was available as a 6-passenger or 9-passenger model. The roof rack was optional. Wheelbase was 122 inches, which was common to all Chrysler Corporation big wagons.

The Plymouth Belvedere 4-door, 6-passenger wagon. There was very little difference between this model and the more deluxe Belvedere I. A roof rack was an available option. The vent-type rear door windows were not functional.

The Plymouth Belvedere I wagon was the mid-size Plymouth wagon and was available in two models. The Belvedere I was the deluxe version, while the Belvedere was the plain model. The difference was in trim, and very little of that. Pictured here is a 6-passenger model. Full wheel covers were standard.

The Plymouth Fury Emergency Wagon. This was a basic Fury I wagon with special options qualifying it for police work. These wagons were outfitted with performance packages and suspension packages. They were painted according to order and included such hardware as sirens and flashing lights. The cargo area provided over eight feet of floor space, so a wagon could double as an emergency ambulance. All carried stretchers.

The American Motors Ambassador Cross Country wagon was a 4-door, 6-passenger model. Simulated wood grain siding graced its slab sides. The roof rack was standard. Wheelbase of the Ambassador was 118 inches with an overall length of 202.5 inches. Standard equipment included a Ceramic-Armored muffler and tail pipe.

The American Motors Ambassador 990 Cross Country Wagon had reclining front seats with breathing vinyl, a standard roof rack, improved rear suspension, energy absorbing steering column, choice of tail or door gate, 91 cubic feet of cargo space, and optional mag-type wheels among some of its features.

American Motor's mid-size wagon was this Rebel 770. It was available as a 6 or 9-passenger model. The wood grain siding was standard, as was the roof rack. There was a choice of tail or door gate. The wheelbase of the Rebel wagon was 114 inches, with an overall length of 198 inches. Three six-cylinder and four V-8 engines were available. Options included a 4-speed transmission, power disc brakes, positraction rear ends, column or console mounted gear shifts.

The Rambler American continued to be the compact size American Motors wagon. There were two models. Pictured here is the deluxe version 440. A roof rack was standard on the 440, optional on the 220 model. Reclining front seats were available options on both models. Wheelbase of the American was 106 inches, with an overall length of 181 inches.

The Jeep Super Wagoneer was a deluxe model equipped with 4-wheel drive, a V-8, vinyl covered roof, a roof rack, mag wheels, simulated wood grain feature strip, and white wall tires. Jeep was upgrading its models to compete with the passenger car-type wagons.

In February of this year, American Motors introduced specially trimmed Rebel wagons, designed for different sections of the country. At the left is the Briarcliff, of which 400 were built and sold in the east. At the top is the Mariner, of which 600 were built and sold in coastal areas. At the right is the Westerner, of which 500 were built and sold in the midwest and southwest.

The Jeep standard Wagoneer featured a V-8 engine, automatic transmission, roof rack, side view mirror, white wall tires and seating for six, with lots of cargo space. The vent-type window in the rear door was not functional.

Ford introduced the Torino Wagon. The Torino Squire, as it was officially called, was the deluxe version of the Fairlane wagon. The Falcon wagons received the optional 'doorgate', and the Falcon Squire model was discontinued. Ford also introduced the Bronco this year. The Bronco was a 2-door utility type vehicle which competed with the Jeep and International Scout. There were nine passenger car type wagons available from Ford this year in addition to the Bronco and the Van type wagons.

Chrysler finally offered the simulated wood applique on the Town and Country wagon. In spring, optional wood grain siding was made available on Newport 2-door hardtops and convertibles. This was an attempt at reviving the lure of the old Town and Countries of the 1940's and 50's. The option met with little success, making those few hardtops and convertible with the option collector cars today.

Chevrolet first introduced the Camaro in 1967 as their answer to the Ford Mustang. This year one of Chevrolet's show cars was the Camaro Waikiki Convertible. The Waikiki was basically a Camaro convertible with real teakwood used in the carved grille, custom squared headlights and teakwood applique siding. The teakwood siding treatment was not passed on to the production models.

Mercury introduced a 2-door Park Lane Hardtop and a convertible with wood applique siding. The applique was similar to that used on the Colony Park wagons and was called 'yacht paneling'. The woodie treatment was probably the least popular option available from Mercury. Few cars were sold with this option, once again creating a very collectable car.

Even though the auto makers were caught up in a woodie binge, the public was not ready. But the urge to apply wood grain applique to models other than wagons would presist, and later the public would be buying. The woodie fever would also spread to foreign shores and imported cars would begin to feature the woodie look. All of this became part of a nostalgia craze of the middle 1970's.

Buick continued to offer the simulated wood grain trim first introduced in 1967. This was the DeLuxe version of the Sportwagon. There were no large Buick wagons. All wagons were based on a 121-inch wheelbase and had the appearance of the Special series, although they were in a series of their own.

A rear view of the Buick Sportwagon, deluxe version. The simulated wood trim helped accent the sweep of the body panel. This same trim was also found on the tailgate and was a distinctive feature. Two versions of this wagon were available, a six-passenger and a nine-passenger model, selling for $3,341 and $3,499, respectively.

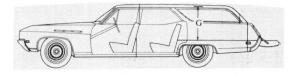

The Buick Sportwagon is shown less the deluxe simulated wood trim. There were two versions of this standard model, a six-passenger and a nine-passenger. All Sportwagons featured the domed vista roof, which was shared with Oldsmobile.

Lowest priced of the Buick wagons was this Special DeLuxe 4-door, 6-passenger model. It sold for $3,001. It was available only with a V-8 engine. Standard equipment included a 3-speed manual transmission with column mounted shift selector.

The Chevrolet Caprice Station Wagon continued to feature simulated wood trim. It was available as a 6 or 9-passenger wagon. It sold for $3,570 in 9-passenger form and $3,458 as a 6-passenger. The basic body design was unchanged from the previous year.

A rear view of the Chevrolet Impala Station Wagon. Shown here is the 4-door, 6-passenger model. It was also available as a 9-passenger wagon. The roof rack was optional. The 9-passenger version sold for $3,558 while the 6-passenger model sold for $3,245.

The Biscayne Station Wagon was Chevrolet's lowest priced full size wagon. It sold for $3,062. It is shown here with optional roof rack, wheel covers and unique fender mounted spot light. In addition to the full size models, Chevrolet also continued to offer the mid-size Chevelle wagon.

One of Chevrolet's show cars this year was the Waikiki. This was a basic Camaro convertible with simulated wood siding, and a real teakwood carved grille. Rectangular headlamps and chrome wire wheels were more of its special features. The car was never put into production. But who knows, with these distinctive features it might have sold.

The Chevrolet Series CS Carryall was unchanged. But it was a popular super size station wagon.

The Chevrolet Series 180 Sport-Van. Vans were beginning to come into their own, not only as work vehicles, but were popular super station wagons.

The Checker Marathon 4-door, 6-passenger Station Wagon. Checker, the traditional cab company, continued to offer a station wagon. This one came equipped with an optional V-8 engine, roof rack, full wheel covers, and white walls. Because of its height, the roof rack had to be placed on the forward section of the roof, in order to be accessible by stepping on the door sills.

For the first time since 1950, Chrysler featured simulated wood grain siding panels. Chrysler wagon sales jumped this year and a total of 22,141 units were built. The 6-passenger version sold for $4,418 and the 9-passenger for $4,523, making it the most expensive production wagon in the United States. A roof rack was optional.

Hot on the heels of having successfully reintroduced wood grain panels to its station wagon models, Chrysler introduced a wood grain option for its Newport 2-door hardtops and convertibles. These options were first shown at the Chicago Auto Show in February. It seems this was an attempt at reviving a modern day Town and Country, although there is no mention of this by the company. It's just as well, since the option enjoyed little success, which makes these vehicles collector cars today.

Dodge Coronet 500 station wagon (2-seat and 3-seat models)

The most expensive of the 500 Series Coronet models was the station wagon. These cars featured imitation wood grain side trim that readily identified them as the most luxurious wagons in the Coronet model range. Available as a 3-seat, 9-passenger wagon for $3,140 or as a 2-seat, 6-passenger car for $3,030, the 2-seat wagon weighed 3,585 pounds and was designated a Model WH45 while the 3-seat version, Model WH46, tipped the scales at 3,680 pounds.

Dodge Coronet Deluxe station wagon (2-seat model only)

Only a 2-seat, 6-passenger wagon was offered in the Coronet DeLuxe Series, Dubbed a Model WL45, this car cost $2,816 and weighed 3,455 pounds in its 6-cylinder form. The V-8 version of this inexpensive little wagon went for $2,910 and weighed 3,590 pounds. Like all 1968 Coronet station wagons, the DeLuxe version offered a full 88 cubic feet of cargo space behind the driver's seat.

1968

Polara station wagon
(2-seat and 3-seat models)

Offering a full 96.9 cubic feet of cargo space, the large Polara station wagon was available in both 3-seat, 9-passenger and 2-seat, 6-passenger form. Like all Polara models the wagon was powered by the 2-barrel version of the 318 cubic inch V-8 engine. As a 3-seat wagon, the Polara sold for $3,454, weighed 4,210 pounds and was designated a Model DL46. The straight 2-seat version cost $3,388 and tipped the scales at 4,155 pounds. The latter version was called a Model DL45.

The Ford Country Squire enjoyed a new body this year and some new features. The Squire was now referred to as the LTD Country Squire, and sported a LTD front end, which included hidden head lights. Ford's top of the line wagon was available in eight 6 or 9 passenger versions. It sold for $3,600 in basic form.

The most expensive car in the Monaco model line was the magnificent Monaco station wagon. This luxury wagon was quickly identified by its imitation wood grain side trim. It offered a full 96.9 cubic feet of cargo space behind the front seat and was available in either 2-seat, 6-passenger form or as a 3-seat, 9-passenger wagon. The 3-seat version, Model DH46, sold for $3,835 and weighed 4,360 pounds. The 6-passenger version, called a Model DH45, carried a price tag of $3,702 and tipped the scales at 4,295 pounds.

One of the more popular Ford wagons was this Country Sedan model, available as a 6 or 9-passenger wagon. It featured the "Magic Doorgate," Galaxie grille, and optional roof rack. The price tag for this model was $3,375.

In Ford's mid-size range, this Fairlane Torino Squire Wagon was the top of the line. It was available in both 6-passenger and 9-passenger versions. The "Magic Doorgate" was standard, as it was on all Fairlane wagons. With optional roof rack the Torino Squire sold for $3,115.

The Ford 4-door, 6-passenger Ranch Wagon was the lowest priced full size Ford wagon at $3,100, which was $38 more than a comparable Chevrolet wagon. As on all full size wagons, the "Magic Doorgate" was standard.

The Ford Falcon Futura Wagon was Ford's compact series station wagon. Prices started at $2,700. The "Magic Doorgate" was standard on Falcon wagons for the first time this year.

The Mercury Colony Park was Mercury's most expensive wagon. It was available as a 6 or 9-passenger model. The Colony Park was one of the wagon series offered by Mercury this year. The roof rack and vinyl roof were optional. Cost of the Colony Park was $3,888 in base form. Mercury also introduced optional simulated wood siding for two other models this year which were not station wagons. The wood graining was available on the Park Lane 2-door hardtop, and the Park Lane convertible. This was probably an attempt at reviving the old Sportsman model of 1946. It was a poor attempt as the option did not sell very well. The few that did sell are, of course, collector cars today.

The wood-grain applique accessory was available this year only in the Park Lane series. Here the Park Lane Convertible sports the walnut-type paneling. The car also has been equipped with the optional wire-type wheel discs. The paneling was probably the least popular accessory in Mercury's book.

The Oldsmobile Vista-Cruiser Custom with simulated wood grain siding. The Vista-Cruiser style provided more headroom for the second and third seat passengers because of the domed roof. The wheelbase was 121 inches. The roof rack was optional.

The heaviest vehicle in the Montego series was the Montego MX Station Wagon, a 6-passenger car weighing 3,584 pounds. It sold for $3,074. The model shown here is equipped with accessory roof rack and wire-spoke wheel discs. The dual action tailgate was available on this model for an extra $45. The Montego wagons used a 113-inch wheelbase.

The Oldsmobile DeLuxe Vista-Cruiser. This 4-door wagon was available as a 6 or 9-passenger model. Standard engine was a 350 cubic inch Rocket V-8, with 2-barrel carburetor. Styling was sleek. All Oldsmobile wagons were based on the F-85 series.

The Oldsmobile Cutlass Station Wagon was a 4-door, 6-passenger model. There were three engine options available—a six, 350 Rocket V-8, or High Performance Rocket V-8 that used premium fuel. Wheelbase was 116 inches with an overall length of 212.5 inches. Cargo capacity was 87.5 cubic feet.

The Plymouth Sport Suburban Wagon was the top of the line. It is pictured here with the Custom Suburban and the Suburban. The Custom and the Sport Suburban wagons were available in 6 or 9-passenger form. The Suburban came only as a 6-passenger model. The roof rack was optional. Wood grain siding was standard on the Sport Suburban.

Topping Plymouth's mid-size wagons was this Satellite Sport Wagon. The wood grain siding was standard. The Sport wagon was available in either 6 or 9-passenger form. The third seat faced to the rear. The tailgate window was power operated. The vent-like windows in the rear doors were fixed.

The lowest priced Plymouth mid-size wagon was this Belvedere model. Capacity of the cargo area was 88 cubic feet. A choice of engines included a 225 cubic inch six or 273 cubic inch V-8, depending on whether the customer wanted economy or performance. The two-way Tailgate was first introduced on Plymouth wagons this year and it was offered as standard equipment on all models.

Following Ford's lead, Plymouth introduced the two-way tailgate this year. It was available on all Plymouth wagons as standard equipment. It was almost identical to the Ford "Magic Doorgate."

Pictured here are two of the six wagons available from Pontiac this year—the Bonneville 9-passenger wagon and the prestigious Executive Safari 9-passenger model with simulated wood grain siding. Roof racks and vinyl covered roofs were optional on both models.

1968

Pictured here are the Pontiac Tempest Custom and Tempest Safari Station Wagons. The Safari was the top of the line and featured simulated wood grain siding. It was proportionately applied, which enhanced the lines of the wagon. Both models were available only in 4-door form. The roof rack was optional on both wagons.

Pontiac's Catalina wagons were available in either 6 or 9-passenger form. The third seat of the 9-passenger wagon faced to the rear. The roof rack on both models was optional. The lines of the 1968 Pontiac station wagon were streamlined and pleasing to the eye.

The American Motors Rebel 770 model 6818 is pictured here as the 6-passenger model. A 9-passenger version was also available. Simulated wood siding and roof racks were standard. Standard on all Rebel models was the 232 cubic inch six-cylinder engine. Optional was the 290 cubic inch V-8.

The basic body design was unchanged for American Motors this year. The top of the wagon line was this Ambassador DPL model 6888. It was available as a 6 or 9-passenger wagon. Simulated wood siding was standard. The roof rack also was standard. The Ambassador wagon offered optional front sway bar and heavy-duty springs and shocks.

The 1968 Jeep Jeepster with optional hardtop was sporty, with room for four. It had the look of a wagon but in strict definable terms it was a two-door sedan. Note the sporty wheelcovers and rackish cut of the door, reminiscent of the roadster.

The American Motors Rambler American 440 Deluxe wagon, model 6808, was a 4-door, 6-passenger model. Deluxe body side moulding, full wheel covers, and a roof rack were standard. Also standard were an economical six cylinder engine and manual shift transmission.

The Buick Sportwagon wood grain trim for this year followed the contour line of the body, being placed above it. This wood grain trim was framed by a stainless steel strip. Buick continued to share the Sportwagon body with the Oldsmobile Vista Cruiser. Light colored cars had dark wood grain while the dark colors used a light wood grain. This was the first year for Buick to incorporate the doorgate.

The 1960s saw the return of the woodie wagon, if only in simulated form. At the close of the decade every wagon manufacturer offered wood grain siding, if not as standard trim for their top of the line models, then as an option. Only one manufacturer had faith in a woodie wagon (real or simulated) prior to 1969. That was Ford. Since 1929 Ford had consecutively offered a woodie. When real wood was no longer practical, Ford switched to a simulated version. The Squire model wagons have always been very popular. Apparently their persistence in holding on to a woodie paid off. Ford has consistently been the leader in wagon sales. Maybe that little bit of plastic and decal film helped.

This year saw the introduction of the Chevrolet Caprice Kingswood Estate Wagon. The new name, 'Estate' designated the wood grain siding, and was similar to the Ford Squire designation. Another new entry from Chevrolet this year was the introduction of the Blazer. This all-terrain vehicle was competition for the Ford Bronco. Only the Blazer was bigger. It featured a 4-wheel drive option and a removable top. It could be converted into a station wagon, panel truck, or pick-up.

The rest of the General Motors Divisions remained unchanged. Buick and Oldsmobile continued to offer station wagons based on their Special and Cutlass series respectively. Neither Buick or Oldsmoblie offered a large or so-called full-size wagon. Pontiac, on the other hand offered the mid-size Tempest wagon as well as the full size Catalina and Bonneville wagons. Only Buick and Pontiac adopted the dual action tailgate/doorgate.

Mercury re-named its big luxury wagon the Marquis Colony Park. It led a three wagon series which included the Monterey and the Montego, in addition to the Marquis. The Monterey used the same wheelbase and body shell as the Marquis, less the simulated wood grain. As a matter of fact, both the full size Ford and Mercury wagons shared the same body shell. The Montego was a mid-size wagon featuring simulated wood grain as an option.

Chrysler Corporation wagons were unchanged in body design. All divisions featured the dual action tailgate/doorgate, on both the full size and mid-size models. Chrysler took up Ford's lead. All full-size top of the line wagon models dominated their respective series in price. The Chrysler Town and Country remains the highest priced station wagon in the United States at $4,699. The Town and Country shared its body shell with the Dodge Monaco and Plymouth Fury wagons. All wagons featured simulated wood grain siding on their top of the line models.

American Motors wagons were unchanged. The fifth door was still featured on all 9-passenger models as standard equipment. It was an option on the 6-passenger wagon. The luxury wagons were part of the SST designation. All featured simulated wood grain siding. And once again the roof racks were standard. American Motors was the only manufacturer to offer this feature as standard equipment. Jeep, International, and Checker were all unchanged, and still offered the same models.

Top of the Buick station wagon line was this Sportwagon. Note the contrast of the dark color with the light wood grain. The Sportwagon was available in either 6 or 9-passenger version. In 6-passenger form, with wood grain siding, it carried a price tag of $3,575.

The Buick Sportwagon is shown without the wood grain trim. This version of the Sportwagon was also available as a 6 or 9-passenger wagon. Cost of the 6-passenger model was $3,465, while the 9-passenger version had a price tag of of $3,631. The Buick wagons continued to have their own chassis of 121-inch wheelbase.

Buick's import, the Opel Kadett Station Wagon, carried a price tag of $2,110. This was a 5-passenger wagon. The roof rack was an option. The tailgate was of the hatchback design.

The Buick Special Deluxe Wagon was Buick's lowest priced station wagon. It, too, featured the doorgate. The power plant was a 230 horsepower V-8. The Special Deluxe was available only as a 6-passenger wagon. It was also placed on a shorter 116-inch wheelbase chassis. The price tag was $3,092.

The lowest priced full size Chevrolet wagon was this Brookwood model. Available only as a 6-passenger wagon, it had a price tag of $3,152. Chevrolet continued to feature the tailgate with self-storing window. This wagon was part of the Biscayne series. It was designated the model 15436.

The Chevrolet Kingswood Caprice Estate Wagon was Chevrolet's top of the line wagon. It was available in 6 or 9-passenger form. As a 6-passenger wagon it sold for $3,548. In 9-passenger form it carried a price tag of $3,661.

Chevrolet's mid-sized wagon, the Chevelle Concours Station Wagon, was now their smallest wagon. This was the top of the Chevelle wagon line, which included the Greenbrier and the Nomad wagons. The Concours wagon was available in either 6 or 9-passenger version. As a 9-passenger wagon it cost $3,136, only $16 less than the lowest priced full size model.

A rear view of the Chevelle Concours Estate Wagon. Chevrolet still had not adopted the doorgate, as Buick had done this year. But coming or going, the Chevelle Concours with wood grain siding was a very attractive station wagon.

New from Chevrolet this year was the Blazer. This was competition for the Ford Bronco. The Blazer, however, was the larger. It could be converted to station wagon, pick-up, or panel truck. The top was removable.

Chevrolet continued to offer the Suburban Carryall. It is shown here with an ambulance conversion by Wayne Cork. The Carryall was a popular base for this type of conversion. In this form it was called the Sentinel Ambulance.

Shown here is the Chevrolet Sport-Van converted to a Travel Cruiser, complete with full lift top, which allowed the added headroom to be able to stand erect. The Travel Cruiser could sleep four. It was equipped with stove, refrigerator, toilet, 80-inch long bed, and dinette table.

The Chrysler Town and Country Station Wagon was restyled for this year, and hit a record in sales, topping 24,516 units. The Town and Country was available in both 6 and 9-passenger form. As a 6-passenger wagon it sold for $4,583. As a 9-passenger model it carried a price tag of $4,669, and remained the highest priced wagon in the United States. One of the features of the Town and Country was the doorgate. The roof rack was optional.

Stageway Coaches of Fort Smith, Ark., continued to use the Town and Country as a base for their 12-passenger airport wagons. The standard luggage rack also doubled as a roof brace.

The heaviest and most expensive of the 1969 Dodges was the attractive and luxurious Monaco station wagon. Available in both 3-seat and 2-seat versions, these cars wore the imitation wood grain side trim that immediately identified them as the top wagon in the Dodge range. As a 3-seat wagon the Monaco was classified as a Model DH46, sold for $4,046 and weighed 4,361 pounds. The 2-seat version of this car cost $3,917 and tipped the scales at 4,306 pounds. The cornering lights seen built into the side trim on the front fender were optional at extra cost.

Photographed at Chrysler's test track at Chelsea, Michigan, is an attractive example of the 1969 Polara station wagon. This car was also offered in 2 or 3-seat versions. The Model DL46 was a 2-seat, 9-passenger wagon that sold for $3,629 and weighed 4,211 pounds, while the Model DL45 was the 2-seat version and went for $3,522, tipping the scales at 4,161 pounds. These large wagons offered a full 93.1 cubic feet of cargo space behind the front seat.

The Coronet DeLuxe station wagon was offered as a 6-passenger, 2-seat vehicle only, with either a V-8 or a 6-cylinder power plant. The standard 6-cylinder version of this wagon went for $2,922 and tipped the scales at 3,498 pounds. The V-8 wagon cost an additional $103 and weighed 3,606 pounds. The Coronet DeLuxe was the least expensive Coronet wagon available for 1969.

The Ford LTD Country Squire was still one of the best selling wagons in the industry. The wood grain siding was synonymous with the Country Squire. This was the top of the line, and was available as either a 6 or 9-passenger wagon. The roof rack was, as always, optional. Utilizing the LTD front end with its hidden headlights made this a very attractive wagon.

Offering a full 84.9 cubic feet of cargo area, the most expensive of the Coronet 500 models was the station wagon. Distinguished by an attractive wood grain overlay on the body sides and across the tailgate, the Coronet 500 wagon was available in either 2 or 3-seat versions. The 2-seat, 9-passenger model, called the Model WP46, cost $3,392 and weighed 3,676 pounds while the 2-seat, 6-passenger version went for $3,280 and tipped the scales at 3,600 pounds.

Available in either 2 or 3-seat versions, the Coronet 440 station wagon was the line's medium priced entry. This car, like all Coronet wagons, offered 84.9 cubic feet of usable space behind the driver's seat and had a total glass area of 4,877 square inches. The 6-passenger, 2-seat version of this car was available with a choice of engines. The 6-passenger, 6-cylinder cost $3,033 and weighed 3,503 pounds while the V-8 version of this car went for $3,136 and weighed 3,606 pounds. The 3-seat V-8 wagon sold for $3,246 and weighed 70 pounds more than the 2-seat V-8 wagon.

A rear view of the Ford Country Squire. Ford pioneered the doorgate, which was a feature on the Country Squire. The optional roof rack incorporated a wind deflector to help keep the rear window clean. The third seat of the 9-passenger wagon was actually two opposing seats.

The lowest priced full sized Ford wagon was this Ranch Wagon model, available only in 6-passenger form. It, too, featured the doorgate. Both six and V-8 power plants were available. In addition to an optional roof rack, accessories included tilt steering wheel, auto speed control, auto ride control, and factory air.

The Ford Torino Squire wagon was the top of the mid-size wagon line. Trailer and boat towing packages were also available. The roof rack was optional. The doorgate was standard on all Torino wagons.

The Ford Torino Fairlane 500 wagon was the lowest priced mid-size Ford wagon. The doorgate was standard. The roof rack was optional. This model was available only in 6-passenger form. The vent styled window in the rear door was not functional.

This is one of two Ford Falcon wagons available for 1969. The Falcon wagons provided 85.2 cubic feet of cargo area. Slect-Shift Cruise-O-Matic transmissions and power steering were among some of the options available on the Falcon wagon.

A rear view of the Ford Falcon wagon shows the doorgate that was standard. The Falcon wagons were available only in 6-passenger form. The roof rack was optional. Price tag for the Falcon wagon in base form was $2,750.

The Ford Cortina Wagon. This little wagon was manufactured in England. It was not imported by Ford dealers in this country. Unlike other foreign manufactured wagons, this one was a 4-door model.

Still quite popular in spite of competition from the Chevrolet Blazer was the Ford Bronco, shown here in station wagon form. The top was removable.

The International Travelall station wagon was popular with sportsman as a go-anywhere wagon. It had the capacity for big loads, was rugged, and gave passenger car comfort.

The top of the Mercury wagon line was the Marquis Colony Park. It sold for $2,878. Unlike the Ford Country Squire, which shared the same body, the wood grain trim on the Mercury was framed in stainless steel instead of fiberglass. The vinyl roof and a roof rack were optional.

Lower in price, but the same full size as the Marqis Colony Park, was this Mercury Monterey wagon. The roof rack was optional. The doorgate was standard. Price tag for this model was $3,519.

The International wagon had lots of ground clearance. With four-wheel drive it made a great off the road vehicle. It could be used for work or play.

The Mercury Montego Station Wagon was Mercury's compact series station wagon. It is shown here with optional wood grain siding. The Montego wagon could be ordered in either 6 or 9-passenger form. The doorgate was standard. The roof rack was optional.

This Monterey Station Wagon has been converted into an economy-priced ambulance known as the Amblewagon. The conversion was available on special order through many L-M dealers. The unit features a blanked-in rear quarter with dummy landau irons, and removable siren and flasher bar.

The Oldsmobile Vista-Cruiser continued as part of the Cutlass series. It was the only size Oldsmobile wagon, and it was virtually unchanged. Oldsmobile and Buick shared the same station wagon bodies, the difference being in that Buick offered the doorgate and Oldsmobile maintained the tailgate.

The Oldsmobile Vista-Cruiser with optional trailer towing package and optional roof rack. Oldsmobile also offered factory air, tilt steering, power brakes, power steering, power windows, and a choice of V-8 engines.

Shown here are the Oldsmobile Vista-Cruiser and the standard Cutlass station wagon. The Vista-Cruiser would be discontinued after this year. Both model station wagons were available as either 6 or 9-passenger wagons.

As part of the Fury line, Plymouth offered three distinct wagons. Pictured here is the top of the line Sport Suburban, complete with wood grain siding and a doorgate. The roof rack was optional. Fury wagons provided 93.1 cubic feet of cargo area.

The Plymouth Custom Suburban Wagon had the same basic features as the Sport Suburban including the door gate, built-in wind deflector, and choice of 6 or 9-passenger models. The difference was the absence of wood grain siding and interior trim.

At the top of the mid-size Plymouth Satilite series was the Sport Satelite Wagon, available in 6 or 9-passenger form. The wood grain siding and dual action doorgate were standard. The roof rack was optional. Plymouth wagon ceilings were lined with acoustic panels. The Satelite wagon had 88 cubic feet of storage space.

The Pontiac Executive Safari wagon. Styling of the Pontiac wagons was unchanged. They presented a very attractive package. Vinyl covered roof and roof rack were optional items. In addition to its full size wagons, Pontiac also offered the compact Tempest wagon.

Pontiac introduced the 'Swing Gate' this year. It was a dual action, dual hinged tailgate, following Ford's lead. Pontiac and Buick were the General Motors Divisions to introduce this type of tailgate. One distinct feature of the swing gage was the unique step plate. A section of the bumper was fastened to the bottom of the tailgate, and when opened like a door; it swung away to provide a step.

The Jeep Wagoneer equipped with four-wheel drive was a favortie work wagon. It had the same off the road reputation as the Jeep CJ models. The roof rack was optional. Jeep wagons were available in 6-passenger form only.

One of the most popular American Motors Wagon models for 1969 was this Rebel SST, model 6918-7. Standard features included wood grain siding and a roof rack. Optional V-8 engines were available, as was factory air, power windows, power steering, power brakes, tilt back seats, and fifth door (on 6-passenger models).

The Jeep Wagoneer was promoted as a 2-car car, at home in any situation. Cargo area was a large 100 cubic feet. The roof rack was optional. The vent like windows in the rear doors were not functional.

Returning to Buick's line-up this year was a "Big" station wagon. Joining the Electra series was this luxury Estate Wagon. Its wheel base was 124 inches and the power plant was a whooping 455 cubic inch V-8. The wood grain paneling and vinyl roof covering were optional.

Buick's new big wagon for 1970 was available in 6 and 9-passenger form. It is shown here without the optional wood grain paneling. The price tag for the 6-passenger version was $3,923, while the 9-passenger model sold for $4,068. Full wheel covers and chrome rocker mouldings were standard.

For the first time since its introduction, the Buick Sportwagon did not feature a skyroof. With the return of the big wagons, the Sportwagon became Buicks mid-size wagon. All models were 6-passenger wagons, mounted on a 116-inch wheelbase. The price tag was $3,210. The roof rack and steel styled wheels were optional.

Buick opened the new decade with the introduction of its big new Estate Wagon. For the first time since 196_ Buick was once again offering a 'Big' wagon. Based on the new LaSabre 124-inch chassis, it had an overall length of 223.3 inches. The new wagon was available in both 6 and 9-passenger form. A dual-action Tail/Door gate was standard. In addition to this big wagon Buick also continued to offer the Sportwagon, based on the small 116-inch chassis. This year the Sportwagon no longer featured the domed skyroof.

All General Motor Divisions now featured the dual action tail/door gate. Chevrolet finally succumed to this innovation, being the last division to hold out. Chevrolet Blazer continued to rise in popularity beating out its arch rival, the Ford Bronco. This also marked the last year for the Oldsmobile Vista-Cruiser. This domed skyroof model would be discontinued after this model year. Oldsmobile was the only General Motors Division not offering a large full size wagon.

The Ford lines continued unchanged. All top-of-the-line models featured simulated wood siding. This trim package was referred to as the 'Squire Package'. Ford continued to outsell all other makes in station wagons. The Squire Package was attractively applied and became very popular. Mercury's Colony Park Marquis wagon was so luxury appointed, that it was referred to as the wagon Lincoln Continental would have built, if it had built a wagon. Ford continued to offer a mini-bus type wagon, which was designated the Econoline Window Van. This model would become very popular in the later 1970's.

Chrysler's famous Town and Country wagon saw a drop in production for this year. Dodge Monaco, Plymouth Fury and Chrysler Town and Country all shared the same body shell. All top of the line Chrysler Corporation wagons featured simulated wood siding. One of the features common to all Chrysler Corporation wagons was a built-in wind deflector on the large wagons. The wind deflector was located on the roof panel above the tailgate window. It helped to keep the window clear. Build-in assist handles were also a common feature of the large wagons. A dual-action tail-gate was standard.

American Motors introduced the Hornet Sportabout. This new wagon combined the utility of a station wagon with the styling of a Hornet sedan. Instead of a tailgate, a hatchback was used. The Sportabout would become AMC's most popular wagon. American Motors also made air conditioning standard on all Ambassador wagons.

The International Travelall and the Jeep Wagoneer were unchanged from previous years.

With the reintroduction of the big wheelbase wagon, Automotive Conversions of Troy, Mich., once again made available a professional Buick wagon. One of the main features of the Amblewagon, as they were called, was the low cost, since this was a stock wagon with minor alterations.

The Opel Kadett wagon was Buick's little import wagon, now available in standard and deluxe version. The deluxe version featured wood grain siding and a roof rack. The cost of this model was $2,159 in base form.

The Chevrolet Blazer continued to rise in popularity. This rugged vehicle, available with 4-wheel drive, made an excellent off the road wagon. The top was still removable.

The top of the line mid-size Chevrolet wagon was this Chevelle Concourse Estate. There were four models available in the Chevelle series. In addition to this one there was the Concourse, the Greenbrier and the Nomad. Engine options included a 155 horsepower Six and a 200 horsepower V-8.

The Chevrolet Kingswood Estate wagon was the top of the line wagon for Chevrolet. It was available in both 6 and 9-passenger form. For the first time this year Chevrolet adopted the dual-action doorgate. The 9-passenger wagon carried a base price tag of $3,866.

The Chrysler Town and Country Station Wagon suffered a production drop this year, with only 15,269 units being produced. Once again the Town and Country was available in both 6 and 9-passenger models. The 6-passenger had a price tag of $4,738, while the 9-passenger model sold for $4,824.

Automobile Conversions of Troy, Mich., offered this converted Chevrolet Suburban Carryall in hearse form. Some of the deluxe features were a woodgrain rub strip above the rocker section and rear wheel skirts. The hubcaps were a deluxe truck accessory. The rear Landau panel could be removed.

Not many changes were made to the Chrysler Town and Country wagon for 1970. Most changes were subtle. Two of the standard features of this wagon were the assist grabs on the tailgate posts, and the wind deflector built into the roof panel just above the tailgate window. The roof rack was optional.

A total of 6,620 Polara station wagons were built this model year. Of these, 3,074 were of the 6-passenger style. They sold for $3,670 and weighed 4,220 pounds. The 9-passenger version cost $3,778, weighed 4,270 pounds, and had a production run of 3,546.

The Coronet 440 station wagon had a total production run of 7,736 units, of which 3,964 were 6-passenger and 3,772 were 9-passenger. The 6-passenger 6-cylinder wagon carried a price tag of $3,156 and weighed 3,585 pounds, while the V-8 version went for $3,258 and tipped the scales at 3,650 pounds. The 9-passenger wagon was only offered with a V-8 engine. It went for $3,358, weighed 3,720 pounds.

The most expensive car in the Monaco Series was the station wagon, available in two versions. A total of 5,475 of these wagons left the factory. Of these, 2,211 were the 6-passenger style and 3,264 were in 9-passenger form. The 6-passenger version cost $4,220 and weighed 4,400 pounds. while the 9-passenger model cost $4,242 and weighed 4,460 pounds. These wagons shared the same 122-inch wheelbase as other standard size Dodge passenger cars but had a length of 223.6 inches over-all. Wood-grain side appliques were standard equipment.

The Coronet 500 station wagon, like the Monaco wagon, was available in both 6 and 9-passenger versions, and adorned with phoney woodgrain appliques on the body sides. A total of 3,436 Coronet 500 wagons were built during the model year. Of this total, 1,657 were 6-passenger wagons that went for $3,404 and weighed 3,640 pounds. The additional 1,779 cars were 9-passenger vehicles which sold for $3,514 and weighed 3,705 pounds. Coronet wagons, like other body styles, utilized a wheelbase of 117 inches but had an over-all length of 211.7 inches.

Ford's top of the line wagon, the Country Squire, is shown here demonstrating the door/gate pioneered by Ford in 1966. The vinyl roof covering and the roof rack were optional. The Country Squire was available in both 6 and 9-passenger form.

The Ford Torine Wagon, with Squire trim, was officially known as the Torino Squire. Squire trim, or the Squire Option as it would later be called, was very popular among wagon buyers. It was a sign of prestige. Torino wagons were available in both 6 and 9-passenger form. The roof rack was optional. The door/gate was standard.

At the bottom of the Ford wagon line-up was this Falcon wagon, available only in 6-passenger form. The door/gate was standard on this model, and on all other Ford wagons. The vent style window in the rear door was not functional.

The Ford Custom 500 Ranch Wagon was Ford's lowest priced full size wagon. It was available only in 6-passenger form. The door/gate was standard.

Unchanged from the previous year, when this body design was first introduced, was the Ford Econoline Wagons. Their passenger and cargo capacities were of course larger than a sedan type vehicle, more like a mini-bus, but they were still classed as wagons by the manufacturer.

The International Harvester Travelall, in the Custom series, had the wood trim as standard. But the roof rack and vinyl roof covering were optional. The Travelall was competition for the Chevy Carryall Suburban.

A stripped down International Travelall, equipped with 4-wheel drive, was promoted heavily for commercial use. The second and third seats could be removed for greater load capacity. The 4-wheel drive Travelalls were also available with automatic transmissions.

Equiped with four-wheel drive, the International Travelall was a favorite with the camping and hunting set. It was a go anywhere rugged off the road vehicle. An option was air-level ride, which prevented rear end sag when a heavy load was carried.

The Mercury Montego MX Villager wagon, with wood grain siding, was the deluxe mid-size Mercury wagon. A companion to this wagon was the Montego MK Station Wagon. It was the same body without the wood grain and other luxury appointments.

The Mercury Marquis Station Wagon was the top of the line model, available both in 6 and 9-passenger form. It was advertised as the wagon Lincoln Continental would have built, if Lincoln had built a wagon. Luxury and prestige were the selling points. It weighed 4,488 pounds and cost $4,123. Two other full size Mercury wagons were part of the Monterey series.

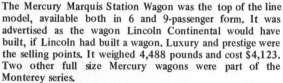

The Oldsmobile Vista Cruiser and standard Cutlass Station Wagon. This was the first year Oldsmobile adopted the dual-action tailgate. This would be the last year Oldsmobile would confine its wagon models to the Cutlass series size.

The 1970 Oldsmobile Vista Cruiser was available in either 6 or 9-passenger form. A new treatment of the simulated wood grain to the sides and tailgate accounted for the major part of the styling changes for this year. This would be the last year for the vista type roof.

A wind deflector built into the roof panel above the tailgate was a feature of all Big Chrysler Corporation wagons, including this Plymouth Fury. Grip assist handles were also standard. The third seat of the 9-passenger models faced to the rear.

The Plymouth Fury Sport Suburban, the top of the line Plymouth wagons, shared its body shell with the Chrysler Town and Country as well as the Dodge Monaco wagon. The roof rack was optional. A door/gate was standard. Disappearing headlamps were one of the styling features this year.

The Plymouth Belvedere Sport Satelite had wood grain paneling and dual-action door/gate as standard features. The roof rack was optional. The Sport Sattelite was available in both 6 and 9-passenger form. A popular option was a rear window washer.

The Pontiac LeMans Safari and LeMans Wagon. The dual-action tailgate was standard on all Pontiac wagons. A unique feature of the Safari wagons was a reflective type wood grain material that was used on the tailgate. It would reflect headlights at night as a safety feature, while during the day it looked like the side panel material. Standard power was a 250 cubic inch Six, while 350 and 400 cubic inch V-8 engines were available at extra cost.

The Pontiac Executive Safari Wagon was available only in 9-passenger form. This was Pontiac's top of the line wagon. The roof rack was optional.

The American Motors Ambassador SST. One of the outstanding features of this model was standard air conditioning. Roof rack and power tailgate window were also standard. The optional fifth door was available on 9-passenger models.

The American Motors Rebel SST wagon was available with AMC's high performance 390 cubic inch V-8 engine, which developed 325 horsepower. The roof rack was standard. Tailgates were available with standard crank type windows or optional power windows. Head rests were also featured on the backs of the front seats. These seats were split with a recliner option.

The Jeep Wagoneer was virtually unchanged from the previous year. The 4-door 6-passenger wagon was available with V-8 engine and 4-wheel drive. The cargo area was very large. The roof rack was optional. It was a popular vehicle among sportsmen, rural dwellers, and commercial users.

Introduced for the first time this year was the new American Motors Sportabout. Based on the Hornet chassis, and made part of the Hornet series, the Sportabout combined the utility of a station wagon with the styling of a sedan. This model featured a hatchback, rather then a tailgate. The roof rack was standard. This would become the most popular AMC wagon produced.

The Buick Estate Wagon was still considered a series of its own. There were two models available, a 6-passenger and a 9-passenger. The 6-passenger cost $4,640, while the 9-passenger carried a price tag of $4,786.

Many Buick Estate Wagons were ordered with the optional wood-grain trim. This trim covered the side panels and the tailgate. A thin chrome strip topped the upper edge of the trim, while a wide chrome band ran along the rockers and the door bottoms.

New for this year was General Motors introduction of the "Clam-Shell" tailgate. It was a completely new innovation in tailgate design. Not to be outdone by Ford, with its "magic" doorgate, GM continued to develop a tailgate design all its own while adopting the doorgate. The "Clam-Shell" design feature was one of self-storing by moving both the tailgate window and the tailgate itself out of the way. With the press of a switch (on the inside) or the turn of a key (on the outside), the tailgate window slid up into a storage area behind the headliner. When it was completely stored the tailgate lowered itself into a storage area beneath the floor. But, this design was not without problems. For one thing, if a buyer did not order a fully automatic gate, the gate had to be pushed down into the storage area, and had to be lifted back out. Now the pushing down was not all that difficult, but the pulling up took some strength. Secondly, jambing of the window in the stored position prevented the gate from coming up. Thirdly, with the tailgate now stored beneath the floor, additional cargo area was lost without the use of the tailgate, a factor competition soon jumped on. Nevertheless, the "Clam-Shell" design was new and novel. It gave Ford considerable concern.

New from Oldsmobile this year was the introduction of the Custom Cruiser. This was a full size "Big" wagon based on a 127-inch wheelbase, the same chassis used for the Ninety-Eight series. Features included wood-grain paneling and the "Clam-Shell" tailgate. Cargo area was discribed as large enough to stack 4 x 8 sheets of plywood.

The Chrysler Town and Country took an upswing in production this year with a total of 16,612 units being built. The Town and Country, the Dodge Monaco and the Plymouth Fury Sport Suburbans continued to share body shells. Basic design for all divisions remained unchanged.

Ford made slight changes to its basic design. The Torino wagon with Squire Package featured hidden headlamps while a new touch was added to the Torino Ranchero. The Ranchero was a pick-up with passenger car features. This year there was a Ranchero Squire, which meant that wood grain paneling was added to the side panels and the tailgate. Ford referred to it as "the most comfortable, most luxurious pick-up of them all, with rich woodtone paneling inside and out and deep pile carpeting and breathable vinyl upholstery. It was a classy looking vehicle.

The most significant move made by the auto industry came about this year with the introduction of sub compacts by all makers. From General Motors to American Motors each manufacturer introduced a small car. The Pinto, the Vega, the Gremlin and the Colt would become auto by-words in the next few years. With the introduction of the Vega, Chevrolet offered three models one of which was a station wagon called the Vega Kamm back. A hatch was used instead of a tailgate. The Dodge Colt was also available in a wagon model, while Gremlin and Pinto were only 2-door coupe type cars. These sub compacts would become very popular and by the end of 1976 would influence the scaling down of all models.

A rear view of the Buick Estate Wagon. Note how the wood-grain trim and chrome accent moulding follow the body contour from front fender to tail light. The roof rack and vinyl roof treatment were optional. Introduced for the first time this year was GM's "Clam-shell" tailgate. This was a new innovation in tailgate design.

Buick continued to offer the Sport Wagon, a mid-size wagon, utilizing the 116-inch wheel base chassis. Body design followed the Skylark series. Only one model was available, a 6-passenger. The cost of this wagon was $3,515. The roof rack was optional.

Buick continued to import the Opel line. This little wagon was the Series 1900 Station Wagon. It cost $2,289.

The Deluxe version of the Buick Opel 1900 series station wagon cost $2,438. Features included ventless door windows and wood grain paneling.

The Chevrolet Caprice Kingswood Estate Wagon was the top of the line. Note the slight rise of the roof panel over the cargo area. This was necessary to accomodate the self storing tailgate window. The price tag for this model was $3,800.

General Motors newly introduced "Clam-Shell" tailgate is demonstrated here on a Chevrolet Caprice Kingswood Estate Wagon. The window glass was stored in the roof area, while the tailgate was stored in the floor.

The Chevrolet Caprice Kingswood Estate Wagon in rear view. The photo demonstrates the "Clam-Shell" tailgate. With this type of tailgate design, the tailgate window opening was reduced. Note the vent louvers on the tailgate. This was part of General Motors flow-thru ventalation system.

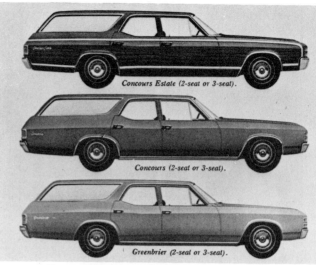

While the "Clam-Shell" tailgate was used on the full size wagons, the mid-size Chevelle continued to use the doorgate, and the Vega used a hatch. All three types of tailgates are shown here.

A line up of Chevrolet Chevelle model wagons, the Concours, the Concours Estate and the Greenbrier. All were offered in 6 and 9-passenger form.

Newly introduced this year was the Chevrolet Vega 2300 Kammback Wagon. This neat little wagon used a hatch instead of a tailgate. Seating capacity was for five, with the use of bucket seats in the front.

A version of the Chevrolet Vega Kammback was this Panel Express, which was the same vehicle with steel panels in the quarter window openings, and the rear seat removed. It made a great little delivery truck.

Still popular was this Chevrolet mini-bus type wagon called the Sportvan. The basic power pack was a 250 cubic inch six cylinder engine. Prices ranged from $3,304 to $3,747.

The Chevrolet Carryall Suburban was priced at $3,800. It was advertised at being strong like a truck yet roomy as a wagon. With second and third seats removed, the cargo area was 180 cubic feet.

The Chrysler Town and Country Station Wagon was available as a 6 or 9-passenger wagon. In 6-passenger form it cost $4,951 and as a 9-passenger wagon the cost was $5,037, which made it the highest priced wagon in the United States. Production was increased to 16,612 units this year.

A rear view of the Chrysler Town and Country Station wagon. The roof rack was optional, but very few wagons were delivered without it. Note the standard doorgate and assist grip handles built into the rear window posts.

The Dodge Coronet Station Wagon was available in both 6 and 9-passenger models. The doorgate was standard, as was the wind deflector above the rear window.

As camping became very popular, many Dodge Coronet wagons were sold with trailer towing packages, which included heavy-duty suspension.

A prototype Chrysler Town and Country Station Wagon had Imperial side marker lights and a New Yorker grill. Otherwise the car was a stock wagon.

The Dodge Monaco wagon was the top of the line and shared the same body shell as the Chrysler Town and Country. Note the placement of the wood grain paneling on the upper third of the side, while it appears on the lower third of the tailgate.

The Dodge Coronet Crestwood station wagon. Wood grain paneling trim designated this model to be the top of its line. Cost of the Crestwood was $3,601 in 6-passenger form. As a 9-passenger wagon it was priced at $3,682. A total of 6,566 Crestwood wagons were built this year.

The Dodge Love Machine was a one-off show car, mounted on a 108-inch Dodge Sportsman van chassis. It was conceived and constructed by customizer George Barris of North Hollywood, Cal. It was finished in 40 coats of sunray yellow candy lacquer.

The Dodge Colt wagon had a wheelbase of 95.3 inches, and it was powered by a 97.5 cubic inch, 85 horsepower 4-cylinder engine. This little 4-door wagon was attractive, and with the rear seat folded, provided added cargo space.

The Ford Country Squire, LTD. The hidden head lights were gone for this year. Otherwise the basic design was unchanged. The Country Squire was available in both 6 and 9-passenger form.

The Dodge Custom Sportsman wagon had a wheelbase of 108 inches and was sometime referred to as a Maxiwagon. The cost of this wagon with a six cylinder engine was $3,438.

Lowest price full size Ford Station Wagon was this Custom 500 Ranch Wagon. The doorgate was standard, as it was on all Ford Station Wagons. The Range Wagon was available in either 6 or 9-passenger form. One of the styling features of the Ford this year was the hidden wipers. The cowl was lowered, the hood extended to within a few inches of the windshield, and the wipers were permitted to rest below the hood line.

A rear view of the Ford Country Squire. It was available with dual facing third seats, and the standard "magic" doorgate. Note the wind deflector on the back edge of the optional roof rack.

The Ford Torino Squire Station Wagon was unchanged from last year. Hidden head lamps, wood grain siding, and the doorgate continued to be featured.

The Ford Bronco continued to be a popular off and on the road vehicle. It is shown here with a hardtop, which classed it as somewhat of a wagon. Front wheel drive and deluxe wheel covers were optional. Note the two gas caps. An optional auxillary tank was added to this model.

The Ford Ranchero Squire incorporated many of the features of the Torino Squire wagon, including the wood grain siding and the hidden head lamp grill. The vinyl roof covering was optional. A total of six engine options were available.

The Ford Econoline Window Van continued to grow in popularity as a extra large wagon. Note the deluxe wheelcovers and chrome grille.

The International Travelall in 6-passenger form. This model is equiped with special trailer towing package, and 4-wheel drive.

This is the International Travelall DeLuxe model in 9-passenger form. Some of the features included wood grain siding, vinyl roof covering, roof rack, and full wheelcovers. This was the 1000 Series. Note the west coast mirrors, handy for trailer towing.

Custom body builders were even turning Lincoln sedans into station wagons. The body builder for this conversion is unknown, but the job was nicely done.

The Mercury Marquis Colony Park was the top of the line Mercury wagon. Its outstanding features were the Lincoln-like luxury interiors. Also note the Lincoln style wheel-covers. This model was available in 10-passenger form with dual facing third seats.

The Montego MX Station Wagon featured Mercury's novel dual-action tailgate, which would either open from the side as a conventional door, or lower in tradtional tailgate fashion. Two seats were standard, but a rear-facing third seat could be ordered. In base form, the wagon weighed 3,563 pounds and cost $3,215 with the 6 or $3,341 with the V-8.

The Mercury Montego Villager Station Wagon was a 6-passenger model. The roof rack was optional, the doorgate was standard. The Villager carried a price tag of $3,545, as compared to the Colony Park Marquis at $4,766. There were two other Montego wagon models, the Montego MX and the MX Brougham.

The Oldsmobile Custom Cruiser was newly introduced this year. It was Oldsmobile's entry into the "Big" wagon field. The Custom Cruiser was built on a 127-inch wheelbase chassis, the same one used for its Ninety-Eight Series.

A rear view of the Custom Cruiser by Oldsmobile. The Clamshell tailgate was standard. Advertising for this model boasted that 4 x 8 sheets of plywood could be stacked in the cargo area.

A rear view of the Plymouth Fury Custom Suburban Station Wagon. This model was one step down from the Sport Suburban. It was available in both 6 and 9-passenger form. The dual-action doorgate was standard, along with the built in roof wind deflector.

The Plymouth Sport Suburban was the top of the line wagon in the Fury series. It shared its body shell with the Chrysler Town and Country and the Dodge Monaco. Hidden head lamps were one of its features. The roof rack was optional. The Sport Suburban was available in both 6 and 9-passenger models.

The Plymouth Satelite station wagon was a 6-passenger model. A 225 cubic inch six or 318 cubic inch V-8 were engine choices. Cargo carrying capacity was 91.3 cubic feet.

A rear view of the Plymouth Custom Satelite. The doorgate and wind deflector were standard, as was the simulated wood siding.

The Pontiac Grand Safari Wagon model became the top of the line this year. It was available only in 9-passenger form. It differed from the other full size Pontiac wagons only in luxury appointments.

The Pontiac Safari 6-passenger wagon with wood grain option and the Pontiac Safari 9-passenger wagon without the option. Roof racks on both models were optional. The Clam-shell tailgate was standard on both models.

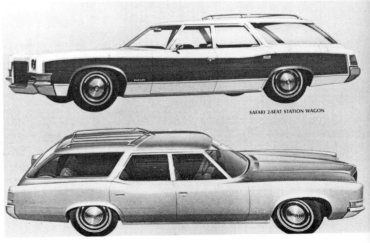

Pontiac LeMans wagons were available in both 6 and 9-passenger models. Both used the doorgate instead of the Clam-shell tailgate. The 6-passenger model is shown with optional roof rack and wood grain paneling.

The American Motors Ambassador wagon was AMC's luxury wagon. Roof rack, factory air conditioning, and reclining front seats were standard on this model.

The American Motors Hornet Sportabout was fast becoming AMC's most popular wagon. Instead of a tailgate, a hatch was used. Passenger capacity was for 6 adults. The Sportabout was available only as a 4-door model.

The Jeep Wagoneer. This model was all dressed up in a variety of options, which went to prove that it was not a truck. Included are a wood grain accent strip, vinyl covered roof, roof rack, sliding sun roof, and wind deflector, not to mention front bucket seats.

The Jeep Commando was a derivative of the early Jeepster model. Standard power plant was a 232 cubic inch six cylinder engine, with an optional V-8 available. Four-wheel drive was also available. The roof rack as optional, and the roof cab section was removable.

1972

The Buick Estate Wagon, 6-passenger model, was officially designated the Model 4R35. It cost $4,589. Riviera styled wheels and roof rach were options.

For 1972 General Motors continued to make the "Clamshell" tailgate standard on all full size station wagons. The mid-size wagons such as Buick Sport Wagon, the Chevrolet Chevelle, Pontiac LeMans and Oldsmobile Cutlass continued to use the doorgate. The GM sub-compact wagons, namely Chevrolet Vega, used a hatch instead of a tailgate. Two full size wagons, a 6 and 9-passenger Estate Wagon, were offered by Buick. In addition to its mid-size Sport Wagon, Pontiac offered three full size wagons and two mid-size, plus a Vega sized hatchback, the Astra. Oldsmobile had one full size and two mid-size versions. Chevrolet had the biggest selection of station wagons among the General Motors Division — four full size, four mid-size and the Vega Kammback. In addition to this line up there was the Blazer, the Suburban Carryall, and the Chevy Van Mini-Bus wagon.

The big news from Ford this year was the introduction of the Pinto Wagon. Much like the Vega, the Pinto used a hatch instead of a tailgate. Unlike Chevrolet, Ford went one step further with its little wagon. Ford made available the Squire option of attractively applied wood grain decals. The dark wood grain panels with light framing, applied to the side and deck lid, was an instant success. It had the look of a mini Country Squire. At least half of the Pinto wagons sold in 1972 had this option. With the addition of the Pinto wagon, Ford now offered a total of nine station wagons in pleasure car form, plus the Bronco and the Econoline Club Wagon. Some of the safety features incorporated into Ford wagons, and also General Motors Chrysler, and American Motors, complied with standards set by the Federal Government. These included steel guard rails inside doors, seat belt reminder system for front seat belts, locking steering wheel with warning buzzer, and the energy absorbing steering column. All 1972 Ford engines were designed to operate on regular gasoline with an octane rating of at least 91.

Chrysler Division boosted its production this year to a hefty 20,589 units. Chrysler continued to offer one wagon size. The Town and Country was available in both 6 and 9-passenger form. Price increase of the Town and Country was a modest $30 over 1971. Dodge and Plymouth continued to offer a wide range of full size and mid-size wagons. The Town and Country continued to share its body shell with the Dodge Monaco and Plymouth Fury wagons, much like Mercury shared its full size body shell with Ford. New from Plymouth this year was the introduction of the sub-compact Cricket wagon. Cricket and Dodge Colt were the same wagon with different trim. Both were manufactured outside the United States. Chrysler did not have a small car on the drawing board, being a big car oriented company. It was simpler to import one to compete with Chevrolet's Vega and Ford's Pinto.

American Motors still offered the big Ambassador wagon, but it had expanded its Hornet Sportabout into a deluxe version with wood grain siding. The Sportabout was now being offered with a sunroof option. International and Jeep continued to offer the same models unchanged.

The Buick Estate Wagon, 9-passenger, model 4R45, carried a price tag of $4,728. The big Buick wagons were advertised with the following quote, "Aren't you glad your new Estate Wagon is so big and comfortable and secure." Its ironic that just five years hence Buick would be referring to its reduced size big wagons as "the sensible size".

The Chevrolet Kingswood Estate Wagon. This top of the line wagon was available in both 6 and 9-passenger models. As a 6-passenger model it sold for $4,150, and in 9-passenger form the price tag was $4,259. This was an increase of $359 over the previous year, and reflected a two year increase of $393.

A rear view of the Chevrolet Kingswood Estate Wagon. The extreme slope of the rear window added much to the overall design of the wagon, as did the curved quarter windows. Both helped rid the wagon of a boxy look, but cut available cargo space.

The Chevrolet Kingswood Wagon was a step down from the Kingswood Estate. Available in 6 and 9-passenger form, it sold for $3,892 as a 6-passenger and $4,001 as a 9-passenger model.

The Chevrolet Townsman Wagon was the lower mid-priced full size wagon, selling for $3,806 in 6-passenger form and $3,914, as a 9-passenger model. The overall styling was much the same as the Kingswood with a little less frill.

In the Chevrolet Chevelle series the luxury model was this Concourse Estate. It featured wood type trim and a dual-action tailgate. The roof rack was optional. As a 9-passenger model it sold for $3,424 and in 6-passenger form for $3,317.

Lowest priced full sized Chevrolet wagon was this Brookwood model. It was available in 6-passenger form only, and sold for $3,718. The vinyl roof covering was $135 extra. The roof rack was also optional. All full size Chevrolet wagons featured the "Clam-Shell" tailgate.

Lowest priced of the Chevrolet Chevelle wagons was this Nomad model. Once Chevrolet's king of the road prestige wagon, it was now a stripped intermediate selling for $2,832, with 6-cylinder engine and $60 more for a V-8.

Chevrolet's mini wagon, the Vega Kammback, continued to use a hatch instead of a tailgate. The louvers on the rear fenders were not there to disappate engine heat. It was part of Chevrolet's flow through ventilation system.

The Chevrolet Chevelle Concourse Wagon. The prime difference between this model and the Concours Estate model was the simulated wood trim. The roof rack was optional. Price of the 6-passenger model was $3,150 and for the 9-passenger model was $3,150 and for the 9-passenger $3,257.

Chevrolet's go anywhere, on and off the road wagon styled vehicle, was the Blazer. It was a utility recreational vehicle equipped with a 307 cubic inch V-8. The top was removable.

The Chevrolet Carryall Suburban was available in a wide variety of forms, but all models were 3-doors — two on the right and one on the left. The Carryall was also available with 4-wheel drive.

1972 MONACO 4-DOOR WAGON

The heaviest and most expensive of the full size Dodge cars for this year continued to be the Monaco station wagon. Available as either a 6 or a 9-passenger, this car, like all Monacos, had automatic transmission, power steering and Power front disc brakes as standard equipment. The 6-passenger wagon cost $4,570 and weighed 4,570 pounds, while the 9-passenger went for $4,699 and weighed 4,615 pounds. This model had a run of 7,714 of which the most popular was the 9-passenger, with 5,145 built. Only 2,569 6-passenger wagons were built.

With woodgrain body side appliques, the Coronet Crestwood was one of the most distinguished looking of all the intermediate station wagons. This car came equipped with a 318 cubic inch V-8. It sold in 6-passenger form for $3,524, and weighed 3,920 pounds, and in 9-passenger form for $3,603 and weighed 3,960 pounds. The Crestwood enjoyed a production run of 6,471 units.

DODGE CORONET

The Chrysler Town and Country Wagon. Production was increased this year to a total of 20,589 units. This was an increase of nearly 4,000 over the year before. Of the total number produced, 14,116 were 9-passenger models, selling for $4,852. The balance of production was in 6-passenger models with a price tag of $4,768. The dual-action doorgate was standard.

Polara Custom 4-door wagon.

The Polara Custom station wagon was available as either a 6 or a 9-passenger car. The 9-passenger version went for $4,008 and weighed 4,495 pounds, while in 6-passenger form this car cost $3,905 and tipped the scales at 4,445 pounds. The production run tallied up 7,666 9-passenger and 3,497 of the 6-passenger variety.

The Polara station wagon was available in 6-passenger form only. It sold for $3,712, weighed 4,445 pounds. This was the least popular of all the standard size Dodge station wagons, with a production run of only 3,013.

The Coronet station wagon, like the Crestwood, was available with a V-8 engine only, and as a 6-passenger wagon, with no 9-passenger version being offered. A total of 5,452 were built.

Appearing for the second year was the nifty little Dodge import, the Colt. The Colt was manufactured for Dodge by Mitsubishi Industries of Japan. Besides the wagon, three other models were offered. Dodge also offered three full size and two mid-size wagons this year.

Dominating the Ford wagon line this year were the country Squire and the Torino Squire wagons. The Country Squire was available in both 6 and 9-passenger form. Ford continued to lead the industry in wagon sales. A vinyl roof covering and roof rack with built in wind deflector were among some of the optional available this year.

Lowest price full size Ford wagon was the Ranch Wagon, available as a 6-passenger model or with dual facing rear seats. It was the same basic design as all the other full size Ford wagons without the luxury trim. Roof rack and white side-wall tires were optional.

The Ford Galaxie 500 Country Sedan was a step down from the Country Squire. It was available in 6 and 9-passenger form. The roof rack was optional. The "Magic" doorgate and full wheel covers were standard.

The Ford Torino Squire Wagon. This popular top of the line mid-size wagon featured high back front bench seat, dual-action doorgate, center fold front seat arm rest, cloth or vinyl upholstery, power door locks, factory air, tinted glass, rear facing third seat, roof rack with wind deflector, carpeted cargo floor, and many other options.

The Ford Gran Torino Wagon was next in line to the Squire model. It had many of the same features, less the simulated wood trim. Cargo space was a big 83.5 cubic feet. The door-gate could be opened with the window up or down. This was a unique feature not to be found in competitive lines.

1972

A rear view of the Pinto wagon. A hatch instead of a tailgate was used. Front seats were bucket, while the rear seat was a bench. Four adults could sit comfortably, while two adults and three children made this a five passenger wagon. The forward seat of quarter windows pushed out and the rear set were fixed.

The Ford Pinto Squire wagon was new this year. The Squire option was made available in the spring of the year and became an immediate success. The roof rack and body side protective strip were optional.

The International Travelall. The versatile wagon was a favorite with sportsmen. It was roomy, and had a large cargo area. All models were 4-doors. A roof rack and 4-wheel drive were optional.

The Mercury Marquis Colony Park wagon. The Marquis line of Mercury continued to sell very well. The Marquis wagon appealed to the Lincoln buyers looking for a wagon. It portrayed luxury and bigness. The Colony Park was available only as a 9-passenger wagon. Both luggage rack and cornering lights were optional.

The International Scout. The on and off the road vehicle was in the same class as the Chevrolet Blazer. Trailer towing packages, roof rack, and four wheel drive were among the many options. The top was removable.

Runner up to the prestiges Marquis wagon was this Mercury Monterey model. It was available in either 6 or 9-passenger form. The roof rack and vinyl roof covering were optional.

The Mercury Montego luxury wagon was distinctive with its simulated wood siding. The dual-action doorgate was standard, and could be opened with the window up. The roof rack was optional.

The Mercury Montego wagon is shown in prototype form. Note the absence of chrome trim on the front fenders. The production model was pretty much the same without the trim. A dual action doorgate was standard, as it was on all Ford and Mercury wagons except Pinto.

The Oldsmobile Cutlass wagon was a lower priced version of a Oldsmobile wagon, available only in 6-passenger form. A dual action doorgate was standard. The full size Oldsmobile wagons used the "Clam-Shell" tailgate.

The Plymouth Fury Sport Suburban wagon was available in either 6 or 9-passenger form. The Fury wagons continued to share body shells with the Dodge Monaco and Chrysler Town and Country wagons. The dual-action doorgate was standard. The roof rack was optional. The wind deflector was built in as part of the roof panel.

The Oldsmobile Vista Cruiser. This was the last year for the domed vista roof. Simulated wood grain siding was standard, as was the dual-action doorgate. The roof rack was optional.

The Plymouth Fury Custom Suburban wagon was available in both 6 and 9-passenger form. Vinyl roof covering and roof rack were optional. The dual action doorgate was standard. Note the assist grip handles built into the rear window posts.

The mid-size Plymouth Satelite Custom was in the middle price range of Satelite wagons. Note the built in wind deflector. Unlike the one found on the Fury models, this one is added on. The dual-action doorgate was standard.

Lowest priced mid-size Plymouth wagon was this Satelite model. Available only as a 6-passenger model, it was stripped of all trim and deluxe appointments. The roof rack was optional. Note the absence of the wind deflector on this model.

Newly introduced this year was the Plymouth Cricket wagon. The Cricket was basically the Dodge Colt with different trim. Some of its features included a hatch instead of a tailgate, child guard door locks for the rear doors, high back front bucket seats, and automatic transmission. The vent like rear door windows were non-functional. The Cricket wheelbase was 98 inches with an overall length of 116.9 inches.

The Pontiac Grand Safari Wagon. This luxury, top of the line wagon was available in 9-passenger form only. Distinctive wood grain siding set it apart from the other Pontiac wagons. The "Clam-Shell" tailgate was standard, along with flow through ventilation. The roof rack was optional.

The Pontiac Catalina Safari wagon was available in both 6 and 9-passenger form. The "Clam-Shell" tailgate was standard, as were the full wheelcovers. A optional roof rack was available.

This mid-size Pontiac wagon, the LeMas Safari, was attractively packaged in wood grain siding. It had a standard dual-action doorgate, instead of the "Clam-Shell" tailgate of its bigger brother. This model was available in either 6 or 9-passenger form.

Newly introduced this year was the mini Pontiac wagon the Astra. It used the same body shell as the Chevrolet Vega. Instead of a tailgate a hatch was used. Passenger capacity was for five.

American Motors Ambassador wagon's standard equipment for this year included, factory air, automatic transmission, 304 cubic inch V-8, power steering, front disc brakes, white sidewall tires, AM radio, tinted glass all around, undercoating, hood insulation, remote left hand outside mirror, visor vanity mirror, electric wipers, and an electric clock. It was the most complete wagon in the industry, with little to no options left to buy. Note the wind deflector built onto the end of the roof rack. The roof rack was standard.

The hottest AMC wagon was the Hornet Sportabout. It is shown here with an optional sun roof. All models were four door wagons. The Sunroof was a canvas push back type, like the European imports used.

The Jeep Wagoneer is shown here dressed up in fancy trim which included wood grain accent strip, roof rack, full wheelcovers and four wheel drive. Standard engine for the Wagoneer was a 258 cubic inch six cylinder with an optional 304 or 360 cubic inch V-8.

A deluxe version of the American Motors Hornet Sportabout featured wood grain siding and standard roof rack. The Sportabout used a hatch instead of a tailgate. Seating capacity was for six.

The Jeep Commando's standard engine was a 232 cubic inch six cylinder. V-8 options were also available. Front end treatment was newly designed for this year. The roof rack was an option. This model was built to compete with the Chevrolet Blazer and International Scout.

The newest innovation in station wagons this year wasn't really new. It was a throw back to 1961. For 1973, General Motors adapted the hatch for its Buick Century wagon, the Chevrolet Chevelle wagon, the Oldsmobile Vista Cruiser, and the Pontiac LeMas wagon. Every mid-size GM wagon now used a hatch instead of the conventional tailgate. The use of the hatch was put into effect on mid-size and compact size wagons by GM in 1961. It was discontinued in favor of the tailgate in 1964. It can only be assumed that the use of the hatch was a cost factor. A tailgate-liftgate combination or tailgate with self storing window is expensive to produce. The hatch is simpler in construction and easier to maintain. But it does have its disadvantages. For one thing, the window is fixed, and thus the hatch must be opened completely to put in or take out cargo. Also, the added cargo floor of the tailgate is lost. All General Motor cars were restyled for 1973.

Buick continued to offer the big Estate Wagon and the smaller Century wagon, which was now available in both 6 and 9-passenger form. Chevrolet continued to offer the same line of wagon models, as did Oldsmobile and Pontiac. Because of the use of the hatch with its fixed window, a operable vent window was used on all mid-size GM wagons, at the rear end of the quarter glass.

Ford Motor Company wagons were also redesigned for 1973. The line of models however remained the same in all divisions. Ford offered a few new options for the larger wagons, such as the Country Squire and Colony Park Marquis. For one thing, a special spare tire puller was available. This was made of plastic, was fitted under the spare with a handle readily accessible when the spare cover was removed. A pull of the handle brought the spare up out of the well with no full or no muss. Another neat little item available for the same models, was a game table for the third seat area in 9-passenger models. With the third seats being dual facing, a game table could be purchased that fit into brackets between the two seats. A checker board was embossed into the table face. It was great for the kids on long trips.

All Chrysler Corporation cars received styling changes this year, but the wagon model line remained unchanged. American Motors models were unchanged in appearance and in number available. International was unchanged, as was Jeep. However, Jeep did introduce a new model called the Cherokee. It was a 2-door sporty version of the Jeep Wagoneer. It was billed as a rugged and sporty, on or off the road vehicle, available with Quadra-Trac, which was Jeep's automatic 4-wheel drive. Other options available on the Cherokee were automatic transmission, power steering, air conditioning, and power front disc brakes.

The Buick Estate wagon continued to be Buick's prestigue wagon. It was available in both 6 and 9-passenger form. The Estate wagon used the 127 inch Electra·chassis. The 6-passenger model sold for $4,589, while the 9-passenger sold for $4,728.

New for this year was the Buick Century Luxus station wagon, available in either 6 or 9-passenger form. The Century wagon used a 116-inch wheelbase chassis. The vent windows at the rear end of the quarter windows were functional. The roof rack was optional.

General Motors reverted to the hatch on its mid-size wagons for 1973. Shown here is the Buick Century wagon. Loading and unloading was easier, but additional cargo floor was lost with the elimination of the tailgate. The 6-passenger Century sold for $3,587 while the 9-passenger model sold for $3,700.

This custom Cadillac Station Wagon was done by the Custom Craft Division, Automobile Specialty Corp. of Southgate, Mich. It was built using a Fleetwood Brougham as the base. The clam-shell tailgate was from a Buick wagon. This was a 9-passenger wagon, called the Fleetwood Brougham Astro Estate Wagon. Custom Craft also built a station wagon based on the El Dorado, called El Dorado "Astrelia" Station Wagon. It was a 6-passenger model.

The Buick Opel Series 1900 station wagon. The little German import was available only in a two door model in 6-passenger form. It carried a price tag of $2,709. Options included wood grain siding and roof rack.

The Chevrolet Caprice Estate Wagon is shown here with the Clam-Shell tailgate fully opened. Note how streamlined the slope of the roof and curve of the quarter window are with the use of this type tailgate.

The Caprice Estate Wagon continued to be Chevrolet's top of the line wagon. It was virtually unchanged from the previous year. The clam-shell tailgate continued to be used on both 6 and 9-passenger models.

Topping Chevrolet's mid-size wagon line was this Laguna Estate. There were five Chevelle wagons available this year. In addition to the Laguna Estate, there was the Laguna, Melibu Estate, Malibu, and the Deluxe. All mid-size wagons featured a hatch this year instead of the conventional tailgate or doorgate.

The Chevrolet Vega Kammback wagon. New for this year was the optional Estate package, which was wood grain siding. This followed the success of the Pinto Squire by Ford. The Kammback was named after a pioneer in automotive aerodynamics, Dr. W.I.E. Kamm. The Vega was powered by 140 cubic-inch engine, and offered over 50 cubic feet of cargo area. There was also a concealed storage area under the cargo floor. A roof rack was optional.

Ever gaining in popularity were the van type wagons such as this Chevrolet Sportvan. It was available this year with a sliding side door, which was borrowed from the Volkswagon Kombis, introduced in 1969.

The Chrysler Town and Country was basically unchanged for this year. It presented a clean pleasing design with great attention given to details. Quality and luxury were the wagon's two big features. Sales continued to be strong. A total of 20,040 units were built. Both a 6 and 9-passenger model was available, with the former costing $5,181 while the latter carried a price tag of $5,306.

A rear view of the Chrysler Town and Country wagon. The doorgate was utilized by all Chrysler Corporation wagons. The assist handles were standard, the roof rack was optional.

Available as either a 2 or 3-seat wagon, a total of 12,541 Polara Custom station wagons were built. Of these, the least popular was the 6-passenger version of which 3,702 were built. This car sold for $4,390 and weighed 4,415 pounds. As usual, the 9-passenger, or 3-seat wagon, was the most popular. This year, it had a production run of 8,839. This popular wagon carried a price tag of $4,519 and weighed 4,495 pounds. The standard Polara wagon, which looked identical to the Custom on the outside, was available only as a 6-passenger. It cost $4,082, weighed 4,445 pounds. This was the least popular of all standard size Dodge wagons, with a production run of 3,327.

The main styling alteration on the Monaco wagon was the appearance of a new style of woodgrain side applique. Once again the Monaco wagon was available in either 6 or 9-passenger versions. The 6-passenger wagon carried a price tag of $4,646, weighed 4,570 pounds, and had a production run of 2,337. The 9-passenger was the most expensive of the standard size Dodges and sold for $4,775. This car weighed 4,615 pounds and had a production run of 5,579.

A rear view of the Dodge Coronet wagon on the Dodge test track. This is a 9-passenger wagon. Note that the third seat faced to the rear. The roof rack was optional, while the doorgate was standard.

The Coronet was available in three station wagon versions, all with V-8 engines only. The most prestigious was the Crestwood which featured woodgrain side appliques. The Custom had a full length side molding while the inexpensive Coronet wagon was devoid of exterior side trim. The Crestwood cost $3,632 and weighed 4,075 pounds as a 6-passenger wagon and $3,711, weighing 4,115 pounds, as a 9-passenger. The Coronet Custom carried a price tag of $3,382 in 6-passenger form, weighing 4,065 pounds, while the 9-passenger went for $3,460 and weighed 4,110 pounds. The standard Coronet wagon was offered in 2-seat, 6-passenger form only and sold for $3,209 while tipping the scales at 4,065 pounds. The Crestwood had a production run of 8,755 while the Coronet station wagon had a run of 4,874. The most popular Coronet wagon was the Custom which had a run of 13,018.

Continuing for the third year was the Dodge Colt wagon. This little wagon was manufactured in Japan for Dodge, to compete with Pinto and Vega. Its outstanding feature was the four door configuration. The competative Pinto and Vega were two door models.

Called a Medicruiser, this attractive van-type of ambulance was produced by the Wayne Corp. of Richmond, Ind. Wayne built a wide variety of these units on both Dodge and Chevrolet van chassis. The advent of this type of ambulance changed the entire concept of ambulance service during the 1970s, and more and more such vehicles are replacing the more conventional type of ambulance. The reason for the popularity can readily be found in the amount of interior space available. Whereas in conventional ambulances, space is often at a premium, the van-type of unit can be fitted out as a virtual rolling hospital or operating room—in some cases riding complete with doctor and nurse in addition to the regular attendants.

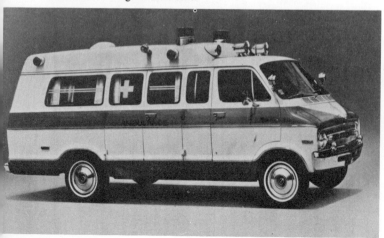

Topping its line up of wagons for 1973 was the ever popular Country Squire. Ford continued to use LTD appointments on this model. It was available, as always, in 6 and 9-passenger form. New for this year from Ford was the introduction of the LTD wagon, which was the same as the Squire without the wood grain siding.

Shown here is an optional game table, available on the Country Squire and LTD 9-passenger wagons. This was a great option for families on long trips.

One of the hottest selling wagons in the country was the Ford Pinto Squire. This sporty little 2-door wagon was likened to a mini Country Squire. The comparison enhanced its sales.

The Ford Torino Squire. This mid-sized Ford wagon became a real hot seller in 1973. Overall appearance was excellent, with the wood graining highlighting the sporty design. The doorgate was standard, while the roof rack with wind deflector was optional.

A rear view of the Ford Pinto wagon. Note how neatly the wood graining was carried out on the rear hatch. The forward section of the quarter window was operational, and pushed out.

Another feature of the Big Ford wagons was the spare tire extractor. As demonstrated here, it made removal of the spare much easier.

The International Traveall was once again unchanged. It is shown here with wood grain siding and optional West Coast clamp-on mirrors, which were great for trailer towing. The Traveall was also available with four wheel drive.

The Mercury Montego Villager station wagon with the Montego MX wagon in the background. This was Mercury's mid-size wagon, available in both 6 and 9-passenger form. It was comparable to the Ford Torino wagons. The roof rack was optional.

The Mercury Marquis Colony Park wagon continued to look like the prestige Marquis, and carried many luxury appointments. It was available in both 6 and 9-passenger form. The roof rack was optional.

The Oldsmobile Custom Cruiser was the big Olds wagon, based on the 127-inch Ninety-Eight chassis. It was available with wood grain siding, in 6 or 9-passenger form. The roof rack was optional.

The Mercury Monterey wagon used the same body as the Colony Park, but without the wood grain siding and luxury appointments. It was available in either 6 or 9-passenger form. The doorgate was standard, as it was on all Ford Motor Company wagons except the compact Pinto.

The Oldsmobile Vista Cruiser. The doomed vista roof was gone but a pop up sun roof, as shown here could be ordered. Vent-like windows at the rear of the quarter windows were functional. Wood grain siding was also available.

The Oldsmobile Cutlass wagon's standard power plant was a 350 Rocket V-8. It was available in 6 and 9-passenger form, with function rear vent window and optional roof rack.

Standard on all mid-size wagons from Oldsmobile and other GM divisions was the hatch, instead of the conventional tailgate. Cargo area was 85 cubic feet. Pictured here is the Vista Cruiser with wood grain siding, and optional roof rack. Note the vent louvers in the rear compartment. This was part of the flow through ventilation system.

The Plymouth Fury Sport Surburban was Plymouth's big wagon. The body shell was shared with Dodge Monaco and Chrysler Town and Country. Wood grain siding and the dual action doorgate were standard. The big wagon was available in both 6 and 9-passenger form.

The Plymouth Satelite Regent wagon was the top of the line mid-size Plymouth wagon, comparable to the Dodge Coronet. It was available in both 6 and 9-passenger form. Wood grain siding was standard on this model.

A rear view of the Plymouth Fury Sport Suburban. The 9-passenger model had a third seat that faced to the rear. The Doorgate was standard, as was the assist grip handles. The roof rack was optional. Also note the rubber step plates on the rear bumper, these were standard on the 9-passenger model.

The Pontiac Grand Safari, with optional wood grain siding, was available in either 6 or 9-passenger form. The third seat on the 9-passenger model faced forward. The standard power plant was a 400 cubic inch 4-barrel V-8. Front disc brakes were also standard, as was power steering and Turbo Hydra-matic transmission.

A rear view of the Pontiac LeMans Safari, with optional wood grain siding. The strips on the hatch are a throw back to the days of the Nomad and original Safari.

The Pontiac LeMans Safari was available in either 6 or 9-passenger models. The third seat of the 9-passenger wagon faced to the rear. Standard engine was a 250 cubic inch six cylinder, coupled with a manual 3-speed transmission.

The American Motors Ambassador station wagon. This was AMC's big wagon. Most everything, including factory air, power steering, brakes, and the roof rack, were standard.

The Hornet Sportabout continued to be American Motors hottest selling wagon. It was available in 4-door form only, and only as a 6-passenger model. The tailgate was a hatch, the roof rack was standard, the wood grain siding was optional.

Jeep became part of American Motors in 1972, and for 1973 there was a continuing program of product improvement. Basic styling remained unchanged but the quality got better. Introduced this year on the Wagoneer models was the Quadra-Trac system, which was a full time four wheel drive. The system increased the go-anywhere capability of the Jeep.

Continuing once again unchanged was the Jeep Commando, whose ancestor was the Jeepster. The Plastic hardtop was removable.

The automobile industry and the great love affair Americans have with automobiles was shaken this year with the awesome reality of the fuel shortage and energy crisis. These two terms, which would become household words for the balance of this decade at least, threw Americans into a tizzy. There were long lines at the pumps, new car sales of big cars dropped, there were Sunday closings, and prices skyrocketed, double and triple over a year ago. Odd and even numbered license tags were used to control consumption in many areas. Summer travel was uncertain. There were charges and counter charges. Rationing was considered. Was it a rip-off or was there really a shortage. The auto industry scrambled to bring out economy cars. EPA ratings and fuel allocations became commonplace terms. Under this vail of gloom, Ford Motor Company ushered in a new model, the Mustang II. It was the first clue to industry-wide scaling down. The 1973 model Mustang was a big car. It had gotten bigger over the years, growing to mid-size status. The wheelbase was 109 inches, with an overall length of 193.8 inches. For 1974, the Mustang II was a small car, smaller than the original Mustang introduced in 1964. Its wheelbase was 96.2 inches with an overall length of 175 inches. Only two models were available, a coupe and a fastback — no wagon. It also marked a continuing trend toward convertible elimination.

All manufacturers were offering the same line up of wagons as in the previous model year, with the emphasis on economy power plants. Station wagon models were still selling utility including more room for the family, more room for carry do-it-yourself materials, convenience of loading and unloading, the doorgate, the clam-shell tailgate, the hatch, and so it went. Pintos were selling, Vegas were selling, Hornets Sportabouts were selling. And so were the hatchback models in every line.

The most surprising outcome for 1974 was the continuing popularity of the van wagon. While production of big full size cars slipped, van production was increasing, a complete contradiction to the uncertinty of the times. But it did reaffirm one thing, American's love affair with the automobile. No matter what, Americans would have a car in any way shape or form, be it mini-wagon or house-like van. The van kindled the urge for individual expression. It was not unlike the custom car era of the 1920's relived again. A Dowdy plain-jane van or van wagon could be turned into a work of art, at least on the inside.

So this was 1974. It was the threshold of change, for the automobile industry. A milestone year, on the brink of a whole new era in automobiles.

The Buick Estate Wagon and the Buick Century wagon. Both wagons were available in either 6 or 9-passenger form. Wood grain siding was optional with each. The Estate wagon used the clam-shell tailgate, while the Century used the hatch. Roof racks were optional on both.

A custom Cadillac station wagon by Custom Craft of Southfield, Mich. This model was based on the El Dorado. It was a 6-passenger wagon called the El Dorado "Astrelia" Station Wagon.

The Chevrolet Caprice Estate Wagon was the top of the line full size Chevrolet wagon. It was available in either 6 or 9-passenger form. The wood grain siding was standard on this model. Chevrolet still maintained the clam-shell tailgate, which made the Chevrolet, along with the other full size GM wagon, the most streamlined in the industry.

The Chevrolet Laguna Estate was the top of the line Chevelle wagon. The rear vent like window was functional. Wood grain siding and parking lights set in the grille were standard for this model. The roof rack was optional. The Chevelle series wagons used a hatch instead of a conventional tailgate or clam-shell tailgate.

The Chevrolet Chevelle Deluxe wagon was the lowest priced Chevelle wagon. Note the use of the hatch on this series. All Chevelle wagons were 4-door models, available as 6 or 9-passenger wagons.

Chevrolet's neat little woody was the Vega Kammback Estate. It did not pan out to be the strong competition for Pinto that Chevrolet had hoped it would be.

Along with the van, the Chevrolet Suburban enjoyed steady production. The Suburban was expanded to a full four door wagon. It became popular for its bigness and ruggedness.

Face lifted for 1974 was the Chrysler Town and Country. The wood grain siding was standard, as was the TorqueFlite transmission. Power steering and power disc brakes.

A rear view of the Chrysler Town and Country wagon. It was available in both 6 and 9-passenger form. The 9-passenger model sold for $5,366.

Topping the line for 1974 was this Dodge Monaco Brougham wagon in 9-passenger form. The Dodge Monaco, along with the rest of the Dodge line, was completely restyled for this year. The hidden head lamps were gone. The overall styling of the front end was stronger.

Next to the Dodge Monaco Brougham was this Monaco Custom. It was the same wagon without the wood grain siding. The door gate was still standard, and so was the built-in wind deflector. The roof rack was optional. The Monaco Custom was available in both 6 and 9-passenger form.

The Dodge Coronet Crestwood was the top of the line mid-size Dodge wagon. Wood grain siding was standard. The Crestwood was available in both 6 and 9-passenger form. The roof rack was optional. However, most wagons were ordered with the rack. A station just did not look finished without it.

The International Scout was competition for the Chevrolet Blazer, although sales never even came close. It was a rugged on and off the road vehicle, which could be ordered with 4-wheel drive. The roof rack was optional.

The Ford LTD Country Squire. This year the Country Squire was named LTD. It was a return to hidden head lamps. In order to comply with safety standards, front and rear bumpers were movable and would push in on crash contact. The gravel pans were made of pliable plastic, painted to match the car color.

The 1974 Ford Torino Squire wagon was unchanged except for grille and the addition of a hood ornament, spring loaded for safety.

Except for new front and rear bumpers, the successful little Pinto Squire wagon was unchanged. The wagon was still very popular with the Squire package of wood grain siding.

The Ford Club Wagon. All van-type vehicles had a new body in 1973, so they were unchanged for this year. The sliding side door was adopted from the Volkswagon vans and buses, the same way Chevrolet did. Vans represented a sizable portion of the station wagon market.

The Oldsmobile Custom Cruiser. This big Oldsmobile wagon was unchanged from last year. It was available in either 6 or 9-passenger form. The roof rack was optional, as was wood grain siding. The third seat faced forward.

The Oldsmobile Cutlass Supreme Cruiser, like the rest of the Oldsmobile lines, was not changed from the previous year. The hatch was still used instead of a tailgate. The roof rack was optional, as was wood grain siding.

The Plymouth Sport Suburban wagon. Styling was new this year for the Fury wagons along with the rest of the Plymouth series. The Custom Suburban is shown in the background. It was a less expensive full size Fury wagon. Both models were available in 6 and 9-passenger form.

Plymouth Satelite Wagons. The model in the foreground is the Regent. The wood grain siding was standard, as was the dual action doorgate. Third seat of the 9-passenger model faced to the rear.

The Plymouth Cricket station wagon. This model was the same as the Dodge Colt. Both were in 4-door form.

Introduced for the first time this year as competition for the Chevrolet Blazer, was the Plymouth Trail Duster. This on and off the road, all terrain vehicle was available with a removeable hardtop or a convertible soft top. It had the configuration of a station wagon, but was not a true station wagon.

The Pontiac Grand Safari wagon was available in both 6 and 9-passenger form. The rear seat of the 9-passenger wagon faced to the front. Wood grain siding was standard, the roof rack was optional.

Newly introduced this year was the Plymouth Voyager wagon. It was the same as the Dodge van wagon. The only difference was in the name plates. Like the Ford, Chevy, Dodge and Volkswagen vans, it too had a sliding side door.

The Pontiac Le Mans Safari wagon was available as a 6 or 9-passenger model. The third seat of the 9-passenger model faced to the rear, unlike the big Pontiac wagons.

The American Motors Ambassador wagon. Standard equipment included factory air, automatic transmission, power steering, power front disc brakes, AM radio, tinted glass, and white wall tires. There was literally nothing extra to buy.

The American Motors Matador wagon had wood grain siding as standard, as was the dual-action doorgate. The cargo area was a whooping 99.1 cubic feet. Standard power plant was a 232 cubic inch six cylinder engine.

The American Motors Hornet Sportabout with D/L package, which included color keyed wood grain side and rear panels, extra quiet insulation, roof rack with wind deflector, reclining front seats and special vinyl trim. The sport wheels were optional.

American Motors Jeep Custom Wagoneer with 4-wheel drive emphasized the versitility of the Wagoneer as a family car in particular. Special interiors were available, even in white vinyl. The tailgate of the Jeep Wagoneer was a bit outdated as compared to other wagons. Jeep still used a tailgate with self storing window. A doorgate may not have been practical.

The sportiest model in the Jeep line was the Cherokee "S", shown here with Quadra-Trac 4-wheel drive. The Cherokee options included: Tilt wheel, power disc brakes, power steering, turbo hydra-matic, Flipper rear quarter vent windows, a roof rack, and aluminum wheels.

Photographed in 1974 in Grenada, the Ilse of Spice in the Carribean, was this Jittney Bus, a real woodie, built on a Morris chassis, and colorfully painted. This only proves that woodies were not really dead.

The year 1975 saw more moves toward economy cars. Ford introduced the Bobcat, which was a Pinto dressed up like a Mercury. This move gave Mercury an economy car, with little or no tooling. Bobcat was available in two models, which included a station wagon. The Bobcat Villager featured a posh interior and wood grain siding.

Chrysler introduced the Cordoba, a new small Chrysler, but this was a personal luxury car. There was no wagon model. Plymouth continued to offer the Trail Duster and Voyager Van., in addition to its passenger car wagons. Dodge's little Colt wagon was now available with wood grain siding. And, taking a page from General Motors, it called the option the Estate Package. In addition to the Colt, Dodge offered six passenger car wagons and the Sportvan.

Chevrolet had available eight passenger car wagons in addition to the Suburban, the Sportvan and the Blazer. The Laguna Estate and Laguna wagon was dropped from the Chevelle series. The top of that series was now called the Malibu Classic Estate. Vega had some new models, the Estate GT and the regular GT. Steel belted radial tires became standard factory installed equipment. Overall body design was unchanged. GMC's General Motors truck Division had a couple of wagon vehicles this year. They were the GMC Suburban and the GMC Jimmy. The Suburban was identical to the Chevrolet Suburban, with a changed grille. The Jimmy was the equivalent of the Blazer, basically the same vehicle with trim changes.

American Motors dropped the Ambassador. The Matador became the big car, while the Hornet became the bread and butter car. The Hornet was available in all models and configurations, including four wagons and four hatchbacks. The International Travelall became a sporty 2-door model with hatch instead of tailgate. Jeep wagoneer models added more wood grain siding. As a matter of fact, woodies and woodie type vehicles were the in thing. Car kits, replicars of woodie wagons, and homemades prevailed. GMC even put wood grain siding on one of its pick-up models, and called it a classic.

The Buick Estate and Century wagons. the Estate wagon shown here has optional wood grain siding, roof rack, vinyl roof covering, and sport styled wheels. Both the Estate and Century wagons were available in either 6 or 9-passenger form. The Estate wagon used the clam-shell tailgate while the Century used the hatch.

The Chevrolet Caprice Estate once again led the line-up of Chevrolet wagons for 1975. Sheet metal and basic trim was unchanged. In addition to the Caprice Estate, there was the Impala and Belair wagons to make up the rest of the full size wagon line. The Caprice wagon was available in 6 or 9-passenger form. The third seat of the 9-passenger model faced forward. The second seat was a 60/40 seat with the smaller split being used to fold down and permit entry into the third seat area.

The Chevrolet Malibu Classic Estate was the top of the line mid-size Chevelle wagon. The wood grain siding was standard. This model was available in both 6 and 9-passenger form. The roof rack was optional. The third seat of the 9-passenger model faced to the rear. Entry was by way of the tailgate.

The Chevrolet Chevelle Malibu wagon was available as a 6 or 9-passenger model. The tailgate was really a hatch. Its release level was mounted on the dash. There was even a tailgate-open warning light. The rear vent like window was functional. The roof rack was optional.

The Chevrolet Vega Estate wagon. Because of the popularity of the competitive Pinto Squire wagon, Chevrolet added wood grain siding to the little Vega wagon. This option however was not as popular as Ford's Pinto Squire package. White sidewall tires and roof rack were optional.

The ever popular Chevrolet Blazer, trimmed in optional two-tone paint, chrome bumper, 4-wheel drive, and 350 cubic inch V-8. West Coast side view mirrors were also optional.

The Chrysler Town and Country station wagon was unchanged. It was once again available in 6 and 9-passenger form. The wood grain siding was standard. The roof rack was optional. The third seat on the 9-passenger model faced to the rear.

The Chevrolet Silverado Suburban was a luxury trimed Suburban. It was available with 9-passenger seating, chrome bumpers, below eyeline West Coast type morrors, special two-tone paint and a 454 4-barrel engine.

The Chevrolet Beauville Sportvan could seat up to 12 people, or it could hold 260 cubic feet of cargo. This was close to three times what a full size passenger car wagon could hold. The Standard sliding door needed only 4-1/2 inches of clearance.

The Dodge Monaco Wagon was the top of the line, available in both 6 and 9-passenger form. Some of its features included hidden head lamps, dual-action door gate, rear facing third seat on 9-passenger models, and optional roof rack. The Monaco wagon still offered a 50/50 split back front seat, and rear window defogger.

The Dodge Coronet Crestwood was the Top of the line mid-size wagon. Features included dual-action doorgate, roof wind deflector, optional roof rack, wood grain siding, color keyed carpeting (including the cargo area), and a cargo area big enough for a 4 x 8 ft. piece of plywood.

The Dodge Colt wagon. This year Dodge added wood grain siding to the popular little wagon. The wood look was in.

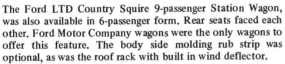

The Dodge Sportsman Van's standard features included a sliding side door, and seating capacity for up to 12 passengers. The two-tone paint combination was optional.

The Ford LTD Country Squire 9-passenger Station Wagon, was also available in 6-passenger form. Rear seats faced each other. Ford Motor Company wagons were the only wagons to offer this feature. The body side molding rub strip was optional, as was the roof rack with built in wind deflector.

The Ford Torino Squire wagon was available in either 6 or 9-passemger form. Wood grain siding and full wheel covers were standard. The dual-action "magic" door gate was standard, as it was on all full and mid-size Ford wagons.

Still the leader in mini woodie wagons was the Ford Pinto Squire. It was offered only as a 2-door wagon with room enough for 4 passemgers. The front seats were bucket seats. The rear seat was a modified bench seat. If needed, it could carry three passengers.

Ford's newly designed Van and Club Wagon continued in popularity. Van production was up. The Club Wagon could carry up to twelve passengers. The two-tone paint was optional.

The GMC version of the Suburban was the same vehicle as the Chevrolet, with only the grille and some trim changed. This model was the Sierra Classic, which featured wood grain siding. The roof rack was optional. It could carry up to nine passengers.

The GMC Jimmy was the equivalent of the Chevrolet Blazer. The two-tone paint scheme was optional. The chrome bumpers were part of a deluxe trim package.

The wood look was in. GMC even trimmed the Series 2500 Sierra Classic pick-up with wood grain siding. This was the 6-passenger, 4-door crew cab, which GMC called the three plus three.

The International Travelall was now available in 2-door form. Features included, optional two tone paint, fancy wheels, roof rack and rear hatch instead of a tailgate.

The Mercury Marquis Colony Park and the Mercury Marquis wagon. The Colony Park was the top of the line. Its features included hidden head lamps, wood grain siding, roof rack with wind deflector, and full wheel covers.

The International Scout is shown here with optional fancy side panel paint job, 4-wheel drive, roof rack and removeable roof.

The Oldsmobile Custom Cruiser. This big wagon was based on the 127 inch Ninety-Eight chassis. Wood grain siding was standard. The Custom Cruiser was available in both 6 and 9-passenger form. The third seat of the 9-passenger model faced forward.

The Mercury Montego MX Villager and Montego MX Station Wagon. The Villager featured wood grain siding full wheel covers and "magic" doorgate as standard equipment. The roof rack was optional. The Montego MX station wagon had some of the same features, less the wood grain siding.

The Oldsmobile Vista-Cruiser wagon's standard features included wood grain siding. Instead of the tailgate a hatch was used on this model. The roof rack was optional. This model was available in both 6 and 9-passenger form.

The Plymouth Gran Fury Sport Suburban styling was all new for this year. Wood grain siding was standard, as was the built in roof wind deflector and grip assist handles for the 9-passenger models. The dual-action doorgate was also standard, as it was on all Plymouth wagons.

The Plymouth Gran Fury Custom Suburban model had the same features as the Sport Suburban, less the wood grain siding. It was available in 6 or 9-passenger form.

The Plymouth Trail Duster was unchanged from last year. Available in either 2 or 4-wheel drive, its load capacity was over 1,800 pounds. Standard power plant was 225 cubic inch six cylinder engine, and 3-speed manual transmission.

The Plymouth Satelite wagons were re-named this year. They were now Plymouth Fury wagons. This was the top of the line Sport Suburban. Features included wood grain siding, dual-action doorgate and full wheel covers. The roof rack and white side wall tires were optional.

The Plymouth Trail Duster with convertible top. Two-tone paint and West Coast side view mirrors were optional.

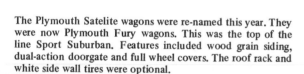

The top of the line Pontiac wagon continued to be the Grand Safari. Features included square head lamps, wood grain siding and clam-shell tailgate. It was available as either a 6 or 9-passenger model. The roof rack was optional.

The lowest priced full size Pontiac wagon was this Catalina Safari wagon. It was available in either 6 or 9-passenger form.

The Pontiac Grand LeMans Safari was Pontiac's mid-sized wagon. Features included wood grain siding, hatch tailgate, and 6 or 9-passenger models. The roof rack was optional. Rear vent windows were functional.

The American Motors Matador Brougham Wagon is shown here with optional wood grain siding and styled road wheels. The roof rack and dual action doorgate were standard.

Once again the most popular American Motors wagon was this Hornet Sportabout. Features included four doors, a hatch tailgate and standard roof rack. Optional wood grain siding was also available. Full wheel covers and white sidewall tires were also optional.

The American Motors Jeep Cherokee made new refinements and convenience options available this year. Some of the new features included electronic ignition system, and new springs and shocks. New options were cruise control, and AM/FM stereo with four speakers.

The American Motors Jeep Wagoneer's new features included wood grain siding, electronic ignition, new power steering and new shocks and new springs. Quadra-Trac full-time 4-wheel drive was standard.

Even the author got into the act with a woodie replicar. Shown here is a 1967 Volkswagen with a woodie kit from Super Plus of California. The 1940 Ford replica hood is plastic, as is the wood-like siding. The author went one step further and added authentic 1940 Ford head lamp doors. Ford script, bumper guards, tail lights, and a spotlight. It was a great little car and turned a lot of heads.

The woodie look was in this year. And it was inevitable that someone would come up with a woodie kit for the Volkswagen chassis. Pictured here is the MiniWOODIE a kit car available from MiniWOODIE, Inc. of California. It used a Volkswagen chassis, a fiberglass 1940 Ford replica hood, and real white ash wood body. The finished product looks like a mini 1940 Ford Wagon. And, its a real wood body car.

The ultimate in woodie cars is probably this Redwood Jaguar. California Jack Wood covered this Jaguar Sedan with 2-inch by 12-inch strips of Redwood veneer, each 1/16th of an inch thick. It took him 1,400 hours to complete his work. The wood was then finished off with ten coats of lacquer. Photo courtesy of Motor Trend Magazine, February, 1975.

Rear view of the MiniWOODIE, a 1940 Ford Woodie replicar, based on the Volkswagen chassis.

All manufacturers were complying with Federal Government regulations, which covered safety, polution and economy. All autos were equipped with 5 mph crash retractible front bumpers, shoulder harness seat belts, catalytic converters, engines which used lead free gasoline, and economy engines with EPA (Environmental Protection Agency) mileage ratings.

Chrysler Corporation introduced two new cars. The Dodge Aspen and the Plymouth Volare. These were entirely new designs in the mid-size class. These two new marquis would compete with the Ford Granada and Mercury Monarch, both of which were introduced a year earlier. Each of the new cars had a wagon in its series. The Dodge Aspen wagon and the Plymouth Volare wagon were basically the same car with different trim. These were 4-door wagons, in 6-passenger form. They had a rather high green house, which gave them superior visability. Instead of a tailgate, a hatch was used. Wood grain options were available to attractively dress up the wagon. A roof rack with wind deflector was optional. Both wagons boasted a load capacity of 1,100 pounds. The standard power plant was a 225 cubic inch six cylinder engine, with automatic transmission. This would be the last year for the Dodge Dart and Plymouth Valiant models.

Chevrolet's little mini car the Chevette, introduced a year earlier, had a woody model available. It was not a station wagon, but the configuration was close to a wagon. All Chevettes were hatch models. The Woody was called the Chevette Woody Coupe. It was attractively packaged, unfortunately it did not sell well. Buick continued to offer two wagon models, the big Estate wagon and the mid-sized Century. The Century was the more popular. Oldsmobile offered three wagon models, the Custom Cruiser, which was based on the large 127-inch chassis, the Vista-Cruiser and the Cutlass Supreme Cruiser, the later two being mid-sized models. Pontiac offered three sizes of wagons, the big Grand Safari and Catalina Safari, the mid-sized LeMans models, and compact Astre wagons.

Ford offered the same line-up of wagons and in addition made available wood grain siding options on the Pinto Hatchback and Bobcat Hatchback models. For the tenth consecutive year, Ford wagons out sold all other wagons. Ford continued to be the Wagonmaster.

American Motors had two Jeep Cherokee models available and two Wagoneer models. Wood grain side paneling was also available on Jeep pick-ups. The big news from American Motors came in the form of an introduction of their new revolutionary small car, the Pacer. Available only in 2-door coupe form it was AMC's new concept of the shape of things to come. The Pacer was shorter and wider, the new small, wide car, as it was advertised. The wheelbase was 100 inches, with a width of 77 inches. Standard engine was a 232 cubic inch six, with single barrel carburator. The Transmission was a 3-speed manual as standard equipment, or a optional Torque-Command automatic. A wagon version of the Pacer would be introduced the following year.

The Buick Century Custom wagon was Buick's best selling wagon. The styling lines were unchanged. The wood grain siding was optional. The hatch tailgate was used instead of a conventional tailgate. The rear window was fixed, but to compensate for this the rear quarter window vents were functional. Roof rack and wire wheel covers were optional.

Topping the long list of wagon models available from Chevrolet this year was this Caprice Estate wagon. It was unchanged from last year. Wood grain siding was standard, as were the full wheel covers. The roof rack was optional. Chevrolet continued to use the "Clam-Shell" tailgate on its full size wagons.

Once again the Malibu Classic Estate Wagon headed the line-up of Chevrolet Chevelle wagons. The wood grain siding was standard. The roof rack, with wind deflector, the full wheel covers, white stipe tires, and deluxe bumpers and guards were optional.

A step down from the Malibu Classic Estate Wagon was this Chevelle Malibu Classic without wood grain siding, which was the only apparent difference between the two models. Body side moulding rub strip, roof rack and white stripe tires were optional.

Chevette Scooter.

The Chevrolet Chevette Woody Coupe was a special trim package available for the compact Chevette. In addition to the wood grain siding, special vinyl upholstery and wood grain dash made up the rest of the package. It gave the little car the look of a mini Estate wagon.

The Chevrolet Blazer for 1976 was unchanged from previous years. The chrome bumpers, roof rack and two-tone paint were options.

The Chrysler Town and Country wagon's cargo area was big enough for a 4 x 8 foot sheet of plywood, layed flat. A 50/50 front bench seat was standard on the Town and Country, with the passenger side being a recliner. There was an abundance of options available on this big wagon, including automatic height control that adjusted the suspension to variations in load.

One of four Chevrolet Vega wagons was this Vega Estate GT Wagon. Features included deluxe interior and upholstery, wood grain siding, GT name plate, roof rack, deluxe bumper guards, deluxe bumpers, and white strip tires. The styled wheels were optional.

The Dodge Coronet Crestwood wagon. Automatic transmission was standard, as was power front disc brakes, and heavy duty suspension. Features included wood grain siding, and dual action doorgate. The roof rack was optional.

New for this year was this Dodge Aspen, a 4-door 6-passenger wagon. This model was the Special Edition, which featured wood grain siding, luxury trim and upholstery. The roof rack was optional. Standard power plant was a 225 cubic inch six cylinder engine, with automatic transmission.

A rear view of the Dodge Aspen Special Edition wagon shows the hatch opening which was nearly four feet wide, and 27.6 inches high. The cargo area was 71.9 cubic feet, with a load capacity of 1,100 pounds. The standard interior of the Aspen was color keyed breathable vinyl white nylon pile carpeting.

The Dodge Ram Charger features included station wagon styling with truck toughness. The wheelbase was 106 inches. It had a turning diameter of 36.9 feet. Optional power steering, LoadFlite automatic transmission and automatic speed control were available. The rugged steel top was removable.

The Dodge Sportsman Wagon. Shown here is the 109-inch wheelbase model, the B-100 with a payload of 1,559 pounds maximum. Dodge Sportsman wagons could seat from 5 to 15 people, depending on the size ordered. Color keyed interiors, high back seats, vinyl and cloth upholstery with colorful stripes, carpeting, automatic transmission and power steering and brakes were some of the options of the Sportsman.

Advertised as the pride of the wagonmaster fleet was Ford's LTD Country Squire. Features included hidden head lamps, wood grain siding, body side moulding rub strip, roof rack with wind deflector and a host of other options. Base price of the LTD Country Squire was $5,523.

The Ford LTD Wagon was available in 6 or 10-passenger form. Some of the features were a lockable storage compartment, carpeted cargo floor, dual-facing third seat, 3-way doorgate, tilt steering, AM/FM stereo with four speakers, 94.6 cubic feet of cargo area, and a floor length of 92.3 inches. The base price of the LTD wagon was $5,207.

The Ford Torino Squire wagon was available in 6 and 9-passenger form. The cargo area was 85 cubic feet. The 6-passenger wagon had 8.1 cubic feet of lockable storage space below the cargo floor. The 3-way door gate opened like a door with the window up or down.

The Ford Club Wagon varied in size from 124 inch wheelbase to 138-inch wheelbase. Standard features included a sliding side door, 300 cubic inch six cylinder engine, solid state ignition system, power front disc brakes, and manual 3-speed transmission.

The Mercury Montego MX Villager was a mid-sized wagon model, available in either 6 or 9-passenger form. The wood grain siding, full wheel covers, and 3-way doorgate were standard.

The Ford Pinto Squire wagon was unchanged, except for grille and bumpers, since its introduction in 1972. It was however still very popular. The base price of the Pinto Squire was $3,671. In 1969 a Country Squire sold for the same money.

The Ford standard Pinto Wagon, even without the wood grain siding, was an attractive package. The cargo area was 57.2 cubic feet. Passenger capacity was for four.

Mercury's compact wagon was unchanged. The Bobcat Villager featured wood grain siding, a 2.3 liter overhead cam 4-cylinder engine, four speed manual transmission, front disc brakes, and high back bucket seats.

The Mercury Bobcat Runabout is shown with optional wood grain siding, roof rack, and steel styled wheels. The wood grain siding was not a popular option.

The Oldsmobile Custom Cruiser is shown here with optional wood grain siding. This large wagon was based on the Olds 98 chassis. Its cargo area was 106 cubic feet. It was available in either 6 or 9-passenger form.

The Oldsmobile Vista-Crusier wheelbase was 116 inches. This was one of two mid-sized wagons available from Oldsmobile this year. The other model was the Cutlass Supreme Cruiser. It could be ordered in 6 or 9-passenger form. The third seat of the 9-passenger model faced to the rear. The tailgate was a hatch.

The Plymouth Gran Fury Sport Suburban was the big Plymouth wagon in full luxury. Full wheel covers, wood grain siding, built-in wind deflector above the tailgate, and the 3-way doorgate were standard.

New for this year was the Plymouth Volare wagon. This was the Premier model. It featured wood grain siding, a roof rack, special color keyed full wheel covers, a hatch tailgate, and deluxe pleated vinyl bench seats. Carpeted floor and cargo area was standard.

The Plymouth Fury Sport Suburban was Plymouth's mid-sized wagon. A 60/40 front bench seat, optional wind deflector, and optional adjustable roof rack were some of its features.

The 1976 Plymouth Voyager with optional sliding side door. The wheelbase was 127 inches. Load capacities ranged from 1,185 to 3,335 pounds. Two-tone paint was optional.

The Pontiac Grand Safari was one of two full sized wagons available this year. Cargo area was a hugh 105.7 cubic feet. The Grand Safari was available in either 6 or 9-passenger form. Wood grain siding and full wheel covers were standard. The roof rack was optional

The Pontiac Grand LeMans Safari. The wood grain siding was standard, the styled wheels and roof rack were optional. This model was available as either a 6 or 9-passenger wagon.

The Pontiac Astre Safari wagon was Pontiac's compact wagon. It was actually a Vega dressed up to look like a Pontiac. The styled wheels were optional, as was the roof rack.

American Motors number one selling wagon was the Hornet Sportabout shown here in the D/L model. All Hornet wagons were 4-door, 6-passenger vehicles with a hatch tailgate and standard roof rack.

American Motors big wagon was this Matador model with optional wood grain siding. The roof rack was standard. The Matador boasted a cargo area of 95 cubic feet.

The American Motors Hornet Sportabout, in standard version was AMC's lowest priced wagon. The hatch provided easy access into the cargo area.

The AMC Hornet Sportabout X featured distinctive side stripes, styled wheels, and raised letter tires as part of its trim package.

The American Motors Jeep Custom Wagoneer, when equipped with standard Quadra-Trac 4-wheel drive, could go anywhere.

The Jeep Cherokee S. This sporty version featured a distinctive top, side strip, and styled wheels. It was the 'Fat Cat' of the Jeep models.

The AMC Jeep Custom Wagoneer is shown here with distinctive wood grain feature strip, roof rack, 4-wheel drive, and 360 cubic inch V-8 engine. The rear door vent-like window is non-functional.

The Jeep Cherokee Chief was a rugged off the road version of the Cherokee. Equipped with big 10 x 15 "Tracker A-T" Goodyear tires, it looked mean and tough, and could virtually go anywhere.

The Buick Estate wagon for this year was reduced considerably in size. It was now smaller than the Century wagon, which was classed as a mid-size wagon. General Motors modified the size of the full size cars but did not proportionately reduce the size of the mid-sized models. This would come in 1978.

The Buick Century wagon was available in both 6 and 9-passenger form. The wheelbase was 116 inches, the overall length 218.1 inches, and the cargo area 85.1 cubic feet. Optional wood grain siding was available. The Century continued to use a hatch tailgate.

The Chevrolet Caprice Station Wagon is shown in optional two-tone paint. Optional wood grain siding was available in the form of an Estate package. This was Chevrolet's top of the line wagon. It was reduced in size, considerably, like all full size GM models. The roof rack and side view mirror were optional.

The year 1977 was one of great change. The bigges change came from General Motors. All full size GM car were reduced in wheelbase and overall length. As an ex ample, the Buick Estate Wagon for 1976 was 231.8 inche in overall length. It had a wheelbase of 127 inches and cargo capacity of 105.7 cubic feet. The 1977 Buick Estate Wagon was 216.7 inches in overall length. It has a wheel base of 115.9 inches and a cargo capacity of 87.3 cubic feet. This was a considerable reduction, but it was a sign of the times. Auto makers were committed to making car smaller and lighter in an effort to increase their fue economy. This would be the last year for big cars.

All GM mid-sized cars were now as big as the so called full sized cars. The Buick Century wagon was as big as the Estate Wagon. The Chevelle was as big as the Chevrolet Caprice, the LeMans as big as the Pontiac Grand Safari and the Cutlass as big as the Oldsmobile Custom Cruiser This would prove to be a difficult year for GM sales in full size cars. Before year's end, Chevrolet would announce the discontinuing of the Vega. The Chevette would more than likely fill the gap.

Chrysler announced two new cars, the Dodge Diplomat and the Chrysler LeBaron. Wagons would be available in both marquis before years end. Chrysler dropped the Plymouth Valiant and Dodge Dart models at the end of 1976. Volare and Aspen filled the vacancy, and were doing very well. Dodge and Plymouth van sales had also im proved.

Ford Motor Company introduced a new small luxury Lincoln, the Versailles. The new Thunderbird was also scaled down from the previous year. The Ford Torino Wagon was replaced by the new Ford LTD II Wagon. The LTD 11 wagon was mid-sized, and used a 118-inch wheel base chassis, with an overall length of 223.1 inches. Mercury dropped the Montego wagon and in its place offered the new Cougar Wagon. The peersonal luxury Cougar was expanded this year to include a sedan and wagon in addition to the personal model. The Cougar wagon was available in two models, the Cougar Villager Wagon and the standard Cougar Wagon, the prime differ ence being that the Villager had wood grain siding. Both were available in either 6 or 9-passenger form. The third seat of the 9-passenger wagon faced to the rear. All Mercury wagons shared their bodies with Ford wagons. Changes to grille and trim were the marked differences.

American Motors announced a new model, the Pacer Wagon. This wagon was an expansion of the Pacer model introduced a year earlier. The Pacer Sedan and Wagon shared the same 100-inch wheelbase chassis, with a differ ence in overall length. The sedan was 170 inches and the wagon at 174 inches. The cargo area of the wagon was 47.8 cubic feet. This was 9.4 cubic feet less than the Ford Pinto wagon, but 1.2 cubic feet larger than Chevrolet's Vega wagon. Wood grain siding was optional, but added a lot to the overall appearance.

The Chevrolet Impala wagon, although reduced in size this year, could still carry a 4 x 8 ft. sheet of plywood flat. The full size wagon for this year was very square in appearance and boxy in design. Because of the boxy design, Chevrolet reverted back to the 3-way doorgate.

Chevrolet's mid-size Chevelle series wagon was actually larger than the so-called full size models. Shown here is the Malibu Classic 9-passenger model. The Classic was also available with Estate wood grain siding. The hatch type tailgate was still retained. Distinctive features included rectangular shaped head lamps.

The Chevrolet Vega Estate Wagon was unchanged from the previous year. Before year's end Chevrolet would announce that this would be the last year for the Vega model. The little Chevette would take its place.

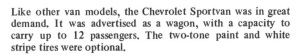

Like other van models, the Chevrolet Sportvan was in great demand. It was advertised as a wagon, with a capacity to carry up to 12 passengers. The two-tone paint and white stripe tires were optional.

The Chevrolet Blazer, unchanged in basic design, grew in popularity to a point that one had to wait four to six weeks for delivery. The model shown here is equipped with optional 4-wheel drive, styled wheels, and West Coast mirrors.

Growing ever popular for its pure utility value was this Chevrolet Suburban wagon. It was the big brother to the Blazer. It is shown here with optional two-tone paint, special trim, and trailer towing package. Passenger capacity was for nine adults.

An artist's rendering of the new Chrysler LeBaron Town and Country. This model would replace the larger Town and Country which was scheduled to be dropped at the end of the 1977 model year. Photo courtesy of Automotive News.

The Chrysler Town and Country Station Wagon. This would be the last year for the large Chrysler wagon. To be introduced later this year would be a scaled down LaBaron Town and Country. It would be the same size as the Dodge Aspen and Plymouth Volare. The Town and Country was available in both 6 and 9-passenger models. The wood grain siding was standard.

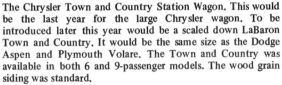

The Dodge Crestwood station wagon is shown here with trailer towing package. It was available in either 6 or 9-passenger form. The wood grain siding was standard. Dodge would discontinue this model at the end of the 1977 model year.

The Dodge Monaco station wagon. This large full size wagon would be discontinued at the end of the 1977 model year. A station wagon would be added to the newly introduced Dodge Diplomat series. It would be in a size comparable to the Aspen.

The Dodge Aspen Station Wagon. This was the Special Edition model with simulated wood grain siding. The wheelbase was 112.7 inches, overall length 201.0 inches, cargo capacity 72.8 cubic feet.

The Dodge Aspen Special Edition wagon is shown here with optional trailer towing package, which included heavy-duty front and rear suspension, heavy duty shocks, wider wheel rims, trailer wiring harness, variable load turn signal flasher, and load carrying trailer hitch.

The Dodge Ramcharger was available with optional 3-passenger rear seat. This was a go anywhere vehicle, equipped with 4-wheel drive for off the road traveling. It was designed to compete with Chevrolet Blazer.

The Dodge Sportsman van was available in two wheel bases, 109-inch and 127-inch, and in three overall length sizes, 176-inch, 194 inch and 212 inch. Seating arrangements could accommodate up to 15 passengers.

The Dodge Sportsman could be outfitted with camper options, including an expanded roof. This would permit standing in the passenger compartment.

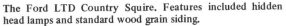

The Ford LTD Country Squire. Features included hidden head lamps and standard wood grain siding.

The Ford Ltd II station wagon was available with wood grain siding as the LTD II Squire Wagon. It could be ordered in either 6 or 10-passenger form.

The Ford LTD II Squire wagon differed from the standard LTD II by its distinctive grille and rectangular head lamps, not to mention the wood grain siding. The roof rack was optional. The LTD II Squire would become the top of the line in 1978.

The Ford Pinto Squire received a new front end treatment this year, which was its only marked difference since its introduction in 1972. The roof rack continued to be an option.

A rear view of the Ford Pinto wagon. Pinto continued to use the hatch tailgate. This made loading and unloading of the little wagon much easier, but put a good many bumps on the heads of tall people.

The Ford Custom Club Wagon continued to be the number one seller in van type wagons. The sliding side door was standard, but the two-tone paint job was optional. The Ford Club wagons were available with either 124-inch or 138-inch wheelbase chassis.

The Mercury Marquis Colony Park was an optional package which included wood grain siding, luxury appointments, cut pile carpeting and electric clock. Other features of the big Mercury wagon were spare tire extractor, lockable storage chest and roof rack with wind deflector. This would be the last year for the Marquis wagon.

New for this year was the Pinto Cruising Wagon. In keeping with the van craze, this new Pinto was dressed up to look like a mini-van. A more accurate discription would have been mini-sedan delivery.

New for this year was the Mercury Cougar wagon. This wagon would become the top of the line Mercury wagon for 1978. Shown here with wood grain siding is the Villager model. There were many luxury options available on the Cougar wagon.

Continuing to spur favorable response from the wagon buying public was the Mercury Bobcat wagon, shown here in optional wood grain siding and roof rack. Though it was popular it did not do as well as its sister, the Ford Pinto.

The Oldsmobile Custom Cruiser. This top of the line Oldsmobile wagon was reduced in overall size this year. The design was new and very boxy. Options included the roof rack, and a 60/40 power front seat. The Custom Cruiser was available in both 6 and 9-passenger form.

A rear view of the new Mercury Cougar Villager wagon. The 3-way doorgate was standard. The roof rack with wind deflector was optional. This wagon shared its body shell with Ford LTD II.

The Oldsmobile Custom Cruiser without the optional wood grain siding. This year marked the return to the 3-way doorgate. With its new boxy design, the Clam-Shell tailgate was no longer practical.

On the Oldsmobile Vista-Cruiser the wood grain siding was optional. The Cutlass size wagon continued to use the hatch tailgate. It was available in either 6 or 9-passenger form. Standard power plant was an improved 350 cubic inch V-8.

The Oldsmobile standard Cutlass wagon, in design and overall appearance, was the same as the Vista Cruiser. The difference was in luxury appointments. The styled wheels and roof rack were options.

The Plymouth Gran Fury Sport Suburban was available in either 6 or 9-passenger form. The wood grain siding was standard. The roof rack was optional. The wheelbase was 124 inches and the overall length was 226.4 inches. The cargo capacity was 102.4 cubic feet, compared to the Chevrolet Caprice at 87.3 cubic feet.

The Plymouth Fury Sport Suburban had a wheelbase longer than the Chevrolet Impala. It was 117.5 inches as compared to 116 inches. But the cargo capacity of the Plymouth was smaller at 84.7 cubic feet as compared to 87.3 cubic feet for the Impala.

Increasing in poluarity was the Plymouth Voyager. It was available in two wheelbase and three overall length sizes. Potential passenger capacity was up to 15 adults. The special two-tone paint and pin stripe were optional.

The Pontiac Grand Safari wagon was newly designed for this year. It is shown here with a 1940 Pontiac woodie in the background for comparison. The new Safari was considerably smaller than the 1976 model. All full size GM cars were scaled down this year. Features included rectangular head lamps and wood grain siding.

The most popular of Plymouth wagons was the Volare. Shown here is the Volare Premier. This was a 4-door 6-passenger wagon. The wood grain siding was standard. The roof rack and wire wheel covers were options. The Volare used a hatch tailgate. The spare was mounted in a compartment below the cargo floor. Cargo capacity was 72.8 cubic feet.

The Pontiac Catalina Safari. With the reduction in size of its full size wagons, Pontiac reverted back to the use of the 3-way doorgate, instead of the clam-shell tailgate. The clam-shell design required a much longer wheelbase. To use it on this size wagon would have meant a great deal of lost cargo space.

Appearing for the last year was the Pontiac Astre wagons. The wood grain siding and styled sheels, along with the roof rack, were options. The wheelbase was 97 inches, with an overall length of 177.6 inches. Cargo capacity was 46.6 cubic feet.

The largest American Motors passenger car wagon was this Matador, available with standard wood grain siding, roof rack, and 3-way doorgate. Tire wheelbase was 118 inches, overall length 215.5 inches and cargo capacity 95.2 cubic feet.

The Pontiac LeMans Safari was the top of the line wagon in the LeMans series. It was unchanged from previous years. The wood grain siding was standard on the Safari model, but the styled wheels and the roof rack were optional.

The Pontiac LeMans wagon had a wheelbase of 116 inches, with an overall length of 215.4 inches. This was compared to 115.9-inch wheelbase and 214.7-inch overall length of the full size wagons. The so called full size wagons were smaller than the mid-sized models.

The American Motors Hornet D/L sportabout wagon was the top of the line Hornet wagon. The wood grain siding was standard as was the roof rack and wind deflector. The Sportabout incorporated a hatch instead of a tailgate. The wheelbase was 108 inches. The overall length 186 inches. Cargo capacity was 62.8 cubic feet.

The newest member of the AMC family was the Pacer Wagon, shown here with optional wood grain siding, styled wheels and roof rack. The vent style window in the rear was functional.

The new AMC wagon was based on the successful Pacer sedan introduced in 1976. The Pacer wagon had a cargo capacity of 47.8 cubic feet. It was powered by a six cylinder engine and had a hefty 22 gallon gas tank.

A rear view of the Pacer wagon. The wood graining was optional, but did much for the overall appearance of the Pacer wagon. With the wood graining the one piece hatch looks like a two piece tailgate.

The Jeep Cherokee S was the fancy-dan of the Jeep wagons. It is shown here with optional paint stripes, styled wheels, and two piece quarter window. The 4-wheel drive Quadra-Trac was standard. This model also had luxury upholstery, which included fancy vinyls and cloth.

The Jeep 2-door Wagoneer was the lowest priced Wagoneer model. Seating capacity was for five. This was actually a stripped down version of the Cherokee S.

About the author

Donald J. Narus, is Director of Operations for the Eaton Oil Co. of Cleveland, Ohio. Eaton Oil is the worlds largest supplier of rustproofing compounds in the auto industry. He is a college history major and graduate Architectural Engineer. He and Lee, his bride of twenty years, reside with their two children Jacqueline 16 and Mark 11, in suburban Parma, Ohio, where Don is active in the Chamber of Commerce and serves as one of the three Civil Service Commissioners to the city.

He has written a number of articles on antique automobiles for various publications and is the author of "Chrysler's Wonderful Woodie — The Town and Country". His love of the automobile dates back to 1936, when as a small boy he helped his grandfather change the oil on his 1932 Plymouth PB sedan. During his adult life, Don has owned 165 cars to date. Including antiques and contemporary transportation.

His love of woodies began in 1948, when he worked summers for a local Chrysler agency, and fondly recalls the car of his dreams sitting on the showroom floor. It was a 1948 Town and Country Convertible, resplendent in its factory fresh maroon paint. Since then he has owned no less than five Town and Country Convertibles. His current pride and joy is a 1949 pepper red model. He also has the distinction of owning a super-rare 1946 Mercury Sportsman Convertible. He also has owned a number of station wagons over the years, including a 1957 Dodge, a 1959 Rambler, a 1967 Ford Country Squire, which was one of his all-time favorites, a Ford Ranch Wagon, and a 1970 Volkswagen Kombi, in which he and his family traveled through five European countries and 22 states. In addition, he has had a 1971 Ford Country Sedan, a 1972 Pinto Squire, which he considers the neatest little wagon around, and a 1973 Pinto Squire.

Don is a member of the Milestone Car Society, The National Woodie Club, The Seventy-One-Society, The Town and Country Owners Registry, The Contemporary Historical Vehicle Association, The Society of Automotive Historians, The Classic Mustang Association International, The Mustang Club of America and the Autoenthusiasts International. His interest ranges from Volkswagen Replicars to the Mercedes Benz 280 SL. His weakness is automobiles, all of them. He is the living example of the line that goes, "Bet you can't have just one!"

The author wishes to dedicate this book to the memory of his parents.